WOLFGANG·PUCK
MAKES IT EASY

Delicious Recipes for Your Home Kitchen

WOLFGANG PUCK

with Martha Rose Shulman

Photographs by Ron Manville

Published by
THOMAS NELSON
Since 1798
www.thomasnelson.com

Published in Nashville, Tennessee, by Thomas Nelson, Inc.

Thomas Nelson, Inc. titles may be purchased in bulk for educational, business, fundraising, or sales promotional use. For information, please email SpecialMarkets@ThomasNelson.com.

Library of Congress Cataloging-in-Publication Data

Puck, Wolfgang.
    Wolfgang Puck makes it easy: deliciously simple recipes for restaurant-quality food from your home kitchen / photographs by Ron Manville.
        p. cm.
    Includes index.
    ISBN-10: 1-4016-0180-4 (hardcover)
    ISBN-13: 978-1-4016-0180-5 (hardcover)
    1. Cookery. I. Title.
TX714.P8328 2004
641.5—dc22   2004016027

Printed in the United States of America

07 08 09 10 11 RRD 12 11 10 9 8

CONTENTS

In memory of my mother, Maria

ACKNOWLEDGMENTS

I want to thank Martha Rose Shulman for her dedication. I don't know if this book would have come to fruition without the passionate work by Martha. She really deserves the credit for this wonderful book.

I'd also like to thank Ron Manville who is not only a very talented photographer, but also an excellent stylist, who, through his enthusiasm, captured the spirit of my food.

To my sons Byron and Cameron who appreciate many of my creations.

To Gelila, whose love is my secret ingredient.

Heartfelt thanks to Sherry Yard for her splendid art direction and her invaluable advice on the dessert recipes.

To Annabelle Topacio and Stella Han for their great assistance in testing and cooking the dishes for the pictures, thank you.

To my partners, Lee Hefter, David Robins, Tom Kaplan, Bella Lantsman, Jennifer Naylor, Carl Schuster, Tracey Spillane, Alex Resnik, my brother and partner Klaus, Thomas Boyce, Mark Ferguson, Mitch and Steve Rosenthal, Joe Essa, Matt Bencivenga, Matt Dickerson, John LaGrone, Christophe Ithurritze, and Jonny Pacheco.

Also to Kevin O'Connor and Bonnie Graves, our talented sommeliers. To Kevin Charbonneau, Norman Kolpas, and Debra Murray.

To all my talented chefs: Ari Rosenson, David McIntyre, Chris Hook, and Suzanne Griswold. To Chris Vasquez, Adam Condon, Michael Beglinger, Eduardo Perez; Luis Diaz and Rene Mata from Chinois; Marian Getz, Hiroyuki "Fuji" Fujino, Daniel Weinstock, Aram Mardigian, Scott Irestone, and Marc Djozlija.

Thanks to Jannis Swerman, who taught us how to communicate. And to Maggie Boone who kept this whole project under control.

INTRODUCTION

This is a recipe collection for the home cook. Even busy chefs like me love to cook at home. We love to cook simple food for our kids, we enjoy backyard barbecues, and we love to cook spontaneously with the ingredients we find at our neighborhood markets. The flavors we seek may be informed by our professional world, but when we cook at home, we have the same constraints as other home cooks: time and money.

Everybody wants to cook great food, but somehow we have it in our heads that great-tasting food requires lots of planning ahead and a brigade of kitchen helpers to prepare the complex stocks and sauces that make restaurant food taste so good. Cook from this book, however, and you'll see that you don't need the personnel and ready access to rare ingredients of a restaurant kitchen to make wonderful meals at home.

Simplicity is the key. My own palate was shaped by the marvelous farmhouse meals that my mother used to prepare for our family in southern Austria. There was nothing fancy about them, and my mother did not need to take extra steps to make them good. When she made a chicken broth it was for chicken soup, not for stock for another dish; it was wonderful because the chicken she used was a free-range chicken, and she simmered the bones long enough to extract all of their rich flavor. When she made a vegetable soup, she used water. But she had fresh, seasonal vegetables to put into that water, and that's why the soup was always so good.

The Principles of Good, Simple Cooking

Simplicity begins with top-notch ingredients. Luckily, today we can find well-stocked farmers' markets and supermarkets all over the country. Certain ingredients have become mainstays in my kitchen, and you will see as you cook your way through these recipes that they are not rare and expensive. I've dubbed them "kitchen helpers," (page 288) because they do the work that I used to spend hours doing every day as a sous-chef in France. These include products like hoisin and barbecue sauce, which I use to make delicious sauces. When a chef makes a sauce in a classical restaurant setting, he relies on reduced veal stock or beef stock for complex flavors and dark, rich color. I might have chicken stock in my home kitchen, but I'm no more likely to store veal or beef stock at home than you are. Nor would I ever spend the time reducing it to a demi-glace just for a good family meal. Still, that never stops me from making a fantastic pan sauce when I sear a peppercorn-encrusted steak (page 173) or pan-cook some thick, moist pork chops (page 188). These sauces can be whipped up in minutes in the same pan I've cooked the meat in, and they can transform a good meal into a great one.

But even a great sauce can't make a dish wonderful if the main ingredients aren't of the highest quality. If you are looking for a way to save money on a meal, don't try to save it on the meat, poultry, fish, or vegetables that are at the heart of your dish. You don't need truffles or foie gras to make a great roast chicken, but you do need the best free-range chicken you can find. Buy local produce in season, either at farmers' markets or at quality supermarkets. Find a good fish market for fresh fish and shellfish. Befriend the butcher in your supermarket. Inspect the food that you buy—touch it, smell it, make sure that it's good. You would never buy a car without looking under the hood and finding out something about the condition of the engine. You should take the same kind of care when you buy ingredients for cooking.

The other thing I urge you to do for yourself is to procure a few good pots, pans, knives, and appliances such as a mixer, a food processor, and a blender. The recipes in this book will be easy if you have some sturdy sauté pans and saucepans, a pasta pot, and a heavy oven-proof casserole. Other tools like the indoor griddle or panini maker will open up a world of indoor grilling and delicious, fun sandwich possibilities. Invest in a pressure cooker, and you'll be impressed not only with the time you'll save but with the incredibly intense flavors of the dishes you'll make in it. I call my kitchen appliances "sous chefs" because they do the chopping, whisking, kneading, and grilling for me.

Making it Easy

When you look at these recipes you may wonder if they really are easy because many of them are quite long. That's because I wanted to explain to you how to do every step. A long recipe is not necessarily a difficult one, and sometimes short recipes can be deceptive—they assume you know more than you do. Because this book is for home cooks and not for chefs, I tell you what pan to use, how to prepare the ingredients, what to look for when you're at the stove. That's why I include photographs and lots of tips. Easy here also means easy-to-find ingredients and recipes that don't require a number of side recipes—recipes within the recipes—to be executed.

I urge you to read the recipes from start to finish before beginning. Then prepare and measure out your ingredients (we call this *mise en place* in restaurant kitchens). Set the table, get out your serving platters and utensils, pour yourself a nice glass of wine, and the cooking should go smoothly. Then you can really enjoy your meal.

BREAKFAST, BRUNCH, AND BREADS

One of the things I love about breakfast and brunch is that they're meals that chefs actually get to cook at home quite often. I will admit, though, that Europeans are sometimes perplexed by the fact that Americans often invite guests for breakfast; we would never consider entertaining our friends so early in the morning!

Growing up in Austria, my breakfasts were quite simple. We didn't have the array of fancy cereals and sweet breads and fruits that are customary at the American breakfast table, though on cold winter mornings I loved eating a bowl of polenta with milk and sugar or semolina with cinnamon and sugar. Normally this was a light meal to get you started with your day. However, at mid-morning we ate a more substantial meal, the *jause*, which usually consists of a sandwich of some kind and juice. Since my mother kept chickens, we always had marvelous fresh eggs. A soft-boiled egg with salt and pepper and toasted country bread or scrambled eggs with onion and potatoes was a Sunday morning luxury.

I've come to appreciate the American breakfast and brunch. In this chapter I've given you a variety of savory and sweet offerings, from great egg dishes to delicious crêpes filled with lemony farmer's cheese, to indulgent chocolate-orange swirl muffins, quick breads, and pistachio-crusted French toast. With this repertoire you can be as creative with your first meal of the day as you are with lunch or dinner.

Strata with Tomatoes and Gruyère Cheese

MAKES 4 TO 6 SERVINGS

A strata is a savory bread pudding. It's one of the most convenient brunch dishes I can think of because it can be assembled the night before. All you have to do in the morning is beat together eggs and milk, pour them in a baking dish, and put the dish in the oven. You can vary stratas in any number of ways.

½	pound stale rosemary country bread or French bread, cut in ¾-inch slices
1	garlic clove, cut in half
1	cup grated Gruyère cheese
2	large, ripe beefsteak tomatoes, sliced
6	eggs, slightly beaten
2	cups milk
½	teaspoon powdered mustard
¾	to 1 teaspoon kosher salt
	Freshly ground pepper

1. Preheat the oven to 350°F. Oil a 12 x 10-inch baking dish or gratin dish.

2. Rub the bread on one or both sides with a cut clove of garlic and place it in the baking dish in one even layer.

3. Sprinkle half the cheese over the bread, and layer the sliced tomatoes on top. Top the tomatoes with the remaining cheese.

4. Beat together the eggs, milk, mustard, salt, and pepper. Pour over the bread mixture.

5. Bake 45 minutes to an hour, until the top is browned and the mixture is slightly puffed.

Wolfgang's EASY TIPS

➤ If your bread isn't stale, toast it lightly before assembling the strata.

➤ Make variations by substituting fontina cheese for the Gruyère cheese and sausage for the sliced tomatoes (see the variation that follows). Or add cooked greens and wild mushrooms sautéed in olive oil with a little garlic to the mix. (See photo on page 5)

Southwestern Strata with Sausage

Though the strata has Mediterranean roots, this Tex-Mex version could become a family favorite.

¾	**pound bulk pork or turkey sausage, mild Italian sausage, or chorizo, casings removed**
½	**pound stale rosemary country bread or French bread, cut in ¾-inch slices**
1	**garlic clove, cut in half**
1	**cup grated pepper Jack cheese**

6	**eggs, slightly beaten**
2	**cups milk**
½	**teaspoon powdered mustard**
¾	**teaspoon kosher salt**
	Freshly ground pepper
1	**cup fresh tomato salsa for garnish**

1. Heat a large, heavy skillet over medium-high heat and add the sausage. Sauté, breaking it up into bite-size chunks with a wooden spoon until cooked through and lightly browned, 5 to 7 minutes. With a slotted spoon, transfer the sausage pieces to paper towels to drain and cool.

2. Oil a 12 x 10-inch baking or gratin dish. Rub the bread slices with the cut clove of garlic and spread in a single layer over the bottom of the baking dish. Sprinkle half the cheese over the bread, top with the sausage, and finish with the remaining cheese. Cover and refrigerate until ready to bake.

3. Preheat the oven to 350°F. Beat together the eggs, milk, mustard, salt, and pepper. Pour over the bread mixture. Bake 45 minutes to an hour, or until the top is browned and the mixture is slightly puffed. Serve with salsa on the side.

Pistachio-Crusted Vanilla French Toast

MAKES 4 SERVINGS

Wolfgang's EASY TIPS

➤ When your bread gets stale, don't throw it out! Stale bread makes great French toast.

➤ Don't soak the bread for too long in the egg mixture or it will fall apart.

➤ A large, heavy nonstick skillet, a tabletop grill, or a panini maker work best for browning the French toast.

➤ Sliced almonds can be substituted for the pistachios.

A crunchy coating of finely ground pistachios transforms this vanilla-scented French toast into something truly extraordinary. Serve it with warm syrup, with your favorite jam, or with a quickly prepared Fresh Berry Compote (page 28).

4	large eggs, beaten
2	cups milk
1	tablespoon sugar
1	teaspoon vanilla extract
⅛	teaspoon freshly ground nutmeg
¼	teaspoon salt
8	(1-inch-thick) slices good-quality white bread, brioche, or egg bread such as challah
2	cups shelled pistachios, coarsely ground in a food processor fitted with the steel blade, or 2 cups slivered almonds
2	to 3 tablespoons unsalted butter
	Powdered sugar for dusting

1. Preheat the oven to 350°F. Butter one or two baking dishes large enough to accommodate the bread in one layer. In a large, wide bowl, whisk together the eggs, milk, sugar, vanilla, nutmeg, and salt.

2. Heat a large, heavy, nonstick skillet over medium-high heat or preheat a griddle. One by one, dip the bread into the egg mixture, turning it and making sure it is completely saturated. Carefully dip the slices into the ground pistachios, coating them evenly on both sides.

3. Add the butter to the hot pan and swirl the pan. When the butter foams, carefully transfer as many pistachio-coated slices as will fit in the pan without crowding. Brown on each side, about 2 minutes per side, and transfer to the baking dish. Place the baking dish in the oven and bake 15 minutes.

4. To serve, cut each slice diagonally in half and arrange the triangles on heated serving plates. Spoon powdered sugar into a fine-mesh sieve and tap the sieve over each serving to dust it attractively with sugar. Serve hot with jam, maple syrup, or Fresh Berry Compote (page 28).

Rolled French-Style Omelet

MAKES 1 SERVING

Wolfgang's EASY TIPS

➤ Omelets should be made to order, which is why this recipe serves one.

➤ It's easiest to make an omelet in a heavy, nonstick omelet pan.

➤ If your omelet pan does not have a nonstick coating, heat a tablespoon of olive oil in the pan before adding the butter.

➤ A perfect omelet should be soft and creamy inside. To assure this, don't use a pan that is too large.

An omelet is one of the simplest, quickest meals you can make. It can be plain, with no filling, or it can serve as a canvas for your own compositions—sautéed vegetables, diced ham or crumbled crisp bacon, cooked baby shrimp, smoked salmon, and, of course, cheeses. The result can be so satisfying that you don't have to serve it just for breakfast or brunch. Omelets make terrific light suppers and lunches.

2	to 3 large eggs	1	tablespoon extra-virgin olive oil, if using an omelet pan without a nonstick coating
⅛	teaspoon kosher salt		
	Freshly ground black pepper	1	tablespoon unsalted butter

1. Heat an 8-inch or 10-inch omelet pan over medium-high heat.

2. While the pan is heating, break the eggs into a mixing bowl, add the salt and a pinch of pepper, and use a wire whisk to beat the eggs until lightly frothy.

3. If using a pan without a nonstick coating, when you can feel that the pan is hot by carefully holding your hand an inch or so above its surface, add the olive oil. Once the oil is hot enough to swirl easily, carefully tilt and swivel the pan to coat the bottom well.

4. Add the butter to the pan. When the butter begins to foam, tilt and swirl the pan to evenly distribute it. Immediately add the eggs. Let them sit for about 10 seconds.

5. Grasp the pan by its handle (using a potholder if necessary to protect your hand) and move the pan forward and backward over the flame while stirring the eggs with a fork or wooden spoon so that the still-liquid egg slips beneath the cooked egg.

6. After 15 to 30 seconds, when the eggs are cooked on the bottom but still fairly moist on top, tilt the pan to about a 45-degree angle by raising the handle so that the cooked eggs fall and gather near the opposite end. Top the eggs with any prepared filling at this time. Hold the far edge of the pan over a heated serving plate and continue tipping the handle up so that the omelet folds over on itself, enclosing the filling, and rolls out of the pan onto the plate. Serve immediately.

Making a French-Style Omelet

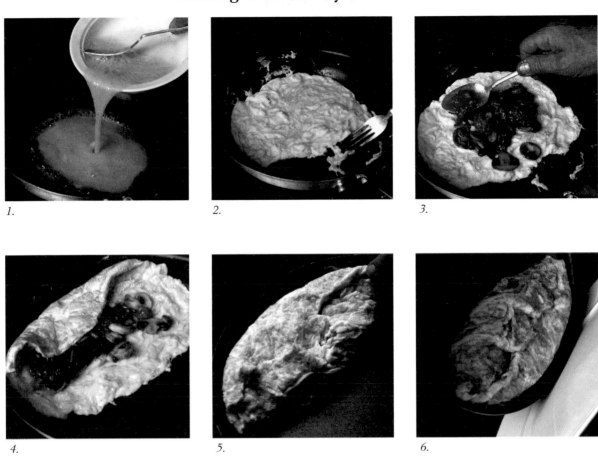

1.

2.

3.

4.

5.

6.

Eggs en Cocotte with Smoked Salmon and Horseradish Cream

MAKES 4 SERVINGS

Serving eggs for a special brunch presents a challenge to home cooks who want to enjoy their company rather than cooking omelets or scrambles to order in the kitchen. That's why I love to make eggs en cocotte. This French term for baked eggs takes its name from the little ovenproof ramekins in which they are made. The English call them shirred eggs. Whatever you call them, baked eggs take almost no time to put together, and the quantities in the recipe that follows multiply easily to serve a larger gathering.

1½	tablespoons unsalted butter, melted		Kosher salt and freshly ground white pepper
6	ounces thinly sliced smoked salmon	2	tablespoons freshly grated horseradish or drained prepared white horseradish
¾	cup heavy cream, chilled		Fresh chervil or parsley leaves for garnish
4	eggs		

1. Coat the insides of four ½-cup ramekins or baking dishes with the melted butter. Line the bottom and sides of each ramekin with the smoked salmon. Reserve 1 piece for garnish, and cut that piece into thin julienne. Top the salmon lining the ramekins with 1 tablespoon of the cream. At this point, if you're working in advance, cover the ramekins with plastic wrap and refrigerate.

2. Preheat the oven to 375°F. Bring a kettle of water to a boil. Line a baking dish large enough to hold the ramekins without touching with a sheet of parchment paper or wax paper. This will prevent the boiling water you'll pour into the dish from bubbling over into the ramekins during baking.

3. One at a time, break an egg into a bowl and transfer to a lined ramekin, taking care not to damage the yolk. Sprinkle each egg with salt and pepper to taste. Place the ramekins in the baking dish and cover with a sheet of buttered aluminum foil. Put the baking dish on the middle rack of the oven. With the oven rack pulled out, carefully pour the boiling water into the baking dish to come halfway up the sides of the ramekins. Carefully slide the rack into the oven and bake the eggs until their whites are set and the yolks are cooked through but still soft, 15 to 20 minutes.

4. While the eggs are cooking, put the remaining ½ cup heavy cream in a mixing bowl and, using a handheld mixer or a whisk, whip until it forms soft peaks when the beaters are lifted out. Stir in salt, white pepper, and horseradish to taste. Transfer the horseradish cream to a sauceboat or small serving bowl.

5. Carefully slide out the oven rack, transfer each ramekin to a serving plate, and garnish each serving with chervil or parsley leaves. Pass the horseradish cream at the table for guests to spoon into their ramekins.

Making Eggs en Cocotte

1.

2.

3.

4.

Savory Crêpes

MAKES 4 TO 6 SERVINGS

Wolfgang's EASY TIPS

➤ Use a nonstick crêpe pan with shallow, curved sides that allow you to flip the crêpes over easily. Traditional iron crêpe pans work beautifully too, as long as they are properly seasoned and never touch water. (Wipe iron pans clean with a paper towel after they cool; they should be used only for crêpes).

➤ For tender crêpes allow the batter to sit for an hour or more so the flour particles can soften.

➤ Crêpes are fun to make with children. But make sure an adult is on hand to supervise, keeping hands or loose clothing away from live flames, turning pot and pan handles toward the work surface so they're less likely to be accidentally knocked off the stove, and using dry pot holders to protect your hands.

➤ Savory crêpes can be used not only as a vehicle for a filling but can be cut into strips and used as a garnish for soup.

I bought my mother a nonstick crêpe pan as a Mother's Day present when I was ten years old, and she used it all the time. In Austria we would fill crêpes with jam and sprinkle them with powdered sugar or fill them with ice cream and drizzle on chocolate sauce. These were my two favorite versions of the Austrian-style stuffed pancakes called *Palatschinken*.

¾	cup all-purpose flour	3	large eggs
¼	teaspoon salt	3	tablespoons unsalted butter, melted
1	teaspoon sugar	1½	cups milk

1. Put the flour, salt, and sugar in the bowl of a food processor fitted with the steel blade and turn the processor on. With the machine running, add the eggs, 2 tablespoons of the melted butter, and the milk through the feed tube. Process for 1 minute. (You can also mix the batter in a blender.) Transfer to a bowl, cover with plastic, and allow to sit at room temperature for 1 hour, or refrigerate overnight.

2. Heat an 8-inch crêpe pan or omelet pan over medium-high heat until it feels hot when you hold your hand above it. Brush lightly with some of the remaining melted butter. Ladle in about 3 tablespoons of batter (½ ladleful) and tilt or swirl the pan to spread the batter evenly. Cook until the crêpe's surface is covered with bubbles and the edges can be easily lifted away from the pan so that you can see if the underside is golden. When the underside is golden, after about 2 minutes, flip the crêpe, using a thin spatula or, very carefully, your fingertips. Cook the other side for 30 seconds and transfer to a plate. Repeat with the remaining batter, stacking the crêpes as you go along. The recipe yields about fifteen 6-inch crêpes or ten to twelve 8-inch crêpes.

3. If you aren't using the crêpes right away, stack them between pieces of parchment or wax paper, wrap them in foil, and refrigerate or freeze.

Making and Filling Crêpes

1.

2.

3.

4.

5.

6.

Crêpes with Lemony Cheese Filling

MAKES 4 TO 6 SERVINGS

These crêpes remind me of the crêpes we used to enjoy for supper in Austria. Shortly before you are ready to serve, the crêpes are wrapped around a sweet cheese filling and baked with a custard glaze. Although we ate them for supper, they make a special brunch dish that's easy enough for a child to make for Mother's Day.

1	recipe crêpes (page 12)
1	egg
3	tablespoons sugar (more or less to taste)
1½	cups farmer's cheese
	Pinch of salt
1	teaspoon finely chopped lemon zest
1	tablespoon fresh lemon juice
½	teaspoon pure vanilla extract

For the custard glaze:

1	egg
2	tablespoons sugar
¾	cup heavy cream
1	tablespoon fresh lemon juice
	Confectioners' sugar for serving (optional)

1. Beat together the egg and sugar. Place a fine-mesh sieve over a bowl and press the cheese through using a sturdy spoon. Add the egg mixture, salt, lemon zest, lemon juice, and vanilla extract and mix together well.

2. About 45 minutes before serving, preheat the oven to 350°F. Butter one or two baking dishes that will accommodate the filled crêpes in a single layer. Lay a crêpe down with the undercooked side showing and place 2 tablespoons of filling across the diameter, leaving a small margin at the edges. Don't worry if the filling is runny; it will stiffen up when the crêpes are baked. Gently fold the edges over the filling, then roll up like an egg roll or blintz, or leave the ends open. Place side by side in the baking dish.

3. For the glaze, beat together the egg, sugar, cream, and lemon juice. Spoon over the crêpes. Place the crêpes in the oven and bake for 30 minutes or until nicely browned. Remove from the heat and serve, sprinkling with confectioners' sugar if you wish. Be careful when you take your first bite; they will be bubbling hot inside.

Wolfgang's EASY TIPS

➤ You can find farmer's cheese in the dairy section of most supermarkets. If you can't, use cottage cheese, but drain it in a cheesecloth-lined strainer for several hours or overnight before using.

➤ This is also excellent with the Raspberry Sauce on page 30.

Caramel-Pecan Cinnamon Rolls

MAKES 12 ROLLS

I grew up on wonderful Austrian pastries made with the brioche-type dough in this recipe. But for sheer decadence, nothing quite matches the American sticky bun. These nutty rolls are one variation. The easiest pan to make them in is a large, heavy muffin pan. But for a more dramatic presentation, try baking them in a round pan or casserole as instructed below.

For the dough:

1	cup milk, heated to lukewarm (80°F to 90°F)
2½	teaspoons (1 package) active dry yeast
⅓	cup sugar
4	cups bread flour or all-purpose flour
3	large eggs
1	teaspoon kosher salt
8	tablespoons (1 stick) unsalted butter, at room temperature

For the topping:

6	tablespoons (¾ stick) unsalted butter
½	cup light brown sugar
2	tablespoons honey
½	vanilla bean, scraped
1½	cups pecan halves

For the filling:

4	tablespoons (½ stick) unsalted butter, melted
½	cup sugar
2	teaspoons ground cinnamon
1	cup coarsely chopped pecans
2	tablespoons milk, at room temperature for brushing before baking

1. For the dough, combine the milk and the yeast in the bowl of a stand mixer and stir to dissolve. Add the sugar and stir together until the sugar is dissolved. Add 2 cups of the flour and mix together using the paddle attachment of your mixer (or with a wooden spoon in a bowl). When the mixture is smooth, cover the bowl tightly with plastic wrap and allow to stand for 1 hour.

2. Add the eggs to the sponge, one at a time, and beat with the paddle attachment until incorporated, scraping down the sides after each addition. Add the remaining flour and the salt. Change to the dough hook and knead at low speed for 1 minute, then at medium speed for 5 minutes, or until the dough comes away from the sides of the bowl.

3. With the mixer at medium speed, add the room-temperature butter, 2 tablespoons at a time, and continue to knead until each addition is incorporated. Turn the dough out onto a lightly floured surface and knead a few times by hand. The dough should be smooth and elastic. Shape into a ball. Rinse and oil your bowl,

Wolfgang's EASY TIPS

➤ This type of dough—brioche—is easiest to make in a stand mixer.

➤ Make sure your ingredients are warm or at room temperature, that the dough is tightly covered with plastic, and that it has a warm, draft-free spot in which to rise.

➤ The cinnamon rolls can be frozen. Thaw them in a microwave as you would a frozen muffin.

➤ To scrape the seeds from the vanilla bean, use the tip of a sharp paring knife to cut the bean in half lengthwise. Scrape the tiny seeds from the pod by running the tip of the knife down the inside of the pod.

return the dough to it, rounded side down first, then rounded side up. Cover the bowl tightly with plastic wrap and place in a warm spot to rise for 1½ hours, or until doubled.

4. When the dough ball has doubled in size, use your fist to punch it down in the bowl. Cover again and set in a warm place to rest for 15 minutes.

5. Meanwhile, make the topping.

If using a muffin tin for the rolls: In a heavy saucepan melt the butter and stir in the light brown sugar, honey, and seeds from the vanilla bean. Stir in the pecan halves and mix well. Spray the muffin tins with pan spray, and spread the mixture evenly over the bottom of each cup.

If using a round frying pan or casserole for the rolls: Combine the butter with the light brown sugar, honey, and seeds from the vanilla bean in a 12-inch chicken-fryer or metal casserole. Stir over medium heat until the butter and sugar have melted. Stir in the 1½ cups of pecan halves and mix well. Spread the mixture evenly over the bottom of the pan, remove from the heat, and set aside.

6. To shape the rolls, lightly flour a work surface. With a floured rolling pin, roll out the dough ball to a rectangle measuring about 9 x 18 inches. For the filling, brush evenly with the melted butter. Combine the sugar and cinnamon and sprinkle over the butter. Sprinkle the chopped pecans evenly over the surface and roll up the dough, starting at a long edge, like a jelly roll. With a sharp serrated knife, cut the log crosswise into twelve 1½-inch thick slices. Arrange them on top of the mixture in the muffin pans or in the pan or casserole. Cover with pan-sprayed plastic wrap and leave at warm room temperature to rise for about 30 minutes. Meanwhile, preheat the oven to 400°F.

7. Uncover the muffin tin or pan. Brush the rolls with milk and bake for 10 minutes at 400°F. Turn the heat down to 375°F and bake 15 to 20 minutes longer, until puffed and golden brown.

8. Unmolding the rolls:

Muffin tins: Place a sheet of parchment on a baking sheet. Remove the buns from the oven and invert immediately onto the parchment. Leave them alone for about 30 seconds, then lift the muffin tin. Do not touch the caramel—it's very hot. Serve the rolls warm.

Pan or casserole: Remove from the oven and invert a large heatproof plate over the casserole. Using oven gloves or pads, hold the casserole and plate securely together with both hands and invert them onto a work surface. Leave them alone for about 30 seconds to give the rolls and their topping time to unmold. Then lift off the casserole and use a spatula to dislodge any of the pecan mixture still sticking to the pan and transfer it to the rolls. Serve the rolls warm.

Chocolate and Orange Swirl Muffins

MAKES 12 MUFFINS

These cake-like muffins could just as easily be in the dessert chapter, but they are certainly welcome on a brunch buffet table.

1½	cups all-purpose flour	½	cup buttermilk
½	cup sugar	½	cup orange juice
2	teaspoons baking powder	1	teaspoon vanilla extract
¼	teaspoon salt	1	teaspoon orange zest
1	egg	2	tablespoons cocoa powder
½	cup vegetable oil or melted butter	½	cup bittersweet chocolate, chopped into chips

1. Preheat the oven to 375°F. Spray muffin tins with nonstick cooking spray and, if you wish, line with cupcake liners. Spray the liners.

2. Sift together the all-purpose flour, sugar, baking powder, and salt.

3. In a separate bowl beat together the egg, oil or melted butter, buttermilk, orange juice, vanilla, and orange zest. Pour the wet mixture over the dry and mix together just until moistened.

4. Divide the batter in half. Sift the cocoa powder into one of the bowls and fold in with half of the chocolate chips. Fold the remaining chocolate chips into the other bowl of batter.

5. Drop spoonfuls of batter into the prepared muffin tins, alternating the orange and chocolate batters. Fill the cups two-thirds full.

6. Bake 12 minutes and turn the pan around. Bake another 5 to 8 minutes, or until a toothpick or knife inserted into the center comes out clean. Remove from the oven and cool in the pans for 10 minutes before removing.

Wolfgang's EASY TIPS

➤ Use the best cocoa and chocolate you can find. I like Penzey's dark cocoa powder and Valrhona bittersweet chocolate.

➤ If you don't have muffin papers, just spray the muffin tins with oil.

Braided Egg-and-Butter Loaf

MAKES 2 LARGE LOAVES

Wolfgang's EASY TIPS

➤ An electric stand mixer will really help when it comes to kneading this large amount of somewhat sticky dough.

➤ If you need to go out, you can slow down the rising process by refrigerating the dough. Refrigerated dough will take approximately 4 times longer to double in size.

➤ This bread freezes well. Wrap airtight in plastic and in foil.

This recipe resembles challah, the rich Jewish loaf traditionally baked for the Sabbath. Unlike challah, however, it includes milk and butter for even richer results. If you want to observe Jewish dietary laws with absolute strictness, not mixing dairy and meat, substitute water for the milk and a half cup of vegetable oil for the butter.

For the dough:

1	tablespoon plus 2 teaspoons (2 packets) active dry yeast
2	cups warm milk (80°F to 90°F)
⅓	cup sugar
6	cups bread or all-purpose flour, plus additional for kneading
6	tablespoons (¾ stick) unsalted butter, melted

3	eggs, at room temperature
2	teaspoons salt
	Cornmeal for the baking sheets

For the egg wash:

1	egg
1	tablespoon water
	Poppy seeds or sesame seeds (optional)

1. Combine the yeast and 1 cup of the milk in the bowl of a stand mixer (or in a large bowl if mixing by hand) and stir to dissolve. Add the sugar and 2 cups of the flour and mix together using the paddle attachment. When the mixture is smooth, cover the bowl with plastic wrap and leave in a warm spot for 45 minutes to an hour, until the mixture is bubbly.

2. Add the remaining warm milk to the sponge and beat in the melted butter. Add the eggs, one at a time, and beat to incorporate. Combine 4 of the remaining cups of flour with the salt and add all at once to the mixture. Mix together using the paddle attachment, then switch to the dough hook. Knead on low speed for 2 minutes then at medium speed for 8 minutes until a smooth dough has been achieved. Add additional flour as needed. Scrape the dough out onto a lightly floured work surface and finish kneading by hand, about 1 minute. Shape the dough into a ball.

(If kneading the dough by hand, scrape it onto a floured work surface. Sprinkle additional flour over the dough and begin kneading it, pushing it forward with the heel of your hand, folding the pushed portion back over onto the dough, and then giving the dough a quarter turn. Continue this process, sprinkling on more flour as necessary, until the dough feels smooth and elastic.)

3. Clean and dry your bowl. Butter or oil it and place the dough in it, rounded side down first, then rounded side up. Cover the bowl with plastic and set it aside in a warm, draft-free place until the dough has doubled in bulk, 1½ to 2 hours.

4. Turn out the dough onto a lightly floured work surface and cut it in half. Cut each half into three equal pieces. Roll each piece of dough back and forth beneath your fingers to form an even strand 18 inches long. Pinch the ends of the three strands together and stretch them out parallel to, and a few inches apart from, each other; then, braid them by alternately lifting the right-hand strand over the middle one and then the left-hand strand over the middle one. Finally, pinch the other ends together and tuck both ends of the loaf neatly underneath. Repeat with the remaining three strands to make a second loaf.

5. Sprinkle a large baking sheet with the cornmeal. Transfer the loaves to the sheet, leaving several inches between them, or use two baking sheets. Beat together the egg and water and gently brush the loaves. Sprinkle with poppy seeds or sesame seeds if you wish. Cover the loaves with pan-sprayed plastic or with one or two clean, damp kitchen towels and leave them to rise until nearly doubled in bulk, about 1 hour. If you are using two baking sheets and have only one oven, place one of the baking sheets in the refrigerator. Remove it after 1 hour.

6. Thirty minutes before baking, preheat the oven to 350°F. Position the topmost rack in the middle of the oven. Place the baking sheet on the middle rack and bake the loaves until they are deep mahogany brown and sound hollow when rapped on the bottom with a knuckle, about 45 minutes. Transfer the loaves to wire racks and cool to room temperature before slicing and serving.

Banana Walnut Quick Bread

MAKES 1 (5 X 9-INCH) LOAF

American quick breads were a revelation to me when I came to the States. This age-old favorite is an easy way to add a delicious fresh-baked treat to your breakfast or brunch.

1	cup shelled walnut halves or pieces	2	large eggs
2½	cups all-purpose flour	¼	cup granulated sugar
2	teaspoons baking powder	½	cup light brown sugar
1	teaspoon baking soda	3	very ripe bananas, puréed in a food processor
1	teaspoon ground cinnamon	¼	cup vegetable or canola oil
½	teaspoon freshly ground nutmeg	1	teaspoon vanilla extract
½	teaspoon salt	½	cup milk

1. Preheat the oven to 350°F. Spray a 5 x 9-inch bread pan with pan spray and line the bottom with parchment. Spray the parchment.

2. Spread the walnuts evenly on a baking sheet or in a baking dish and toast them in the oven until they are fragrant and lightly browned, about 10 minutes. Remove from the oven, allow to cool, and chop coarsely.

3. Sift together the flour, baking powder, baking soda, cinnamon, nutmeg, and salt.

4. Combine the eggs and sugars in the bowl of a stand mixer or in a large bowl with a hand mixer, and beat at high speed until the mixture is thick and forms a ribbon when drizzled from a spatula, 2 to 3 minutes. Add the puréed bananas, oil, vanilla, and milk, and blend well. Scrape down the sides of the bowl. At low speed, add the flour mixture in three additions, scraping down the sides of the bowl between each addition. Fold in the nuts with a spatula.

5. Scrape the batter into the prepared pan and place in the oven. Bake 1 hour and 15 minutes, or until a tester inserted into the center comes out clean. Remove the pan from the oven and allow the loaf to cool in the pan for 10 minutes, then reverse onto a rack. Allow to cool completely before slicing. For the best flavor, wrap airtight and don't slice until the next day.

French Bread

MAKES 2 LOAVES

Although it's not difficult to find good French bread in America now, it's fun to make your own loaves. This dough is easy to work with.

2½	teaspoons (1 packet) active dry yeast	3	to 3½ cups bread or all-purpose flour, divided
1	teaspoon sugar	¼	cup semolina flour
1½	cups warm water (80°F to 90°F)	2	teaspoons salt

1. Combine the yeast and warm water in the bowl of a stand mixer or in a large bowl, add the sugar and whisk together until the yeast and sugar have dissolved. Leave it until the yeast begins to cloud, about 2 minutes. Add 1¾ cups of the bread or all-purpose flour and beat at medium-low speed for 4 minutes to incorporate air into the spongy dough. Cover the bowl with plastic wrap and leave it to rise in a warm, draft-free place for as little as 30 minutes or as long as 2½ hours; the longer it sits, the more open-textured the final bread will be.

2. Combine the semolina flour with 1¼ cups of the remaining bread or all-purpose flour and the salt. Add to the spongy dough and beat together with the paddle attachment just to combine the ingredients. Switch to the dough hook and knead at medium speed for about 10 minutes, holding onto the machine if necessary. Add more flour as necessary. The dough should be soft and elastic. (If kneading by hand, add the flour a cup at a time, and when the dough can be scraped out onto your work surface, flour your work surface and scrape out the dough. Knead for 10 minutes, adding flour as necessary.) Scrape the dough out of your bowl onto a lightly floured work surface and finish kneading by hand, about 1 minute. Shape the dough into a ball.

3. Clean and dry your bowl, spray it with pan spray and put the dough in it, rounded side down first then rounded side up. Cover the bowl with plastic wrap and leave it in a warm, draft-free place until the dough rises to slightly more than double its bulk, 1½ to 2 hours.

Wolfgang's EASY TIPS

➤ If you need to go out before the dough is ready, place it in the refrigerator.

➤ An electric stand mixer with a dough hook attachment makes this a very easy bread to make.

➤ You can make great-tasting variations of this bread by adding herbs like rosemary, thyme, or oregano or ingredients like sun-dried tomatoes or olives to the dough.

4. With a fist, punch down the dough in the bowl. Reach to the back of the bowl under the dough and pull the bottom of the dough up and into the center. Repeat the same action at the front of the bowl. The dough is now ready to shape.

5. Turn out the dough onto a lightly floured board and cut it in half. Shape the dough into a rectangle and place it lengthwise on your work surface. Roll tightly like a sausage or fold one long side towards the center and tuck it in. Then fold the other side over and pinch a seam down the length of the loaf. Roll the dough with both hands to form a long, thick sausage shape. Tuck in and pinch together the ends. Cover with plastic and allow to relax for 10 minutes.

6. Line a baking sheet large enough to hold both loaves with parchment. Spray the paper with nonstick spray and sprinkle with semolina or cornmeal. Uncover the loaves and transfer them to the baking sheet. Cover with pan-sprayed plastic and a damp towel, and let the loaves rise in a warm place until slightly more than doubled, 1 to 1½ hours.

7. A half hour before baking, preheat the oven to 450°F, preferably with a baking stone in it. Position the rack in the middle. Holding a sharp razor or a very sharp knife almost parallel to the surface of the loaves, make three or four diagonal shallow slashes across each loaf. Spray the loaves with water and bake for 10 minutes. Reduce the heat to 375°F and bake until they are deep golden brown and sound hollow when their undersides are rapped with a knuckle, 30 to 35 minutes. For a crunchier crust, spray a fine mist of fresh water from a spray bottle into the oven two or three times during the final 10 minutes of baking. Transfer the loaves to a wire rack to cool before serving.

Making French Bread

1. Sponge

2. Mixing the dough

3. Finished dough

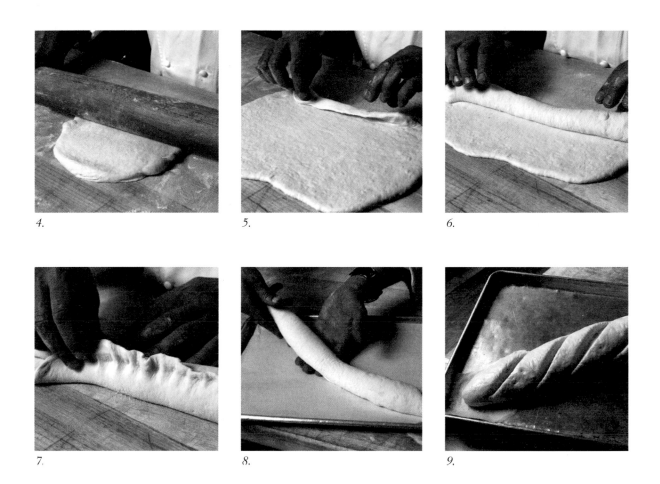

4.

5.

6.

7.

8.

9.

Brioche

MAKES 2 LOAVES

This recipe for brioche comes from my pastry chef, Sherry Yard. Brioche is a rich, buttery breakfast bread that is much loved in France. It has the added value of being the perfect choice for French toast, once the bread goes stale.

Wolfgang's EASY TIPS

➤ Butter must be softened for it to work into the dough. You need to remove it from the refrigerator to allow it to soften, but it should remain cool. Don't let it get so warm that it's mushy. It should yield when you press on it but your finger shouldn't go right through. The temperature of butter that is ready for brioche dough is 65°F to 68°F.

➤ When checking the temperature of the bread stick the thermometer into the bottom of the dough so you won't see a hole.

For the sponge:

2½ teaspoons (1 packet) active dry yeast

½ cup milk, at room temperature

¼ cup sugar

½ cup all-purpose flour

For the dough:

1 cup all-purpose flour

2 cups bread flour

1¼ teaspoons salt

4 large eggs, at room temperature and slightly beaten

½ pound (2 sticks) unsalted butter, softened but still cold (see tip)

For the egg wash:

1 large egg

Pinch of salt (less than ⅛ teaspoon)

1 tablespoon water

1. For the sponge, in the bowl of an electric stand mixer combine the yeast and milk and whisk until the yeast is dissolved. Stir in the sugar and all-purpose flour, forming a thick batter. Cover with plastic wrap and place in a warm environment for 30 to 45 minutes, or until bubbles form.

2. For the dough, place the all-purpose flour, bread flour, and salt on top of the sponge. Add the eggs. Put the bowl on the mixer fitted with the paddle attachment. Mix at low speed for 2 minutes, or until the eggs are absorbed. Increase the speed to medium and knead the dough for 5 minutes. Hold onto the mixer when necessary since it may jump around.

3. Continue to mix on medium speed while you gradually add the softened butter, 2 tablespoons at a time. Stop the mixer and scrape down the sides occasionally. Turn the speed back up to medium and knead until the dough is shiny and smooth, about 5 minutes. Scrape out the dough, wash and dry the bowl, and then coat it lightly with oil.

4. Place the dough in the lightly oiled bowl rounded side down first then rounded side up. Cover with plastic wrap and set it aside to rise at room temperature until doubled in size, about 2 hours.

5. When the dough doubles in size press down to deflate, folding it over itself 2 or 3 times. Cover it with plastic wrap again and place it in the refrigerator for a minimum of 4 hours or overnight.

6. Coat the insides of two loaf pans with nonstick cooking spray. Remove the dough from the refrigerator. Turn it out onto a lightly floured work surface. Divide the dough in half. Cover one piece with plastic wrap while you shape the other one. Dust the top of the dough lightly with all-purpose flour. With a rolling pin roll the dough the length of the pan and double the width. With your hands, starting from the short side, roll the dough up jelly-roll style. Pinch together the seam. Place the dough seam side down in the prepared pan. Gently work the dough into the pan with your fingers so it touches all sides. The dough should fill the mold halfway.

7. Cover the dough with oiled plastic wrap and set it aside at room temperature until it has doubled in size and filled the molds completely, about 1½ hours. Towards the end of the proofing preheat the oven to 400°F and adjust the oven rack to the middle.

8. For the egg wash, whisk together the egg, salt, and water in a small bowl. Gently brush the surface of the dough with the egg wash. Place the loaves in the oven and bake 10 minutes. Reduce the temperature to 350°F and bake 30 minutes longer. When finished the dough will have a dark mahogany crust, an internal temperature of 180°F, and a hollow sound when thumped on the bottom.

9. Remove the brioche from the loaf pan as soon as it comes out of the oven and set it on a cooling rack. When cool, the loaf can be wrapped tightly in plastic and frozen for up to two weeks. To use a frozen loaf, defrost at room temperature, wrap in aluminum foil, and refresh in a 350°F oven for 10 minutes. Tightly wrapped loaves will stay fresh at room temperature for two days.

Fresh Berry Compote

Made in a matter of minutes, this simple sauce can be served hot or cold with Savory Crêpes (page 12) or Pistachio-Crusted Vanilla French Toast (page 6). It's also great spooned over your favorite ice cream or stirred into plain yogurt. Use the ripest berries you can find.

3	cups fresh berries, rinsed	1	teaspoon lemon juice
½	cup sugar		

1. Combine all the ingredients in a nonreactive medium saucepan and bring to a simmer over medium heat. Stir frequently until the sugar dissolves and the berries give up their juices. Continue simmering, stirring occasionally, until the juices thicken to a syrupy consistency, about 5 minutes more. Remove from the heat and chill or serve warm.

Brandied Dried Apricot Jam

You'll find it amazing that something so easy to make could taste so delicious. Serve this as a filling for Savory Crêpes (page 12), as a topping for blinis, as an accompaniment for Pistachio-Crusted Vanilla French Toast (page 6), as a spread for breakfast breads, or even as a topping for good vanilla ice cream.

1 cup firmly packed, dried apricots, cut into small pieces	¼ cup dry white wine
1½ cups water	1 cup sugar
¼ cup apricot or peach brandy	1 cinnamon stick

1. Put the apricot pieces in a mixing bowl, bring the water to a boil, and pour over the apricots. Add the brandy and wine, cover with plastic wrap, and leave in the refrigerator to soak for at least 30 minutes to 1 hour or for as long as overnight.

2. Transfer the apricots and their soaking liquid to a nonreactive saucepan. Add the sugar and the cinnamon stick and bring to a boil over high heat. Reduce the heat and simmer, stirring occasionally, until the mixture has a thick, jam-like consistency, about 45 minutes to an hour. Remove from the heat and allow to cool.

3. Transfer the mixture to a bowl or storage container, remove and discard the cinnamon stick, cover, and refrigerate.

Raspberry Sauce

MAKES 4 TO 6 SERVINGS

This smooth, seedless berry sauce is more tart than Fresh Berry Compote (page 28). You can serve this sauce with Savory Crêpes (page 12) or Pistachio-Crusted Vanilla French Toast (page 6). Or you can use it as a syrup-like sauce for ice cream.

2	cups fresh or frozen raspberries
3	to 4 tablespoons sugar
1	teaspoon lime juice

1. Put all the ingredients in a small nonreactive saucepan and cook over medium-high heat, stirring frequently, for 5 to 10 minutes, or until the berries have given up their juices and are thick and syrupy.

2. Place a fine-mesh sieve over a mixing bowl. Pour the berry mixture into the sieve and with a rubber spatula or the back of a spoon, press the fruit through the sieve to strain out the seeds. Cover the bowl with plastic wrap and refrigerate until serving time.

Wolfgang's EASY TIPS

➤ Use the back of a large cooking spoon to force the raspberry sauce through a sieve.

➤ The sauce freezes well for several months.

APPETIZERS, SOUPS, AND SALADS

I've always believed that when you plan a dinner with more than one course, the first and the last courses are the most memorable. The appetizer course sets the tone for your dinner. If I'm serving an elegant meal I'd begin with the Rich Mussel Soup on page 66 or My Favorite Spring Pea Soup on page 62. If I'm serving an ethnic meal with Asian overtones, I might choose one of the satays on pages 46–49. For a rustic country meal, nothing fits the bill better than a variety of garlic crostini with assorted toppings.

It's very important that the first course be seasoned well; this is when people should start talking about the food. Presentation is also important because the beginning of the meal is the first opportunity your guests will have to feast with their eyes. Remember that the seasons are important. You don't want to serve a really rich or hearty soup like the Robust Minestrone with Lentils and Rice (page 60) on a hot summer day, any more than you'd serve a gazpacho (page 68) or scallop ceviche (page 42) if it's freezing outside.

Today more than ever people like to make a meal out of appetizers. Because I live in California and our food has such a variety of influences, giving an ethnic twist to the first course is always exciting to me. With smaller dishes you can have a diverse meal, serving a few of these appetizers. Or dinner could be just one of these soups served with a simple green salad and some crusty bread.

But if you're serving a multicourse menu, it's important that you serve small portions so that you can whet your guests' appetites without filling them up. When they finish their appetizer, they should want more. Then you know they're ready for the main course.

Artichokes Stuffed
with Fresh Herbs, Breadcrumbs, and Parmesan

MAKES 4 SERVINGS

When you stuff artichokes with breadcrumbs and herbs, you don't have to bother with a dipping sauce, because each leaf is cooked with its own condiment. These make a great impression at the start of a meal, and you could also eat them as a main course. I love using mint to flavor the breadcrumb mixture, but feel free to substitute other fresh herbs that you like, such as flat-leaf Italian parsley or dill weed.

2	cups chicken broth	2	tablespoons extra-virgin olive oil
2	tablespoons lemon juice	2	tablespoons freshly grated Parmesan cheese
	Pinch of salt	1	teaspoon kosher salt
4	jumbo artichokes	1	teaspoon freshly ground pepper
2	garlic cloves		
1	cup fresh breadcrumbs	4	tablespoons unsalted butter, cut into pieces
2	tablespoons chopped fresh mint or basil		

1. Combine the chicken broth, lemon juice, and a pinch of salt in a saucepan large enough to accommodate the artichokes, or in a pressure cooker. With a sharp stainless steel knife, cut off the stems flush with the bases of the artichokes and cut off the top third of the globe. With kitchen scissors, trim off the sharp tips of the remaining artichoke leaves. As you finish trimming each artichoke, place it upside down in the liquid; the acidity of the lemon juice will help keep the cut surfaces from discoloring.

2. Bring the liquid in the pot to a boil, reduce the heat, cover, and cook the artichokes for 30 to 35 minutes, or until they are just about tender. Remove from the cooking liquid and allow to cool until you can handle them.

3. While the artichokes are cooking, make the stuffing. Chop the garlic in a food processor with a stainless steel blade. Scrape the sides of the bowl and add the breadcrumbs, mint or basil, olive oil, Parmesan, salt, and pepper. Pulse several times to combine the ingredients well. Carefully remove the blade and put it aside, leaving the mixture in the work bowl.

4. When the artichokes are cool enough to handle, place them right side up on a work surface. Spread the leaves apart and distribute the bread mixture between the leaves and inside the middle of the artichokes. Pack the mixture in tightly. Return the artichokes to the liquid in the pot with the stuffing side up. Bring to a boil,

Wolfgang's EASY TIPS

➤ Choose artichokes with tightly closed leaves that show no cracks.

➤ I find that kitchen scissors are the perfect tool for trimming the sharp tips of the artichoke leaves quickly and easily.

➤ Look for fresh herbs in farmers' markets.

➤ When working with artichokes, have an acidic liquid to place the artichokes in after you cut them so that they won't discolor. The chicken broth and lemon juice work well in this recipe. In other dishes you would begin by filling a bowl with cold water and adding to it the juice of half a lemon. Have the other half lemon handy for rubbing the cut surfaces, and place the prepared artichokes in the bowl of water as you go along so that they don't discolor.

➤ You can cook the stuffed artichokes in a pressure cooker in just 10 minutes of cooking time (see the instructions on page 34).

reduce the heat, cover tightly, and simmer for 10 minutes, or until you can easily pull off a leaf.

5. Preheat the oven to 200°F. Carefully transfer the artichokes from the pot to an ovenproof platter. Brush them with olive oil and sprinkle breadcrumbs on top. Put them in the oven to keep warm while you complete the sauce.

6. For the sauce, strain the cooking liquid through a sieve into a small saucepan. Over high heat bring the liquid to a boil and continue cooking until it has reduced by half, about 10 minutes. Reduce the heat to medium and whisk in the butter piece by piece. Continue simmering for a few minutes until the sauce reaches a syrupy consistency. Remove the artichokes from the oven and place them on individual serving plates. Spoon the sauce over each artichoke and serve immediately.

Using a pressure cooker: Stuff the artichokes before cooking. Following the manufacturer's instructions secure the pressure cooker lid and bring it to high pressure. Set the timer, reduce the heat to low, and cook the artichokes for 10 minutes. When finished, follow the manufacturer's instructions to release the pressure safely. Proceed as directed above.

Preparing the Artichokes

1.

2.

3.

4.

5.

Finishing the Stuffed Artichokes

6.

7.

8.

Roasted Garlic Crostini with Assorted Toppings

Wolfgang's EASY TIPS

➤ The roasted garlic will keep for up to 3 days, covered, in the refrigerator.

➤ In addition to using the garlic for the crostini, try mixing it into stir-fried vegetables and spooning it onto pizzas; stir it into risottos or your mashed potatoes; add it to sauces for meat, poultry, seafood, or pasta; or purée it with butter to make the best garlic bread you can imagine.

I grew up only about 280 miles west of Transylvania, as the bat flies. So maybe my mother cooked with so much garlic to keep the vampires away from my sisters, my brother, and me. Actually, Austrians, like many Europeans, love the powerful bulb, and as a child I ate more than my share of it in soups, stews, sautés, roasts, and other savory dishes. Only as a professional chef did I learn the secret of roasting garlic. Because its texture is buttery and rich, I like to spread it on crostini. Once you've spread the roasted garlic over your toasts you can choose from a number of toppings.

For the roasted garlic:

4   heads garlic

¼   cup olive oil

For the crostini:

12   slices of baguette or country-style Italian bread, sliced at a 45-degree angle about ½ inch thick

¼   cup extra-virgin olive oil

     Pureed garlic from 4 whole roasted heads of garlic (see above)

     Assorted topping options:

     Shaved Parmesan, dry jack, or Gruyère cheese

     Fresh, creamy goat cheese, at room temperature

Roasted red bell peppers, home-roasted or bottled, cut into thin strips

Prepared tapenade (black olive and anchovy paste)

Oil-packed sun-dried tomatoes, cut into thin strips

Capers, drained

Roma tomatoes, thinly sliced, or halved, seeded, and diced

Fresh basil leaves, cut into fine julienne strips or left whole

Crushed red pepper flakes

Balsamic vinegar

Thinly sliced prosciutto

Anchovy fillets packed in olive oil, drained

Fresh mozzarella cheese, sliced

1. Preheat the oven to 375°F. Put the garlic in a roasting pan and drizzle on the olive oil. Toss to coat thoroughly. Bake for 50 to 60 minutes, or until the garlic bulbs are very tender but not overly brown. Test by carefully giving a bulb a gentle squeeze while protecting your hand with a folded kitchen towel or an oven glove. Remove from the oven and allow to cool.

2. Using a sharp serrated knife, cut each head of garlic crosswise in half midway between its leaf and root ends to expose all the cloves inside. Their pulp will be golden brown and as soft as butter. You

can squeeze it out of each half by hand or scoop it out with a small spoon or knife. Transfer the roasted garlic to a small bowl, pour in any olive oil from the baking dish, and stir and mash with a fork to form a smooth purée. You'll have ⅓ to ½ cup of purée, depending on the size of the garlic heads.

3. To make the Roasted Garlic Crostini, preheat the oven to 375°F. Brush the bread slices with the olive oil and arrange them on a baking sheet. Bake them until golden, 12 to 15 minutes. Remove them from the oven and let them cool to room temperature. Spread the puréed roasted garlic evenly on the tops of the crostini. Top the crostini with any of the options listed above, or make an assortment. Spread some with 1 tablespoon each of goat cheese; then decorate the cheese with strips of roasted bell pepper or a mixture of sun-dried tomato strips and capers, or a smear of tapenade. In place of the goat cheese, top others with diced tomato tossed with some fresh basil, a pinch of crushed red pepper flakes, and a drizzle of balsamic vinegar; with prosciutto and Parmesan cheese; with anchovy fillets and freshly ground black pepper; or with slices of Roma tomato and fresh mozzarella, topped with fresh basil leaves.

Potato Pancakes with Smoked Sturgeon

MAKES 4 SERVINGS, 12 TO 14 LATKES

Wolfgang's EASY TIPS

➤ To ensure the crispest possible results, remove as much liquid as possible from the shredded potatoes and onions. The moment you've finished shredding them, pick them up by the handful and squeeze hard to extract the liquid. You can get even more liquid out if you wrap the potatoes and onions in a clean kitchen towel, twist the towel at both ends and squeeze.

➤ Cook the pancakes right away so the shredded potatoes don't discolor, resulting in gray pancakes.

➤ The smaller the latke, the easier it is to get a really crispy result. That's why I drop the mixture by tablespoons into the hot oil. However, you can also make a big potato galette in an 8-inch pan like the photo on the right.

Hanukkah isn't the only time of year for crisp potato pancakes, or latkes. The irresistible crispy rounds are delicious for all kinds of winter meals and in all kinds of ways, from simple appetizers to side dishes to main courses. These small, crisp latkes make a star opener topped with sour cream or crème fraîche and dill and sprinkled with smoked sturgeon. You can add a little paddlefish caviar or salmon roe to the topping, or if you're feeling extravagant, some nice osetra caviar. Of course they could always be served up at Hanukkah in the traditional way, with applesauce and sour cream.

1 **pound russet baking potatoes, peeled**	½ **cup crème fraîche or sour cream**
1 **small onion, peeled**	1 **teaspoon minced fresh dill**
1 **egg, beaten**	**Lemon juice**
2 **tablespoons all-purpose flour**	½ **pound smoked sturgeon, separated into large flakes, skin and bones removed (you may substitute smoked whitefish, trout, or smoked salmon)**
½ **teaspoon baking powder**	
¾ **teaspoon kosher salt**	
¼ **teaspoon freshly ground black pepper**	
Cooking oil, such as canola, peanut, or safflower	

1. Using the large holes of a box grater/shredder or the grating disk on a food processor, shred the potatoes into a mixing bowl. Grate in the onion.

2. Line a large bowl with a clean kitchen towel. Transfer the mixture to the towel-lined bowl, twist the towel around it and squeeze out as much liquid as you can (alternatively you can pick the mixture up by handfuls and squeeze dry). Transfer to another bowl. Add the egg, flour, baking powder, salt, and pepper. Stir with a fork until well blended.

3. Heat about ¼ inch of oil in a large, heavy skillet or in an electric fryer set at 350°F until it ripples and feels quite hot when you hold your hand over it. With a metal tablespoon, carefully place a spoonful of the mixture into the hot oil. Press down on the mixture with an offset spatula to form an evenly thick pancake about 3 inches in diameter. Add more spoonfuls, taking care not to overcrowd the skillet. Cook the pancakes until golden brown, 2 to 3 minutes per side, turning them over carefully with a slotted

metal spatula. Transfer to a tray or platter lined with paper towels to drain. Continue with the remaining mixture. If not serving right away, allow to cool completely. When ready to serve, preheat the oven to 400°F. Place the potatoes on a baking sheet and heat in the oven until crisp, about 10 minutes.

4. Meanwhile, in a small bowl, stir together the crème fraîche or sour cream and dill. Season to taste with lemon juice, salt, and pepper.

5. To serve, transfer the hot potato pancakes to a platter. Spoon a small dollop of the crème fraîche mixture onto each pancake and top with flakes of sturgeon. Serve immediately.

Wolfgang's EASY TIPS

➤ You can make potato pancakes in advance. Leave the cooked pancakes at room temperature and when guests start to arrive, preheat the oven to 400°F. Spread out the pancakes on a large, dry baking sheet, in batches if necessary, taking care not to overlap them. Bake them until they are once again hot and crispy, about 10 minutes.

Countertop Grilled Eggplant Parmesan

This is a terrific modern—and healthy—take on Eggplant Parmesan. The traditional dish can be very heavy since the eggplant is usually breaded and fried before being topped with tomato sauce and cheese. Here no oil is required. The eggplant slices are grilled on both sides in minutes in a countertop panini maker or double-sided indoor grill. Use your favorite marinara sauce, whether it comes out of your own saucepan or a container from your supermarket's refrigerated case or pasta sauce aisle. I like to serve a little extra sauce on the side and garnish with pretty, fresh basil leaves.

2 to 3 tablespoons olive oil (if cooking in a sauté pan)

1½ cups good-quality marinara sauce, homemade (page 216) or commercial

2 large eggs, beaten

1 large, firm eggplant, trimmed and cut crosswise into an even number of ½-inch slices

1 cup freshly grated Parmesan cheese

1 teaspoon Italian seasoning blend or a mixture of oregano and thyme

1½ cups shredded mozzarella cheese or mozzarella-fontina mixture

Fresh basil or oregano leaves for garnish

1. Preheat a countertop panini maker or double-sided electric grill, or heat 2 tablespoons of the olive oil in a large nonstick sauté pan. Set aside ½ cup of the marinara sauce in a saucepan.

2. Meanwhile, beat the eggs in a mixing bowl. Add the eggplant slices and turn them in the egg to coat them evenly. Leave them to soak in the egg for a few minutes.

3. Spread the Parmesan evenly over a dinner plate. Sprinkle on the Italian seasoning or oregano and thyme, and toss lightly with your fingertips or a fork to blend. One by one, press the eggplant slices into the Parmesan mixture to coat them on both sides, and transfer them to a sheet of wax paper or parchment.

4. Place the eggplant slices in the panini maker, double-sided grill, or sauté pan a few at a time, taking care not to overcrowd them. Cook for 2 minutes on each side, then transfer to a plate and set aside while you cook the remaining batches.

5. Lightly salt all of the grilled eggplant slices. Return half the eggplant slices to the panini maker and arrange them in an even

layer. If there is not room for half, use as many as will fit comfortably. Spoon 1 to 2 tablespoons of the marinara sauce onto each slice (depending on the size of the slice), top with 2 to 3 tablespoons of the mozzarella, and cover with another eggplant slice. Close the lid and cook until the mozzarella has melted, about 2 minutes more.

6. Heat the marinara sauce that you set aside in the saucepan to a simmer. Ladle a spoonful of the sauce onto each plate and place the eggplant stack on top. Garnish with fresh basil leaves or a sprig of oregano and drizzle with the remaining 1 tablespoon olive oil before serving.

Making Grilled Eggplant Parmesan

1.

2.

3.

4.

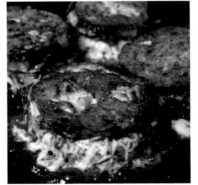
5.

Scallop Ceviche with Jalapeño and Fresh Lime

MAKES 4 SERVINGS

Given the popularity of sushi today, I really wonder why more people don't try ceviche, the zesty Latin American seafood cocktail. Few things I know taste more refreshing, yet some people still resist ceviche because of the notion of raw seafood. But (unlike sushi) the seafood in ceviche is cooked; it's just not cooked by heat. The acidity of the lime juice causes it to turn firm and opaque while highlighting its fresh, clean flavor. Ceviche is incredibly easy to make; the only tool you'll need is a sharp knife.

1	pound fresh sea scallops or bay scallops, cut into ½-inch pieces	2	tablespoons extra-virgin olive oil
⅔	cup fresh lime juice	2	tablespoons chopped fresh cilantro
2	garlic cloves, peeled		Kosher salt and freshly ground black pepper
3	green onions, finely chopped		Cilantro or parsley leaves for garnish
2	medium ripe tomatoes, peeled, seeded, and chopped		
1	medium jalapeño pepper, stemmed, seeded, and deveined, finely chopped		

1. Put the scallop pieces in a glass or stainless steel bowl. Pour the lime juice over them and stir gently to coat them thoroughly. Cover with plastic wrap and refrigerate for 24 hours.

2. Before serving, bring a small saucepan of water to a boil. Add the garlic cloves and blanch them in the boiling water for 1 minute to remove some of their harshness. Drain the cloves well, pat them dry with paper towels, and then chop them finely.

3. Drain most of the lime juice from the scallops and return them to the bowl. Add the chopped garlic, green onions, tomatoes, jalapeño, olive oil, and cilantro to the scallops. Mix well and season to taste with the salt and pepper. Garnish with cilantro or parsley leaves. Serve immediately or cover the bowl and refrigerate until serving time.

Panko-Crusted Scallops with Cilantro-Mint Vinaigrette

MAKES 4 SERVINGS

Wolfgang's EASY TIPS

➤ Try this recipe with shrimp or other seafood as well as vegetables like blanched cauliflower, eggplant, or thick slices of green tomato.

➤ A small, modern countertop electric deep fryer makes the cooking especially easy, eliminating frying odors and ensuring that the right temperature is maintained for extra-crisp, nongreasy results.

➤ If you don't want to make the cilantro sauce, Chinese hoisin sauce makes a great sauce for dipping (your kids might prefer ketchup).

We often fry meat, poultry, and fish with a breadcrumb coating in Austria. In Japan mushrooms and vegetables are also deep fried, and they taste delicious. I love to use the jagged Japanese-style dry breadcrumbs called panko for my deep frying. They're coarser than the crumbs Western cooks use, so they give you a really attractive, even, crunchy coating that contrasts perfectly with tender scallops. You'll find them in Asian markets or the Asian foods aisle of your supermarket.

For the cilantro-mint vinaigrette:

1	egg yolk
	Juice of 2 limes
1½	tablespoons soy sauce
1	medium garlic clove, chopped
¼	cup rice vinegar
½	teaspoon Chinese chile sauce (optional)
1	bunch cilantro leaves, picked and coarsely chopped (about ½ cup)
6	sprigs mint leaves, picked
½	teaspoon kosher salt
	Pinch of black pepper
1½	tablespoons packed brown sugar

1½	cups peanut oil
2	teaspoons sesame oil

For the scallops:

1	pound fresh sea scallops, cut in half lengthwise if very large
	Kosher salt and freshly ground white pepper
2	large eggs, beaten
¼	cup milk
½	cup all-purpose flour
1	cup panko
	Peanut oil or vegetable oil for deep-frying
	Bottled hoisin sauce for serving

1. To make the cilantro-mint vinaigrette, put the egg yolk, lime juice, soy sauce, garlic, rice vinegar, Chinese chile sauce (if using), cilantro leaves, mint leaves, salt, pepper, and brown sugar in a food processor fitted with a steel blade. Purée for about 2 minutes, or until the mixture is smooth. With the machine running, slowly drizzle in the oils and process until the mixture is thick. Refrigerate until ready to use.

2. In an automatic deep fryer or a deep, heavy frying pan, preheat several inches of oil to a temperature of 350°F. (If you don't have an automatic deep fryer, check the temperature by clipping a deep-frying thermometer to the side of the pan.) Meanwhile, pat the scallops dry with paper towels and season them with a little salt and pepper. In a bowl beat together the eggs and milk. Place the

scallops on one plate, the flour on another plate, and the panko
on a third plate.

3. Dredge a scallop in the flour, turning it to coat all sides and then
shaking off excess flour. Dip it in the beaten egg, letting the excess
egg drip back into the bowl. Dip the scallop into the panko,
pressing lightly to help the crumbs adhere on all sides. Gently
shake off any excess crumbs. Place the scallop back on its plate
and repeat with the remaining scallops.

4. When all the scallops are coated and the oil has reached 350°F,
place about 6 scallops in the oil and fry until golden brown, about
2 minutes; flip them over if necessary. Lift them out with the
fryer's strainer basket, or remove with a wire skimmer if using a
frying pan, and let the excess oil drain off; then transfer to paper
towels and immediately sprinkle lightly with salt. Repeat with the
remaining scallops. Serve hot, with the vinaigrette or hoisin sauce.

Curried Chicken Satay with Fresh Mint-Soy Vinaigrette

MAKES 24 SKEWERS, 8 TO 12 SERVINGS

Wolfgang's EASY TIPS

➤ You can find wooden or bamboo skewers in well-stocked markets or kitchen supply stores. The 6-inch length is best for these. Make sure to soak them in water for 30 minutes first so that they won't catch on fire.

➤ You can prepare the skewers several hours ahead and let the chicken marinate in the refrigerator.

➤ You can serve these with rice as an easy dinner.

➤ Your dressing will have a marvelous peanutty flavor if you use roasted peanut oil, which you can find in specialty food stores and some supermarkets.

My son Byron's favorite dinner is chicken satay with rice. The slender Indonesian-style kebab skewers make an easy and attractive appetizer, and they're great party food. Since the poultry is sliced so thinly, it needs hardly any time to soak up flavors during marinating and only two to four minutes to cook on a grill or under a broiler. For an easy family supper, try using a hinged countertop grill or panini maker. But be careful to clean out any juices that might drip into the pan after using.

For the chicken satay:

2	skinless, boneless chicken breast halves
1½	teaspoons curry powder
1	teaspoon freshly ground black pepper
½	teaspoon kosher salt
½	teaspoon ground cumin
2	tablespoons peanut oil or vegetable oil

For the mint-soy vinaigrette:

2	large egg yolks, beaten
¼	cup rice wine vinegar
2	tablespoons finely chopped fresh mint
1	tablespoon soy sauce
½	teaspoon ground coriander
½	cup regular or roasted peanut oil
¼	teaspoon salt
¼	teaspoon freshly ground pepper

1. Soak two dozen 6-inch bamboo or wooden skewers in water for 30 to 60 minutes. With a sharp knife, cut each chicken breast lengthwise into twelve long, thin strips. Thread 1 strip onto each of the skewers, weaving the skewer back and forth along the length of each chicken strip. Arrange them on a large platter or baking tray.

2. To prepare the marinade, in a small bowl combine the curry powder, pepper, salt, and cumin. Spoon the oil over the chicken strips, turning to coat them evenly, and then evenly sprinkle the dry ingredients over them on both sides. Cover the platter or tray with plastic wrap and marinate in the refrigerator for 1 hour or longer.

3. Prepare the Mint-Soy Vinaigrette: In a food processor fitted with the steel blade or a blender, combine the egg yolks, vinegar, mint, soy sauce, and coriander. With the motor running, slowly drizzle in the oil and continue processing until smooth. Transfer the dressing to a bowl, season to taste with salt and pepper, cover with plastic wrap, and refrigerate.

4. Preheat a hinged indoor grill or panini maker, following the manufacturer's instructions, or preheat a broiler, outdoor grill, or stovetop grill pan. Grill the skewers, in batches if necessary, until cooked through and nicely browned, about 2 minutes total on a hinged grill or panini maker, or 2 minutes per side in the broiler, in a grill pan, or on an outdoor grill. If using an indoor grill, take care that the skewers don't prevent the grill or panini maker from closing properly.

5. Serve the skewers immediately, passing the vinaigrette for guests to drizzle over their own skewers or to use as a dip.

Honey-Marinated Beef Satay with Spicy Butter Sauce

MAKES 24 SKEWERS, 8 TO 12 SERVINGS

Wolfgang's EASY TIPS

➤ You can find 6-inch bamboo or wooden skewers in well-stocked Asian markets, in the Asian aisles of supermarkets, and in kitchen supply stores. Always soak them in water for 30 minutes before use, and be sure to refrigerate the skewered meat if you assemble them ahead of time.

➤ When you cook these on an indoor hinged grill, make sure you've set up your pan for catching drips, and clean the rim and crevices well after grilling.

➤ You can make these satays in a grill pan, under a broiler, or on an outdoor grill.

You can make this dish with good quality, tender New York strip or fillet, or with the less costly and more authentic skirt or flank steak that is used in Asian recipes for satay. If you use a quality meat like tenderloin tips or end cuts from a New York strip loin, you can cook the meat medium rare. The recipe, which has long been a favorite of mine, is adapted from the Szechuan beef satay that appeared in my book *Adventures in the Kitchen* (Random House, 1991). Now I make it quite spontaneously using an indoor grill. You could also serve these skewers as a main dish, with rice and vegetables.

For the beef satay:

¾	**pound New York strip or fillet steak, trimmed**
½	**cup soy sauce**
1	**tablespoon honey**
½	**to 1 teaspoon chile flakes**
½	**teaspoon ground cumin**
½	**teaspoon ground turmeric**
2	**tablespoons vegetable or peanut oil**

For the sauce:

2	**garlic cloves, peeled and finely chopped**
2	**plus 2 tablespoons unsalted butter**
1	**teaspoon minced fresh ginger**
1	**whole green onion, finely chopped**
1	**cup chicken stock**
¼	**cup soy sauce**
1	**teaspoon honey**
2	**tablespoons hoisin sauce or your favorite barbecue sauce**
1	**teaspoon chile flakes**

1. Soak two dozen 6-inch bamboo or wooden skewers in water for 30 to 60 minutes. Drain and pat dry. With a sharp knife, cut the steak into twenty-four long, thin strips. Thread 1 strip onto each skewer, weaving the skewer back and forth along the length of each steak strip. Arrange the skewers on a large platter or baking tray. Cover with plastic wrap and refrigerate until needed.

2. About 30 minutes before you wish to grill the skewers, combine the soy sauce, honey, chile flakes, cumin, turmeric, and oil in a small bowl. Pour this marinade over the steak skewers, turning to coat the meat evenly. Leave the steak skewers to marinate at room temperature for about 20 minutes.

3. Preheat a hinged grill or panini maker, following the manufacturer's instructions, or preheat a broiler, outdoor grill, or stovetop grill pan.

4. Meanwhile, make the sauce: Bring a small saucepan of water to a boil. Add the garlic cloves and blanch them in the boiling water for 30 seconds to a minute to remove some of their harshness. Drain the cloves well, pat them dry with paper towels, and chop them finely. In a small skillet, melt 2 tablespoons of the butter over medium-high heat. Add the garlic, ginger, and green onion and sauté just until they begin to soften and smell fragrant, about 2 minutes. Add the stock, soy sauce, honey, hoisin or barbecue sauce, and chile flakes and bring to a boil. Cook for 1 to 2 minutes longer. Pour the sauce through a strainer into a clean pan and, over medium heat, whisk in the remaining 2 tablespoons of butter, a little bit at a time. Keep warm.

5. Grill the skewers (in batches if necessary to prevent overcrowding) until cooked through and nicely browned, about 2 minutes total on a hinged grill or panini maker or 2 minutes per side in the broiler, in a grill pan, or on an outdoor grill—1 minute if you want the meat rare. Take care that the skewers don't prevent a hinged grill or panini maker from closing properly. Transfer to a platter, pour on the sauce, and serve. Or serve with the sauce on the side for dipping.

Chinese Five-Spice Spare Ribs with Pickled Ginger

MAKES 4 TO 6 SERVINGS

These sweet and pungent ribs can be made in a pressure cooker or baked in the oven. They are glazed with the sauce after they're cooked. The pressure cooker will give you an amazingly fall-apart tender result. Make sure you pass lots of paper napkins when you serve these. They make a great main dish as well as appetizer.

3	pounds spareribs or baby-back ribs	1	cup apple cider or apple juice
1	tablespoon Chinese five-spice powder	¼	cup apple cider vinegar
	Kosher salt and freshly ground black pepper	1	tablespoon pickled ginger
		1	garlic clove, peeled and crushed
¼	cup bottled hoisin sauce	2	tablespoons tomato paste
¼	cup bottled Chinese plum sauce	2	teaspoons soy sauce
		1	tablespoon honey

1. Rub the ribs all over with the five-spice powder and sprinkle generously with salt and pepper. Mix together the hoisin sauce and plum sauce, and brush the ribs evenly with a thick coating. Cut the ribs into sections of three to five ribs each.

Using a pressure cooker:

2. Put the cider, vinegar, ginger, and garlic in the pressure cooker and heat over medium-high heat. Add the ribs to the liquid in the pressure cooker. Secure the lid. When high pressure has been achieved, turn the temperature to low and set the timer for 20 minutes.

3. After 20 minutes, follow the manufacturer's instructions to release the pressure. Remove the ribs from the pressure cooker and transfer to a platter. Skim the fat off the surface of the liquid in the pot. Add the tomato paste, soy sauce, and honey to the cooking liquid, set the heat to high and continue cooking the sauce, uncovered, until it reduces to a thick syrup, about 5 minutes.

4. Cut up the ribs into individual pieces, return them to the sauce, turning to coat them evenly, and rewarm them. Transfer to a serving platter and pass any extra sauce on the side.

Using the oven:

2. Preheat the oven to 350°F. Oil a baking dish or roasting pan large enough to accommodate the ribs in one layer (you may need two pans). Place the ribs in the pan, cover tightly with foil, and bake 1 hour, or until tender when pierced with a fork. Transfer the ribs to a platter.

3. Pour off the liquid from the roasting pan and skim off the fat. Pour the liquid into a large pot, add all of the remaining ingredients, and bring to a simmer. Cook over medium heat, stirring often, until the liquid reduces to a thick, syrupy consistency, about 15 minutes.

4. Heat the ribs in the sauce as instructed above.

Chicken Stock

MAKES 2 TO 3 QUARTS

Wolfgang's EASY TIPS

➤ If you don't have time to make stock but do have bones from a roast chicken, put them in the freezer. You can always make the stock on a rainy day.

➤ When making stock it's important to skim it thoroughly and often so that it will be clear and have a pure flavor. Lots of fat and frothy impurities come to the surface while the water is coming to a boil, so most of the skimming will be done early on.

➤ Stock can be stored in the refrigerator for three days, and it freezes well for three months. Lift the fat from the surface of chilled stock and transfer the stock to freezer containers or ice cube trays. Thaw as needed in the microwave.

➤ Although this recipe calls for 5 to 6 pounds of chicken bones, you can make very nice, light stock with as little as 1 to 2 pounds, which is what the carcass of your roast chicken will weigh.

➤ Chefs don't salt their chicken stock because they often reduce it for sauces. But you can salt yours if you are going to be using it for soups.

Stock is so important to chefs that it's the first thing we learn to make. This hasn't changed since I began my apprenticeship at age fourteen. And even though today the home cook can find good quality canned chicken stock, there is still nothing to compare to homemade. Every time you roast a chicken at home, save those carcasses for stock so that it's always on hand in your freezer. And if you want to make it the way chefs do, from raw chicken bones, you can obtain them from the butcher.

5	to 6 pounds chicken bones, including necks and feet, coarsely chopped (or 1 to 3 roast chicken carcasses)
3	to 4 quarts cold water
2	medium carrots, peeled and sliced
1	medium onion, quartered
1	small leek, thoroughly washed and sliced
1	small celery stalk, sliced
½	head of garlic, cut in half (optional)
3	sprigs parsley, with stems
1	bay leaf
½	teaspoon whole white peppercorns
	Kosher salt, if desired

1. Put the chicken bones in a large stockpot and pour in cold water to cover by an inch or two. Bring to a boil over medium-high heat. As the water heats, regularly skim off the fat and froth that rise to the surface. When it finally comes to a boil, skim off all of the froth.

2. Add the remaining ingredients and reduce the heat to low. Cover partially and keep the stock at a bare simmer for 2 to 3 hours. Skim from time to time.

3. Strain the stock through a cheesecloth-lined fine-mesh strainer set over a pot or bowl. Refrigerate uncovered overnight. Discard the hardened layer of fat that forms on the surface. Strain into containers and freeze, or use as needed.

Fish Stock

MAKES 1 QUART

When you want to make fish soup that has a really intense flavor, make this fish stock first. Ask your fishmonger to save bones and heads of white-fleshed fish.

4	fresh parsley sprigs	1	pound fish bones from any saltwater fish except salmon, cut into pieces
1	small handful celery leaves		
1	sprig fresh thyme	1	carrot, sliced
1	bay leaf	1	shallot, sliced
1	teaspoon whole black and white peppercorns	½	onion, sliced
		½	celery stalk, sliced
2	tablespoons olive oil	2	cups dry white wine

1. Prepare a bouquet garni by wrapping the parsley, celery leaves, thyme, bay leaf, and peppercorns inside a square of cheesecloth and tying it securely with kitchen string.

2. In a medium saucepan or small stockpot, heat the olive oil over medium heat. Add the fish bones, carrot, shallot, onion, and celery and sauté, stirring frequently, for 10 minutes. Add the wine and stir and scrape to deglaze the pan deposits. Add the bouquet garni and enough cold water to cover. Bring to a boil, using a large spoon to skim off foam as it rises to the surface. Reduce the heat and simmer for 25 minutes. Strain through a cheesecloth-lined fine-mesh strainer set over a heatproof bowl. You should have about 1 quart of stock.

Wolfgang's EASY TIPS

➤ Never use salmon bones and heads for fish stock. The fish is too fatty and strong-tasting.

➤ Fish stock does not store well. Use within a day of making or freeze in a small container.

Roasted Squash Soup

MAKES 4 SERVINGS

When I first came to America in 1973, I had never eaten pumpkin or other hard-shelled winter squashes. I was familiar with them, though, because back home in southern Austria pumpkins were grown to make dark green pumpkinseed oil, an aromatic seasoning drizzled over food there the same way extra-virgin olive oil is used in Italy. But I was ready to like American squashes. I'm always ready for a culinary adventure. Imagine my disappointment, then, when I first tried a traditional pumpkin soup; it resembled a disappointing dessert, watery and slightly sweet. So I got to work at once and the luxurious soup I developed is a perennial favorite at Spago.

For the cranberry-apple relish:

1	cup whole fresh or frozen cranberries, or dried cranberries
1	apple, peeled, cored, and cut into ½-inch dice
½	cup sugar
⅓	cup water (or soaking water from the dried cranberries)
2	tablespoons lemon juice

For the soup:

1	butternut squash, about 2 pounds
½	kabocha squash, about 1½ pounds
2	plus 2 tablespoons unsalted butter
	Kosher salt and freshly ground white pepper
½	small brown-skinned onion, peeled and finely diced
¼	teaspoon grated nutmeg
¼	teaspoon ground cinnamon
¼	teaspoon ground ginger
⅛	teaspoon ground cardamom
2	teaspoons brown sugar
2	cups good-quality chicken broth or vegetable broth
½	cup heavy cream, crème fraîche, or unsweetened whipped cream for garnish (optional)

1. Make the cranberry-apple relish. If using dried cranberries, put them in a bowl and cover with boiling water. Let steep 15 to 30 minutes and drain over a bowl. Retain ⅓ cup of the soaking water. In a small saucepan, combine the apple, sugar, water, and lemon juice. Cook over medium-high heat, stirring frequently, until the mixture starts to boil. Reduce the heat to a simmer and continue cooking, stirring frequently, until the mixture is thick and the berries have popped open, about 20 minutes, or up to 30 minutes if using dried cranberries. Let the mixture cool and then transfer to a nonreactive container, cover, and refrigerate. You should have about 1½ cups, enough for the soup plus extra to use as a relish for holiday meals.

2. Meanwhile preheat the oven to 350°F. With a large, sharp knife, carefully cut the butternut and kabocha squashes lengthwise in half. With a sharp-edged spoon, scoop out the seeds and strings from the butternut and kabocha squash halves.

3. Melt 2 tablespoons of the butter. Place wire racks on top of a baking sheet large enough to hold the squash halves. Brush the cut side of each squash half with melted butter and season with salt and white pepper. Arrange the squash cut side down on the rack. Cover with foil. Bake until the squash is tender enough to be pierced easily with a sharp knife tip, about 1½ hours. Remove from the oven and leave until cool enough to handle. Pour any liquid in the roasting pan into a bowl and combine with the stock. With a spoon, scoop out the flesh from each squash half into a food processor fitted with the stainless steel blade, or a blender. Process until puréed. You should have about 3 cups or a little more. Transfer the purée to a mixing bowl and set aside.

4. In a medium soup pot, melt the remaining 2 tablespoons butter over medium heat. Add the onion and sauté until glossy but not yet browned, 3 to 5 minutes. Stir in the nutmeg, cinnamon, ginger, cardamom, and brown sugar and stir together for about a minute. Add the squash and continue cooking, stirring occasionally, until heated through.

5. In a medium saucepan, bring the stock and cream to a boil over medium-high heat. Stir the liquid into the squash purée until well blended. Add salt and pepper to taste.

6. If you want a really silky texture, blend the soup before straining. In batches, transfer to a blender or food processor, taking care not to overfill the container, and process until smoothly blended, 1 to 2 minutes. You can also do this with an immersion blender. Transfer each batch to a fine-mesh strainer set over a heatproof mixing bowl and press it through with a rubber spatula. If not serving right away, cover with plastic wrap and refrigerate.

7. In the soup pot over medium heat, bring the soup back to serving temperature. Taste and adjust the seasonings if necessary. Ladle into heated serving bowls and garnish each serving with a spoonful of relish and some crème fraîche or whipped cream if desired. Serve immediately.

Wolfgang's EASY TIPS

➤ In addition to the cranberry-apple relish that accompanies the soup in this recipe, you could garnish it with a swirl of puréed roasted red bell pepper or a teaspoon of imported Austrian extra-virgin pumpkinseed oil, now available in gourmet shops or on the Internet.

➤ The cranberry-apple relish can be made several days ahead and kept in the refrigerator.

Spiced Carrot and Orange Soup with Minty Yogurt

MAKES 4 TO 6 SERVINGS

Wolfgang's EASY TIPS

➤ You can cook this soup on top of the stove or in the pressure cooker. The flavors will be even more intense if you use a pressure cooker.

➤ When shopping for carrots, make sure they are smooth and firm (they should not flex when you bend them). I prefer medium-sized carrots to huge ones, as the large ones can be woody.

➤ If the carrots are sold with their greens still attached, which some shops like to do to emphasize how recently they were picked, the foliage should look brightly colored and fresh. But never leave the greens on once you get the carrots home; they'll continue to draw moisture and nutrients from the roots. As soon as you unpack the vegetables, cut or twist off their greens, and then store the carrots loosely wrapped in a plastic bag in your refrigerator's vegetable bin. Do not, however, keep them near fruit, especially apples, bananas, and peaches, which give off ethylene gas that can quickly turn the carrots bitter.

Here's another gorgeous bright orange soup. I like to complement the natural sweetness of carrots with fresh orange juice and a hint of spices. Carrots are so sweet to begin with, and when you cook them, they sweeten even more. This soup has a dazzling color and a heavenly flavor. You can make it vegetarian by using vegetable broth or water in place of the chicken broth. And you can enrich it by garnishing each serving with a few tablespoons of cream or, as I prefer, a dollop of tangy minted yogurt.

4	tablespoons unsalted butter
2	pounds carrots, peeled, trimmed, and thinly sliced
1	onion, peeled and thinly sliced
1	teaspoon ground cinnamon
1	teaspoon ground ginger
½	teaspoon ground turmeric
2	to 4 tablespoons light brown sugar
1	cup fresh orange juice
	Salt and freshly ground white pepper to taste
6	cups chicken broth, vegetable broth, or water

For the minted yogurt:

1	cup plain yogurt, drained if runny
1	tablespoon finely chopped fresh mint
	Salt and freshly ground white pepper to taste
4	fresh mint sprigs for garnish

1. In a large saucepan, melt the butter over medium heat. Add the carrots and onion and sauté, stirring frequently, until they look bright and glossy, 5 to 6 minutes. Sprinkle in the cinnamon, ginger, turmeric, and 2 tablespoons of the brown sugar and continue sautéing, stirring continuously, for 1 minute more. Add the orange juice and stir and scrape to deglaze any pan deposits. Raise the heat slightly, bring the juice to a boil, and continue boiling, stirring occasionally, until the juice reduces to ½ cup, about 5 minutes. Season lightly with salt and pepper.

2. Stir in the broth and bring the liquid to a boil. Reduce the heat to low, cover the pan, and simmer gently until the carrots are very tender, about 30 minutes.

Using a pressure cooker: Follow step 1 as directed. If you have an electric pressure cooker, the onions and carrots may be glossy in fewer than 5 minutes. Stir in the broth, cover, and bring to high pressure. When pressure has been reached, turn the heat to low and set the timer for 10 minutes. After 10 minutes, release the pressure and proceed with the recipe as directed.

3. Set a strainer over a nonreactive, heatproof mixing bowl. Pour off 2 cups of the cooking liquid and set aside (return any solids that end up in the strainer to the pot). Using an immersion blender, purée the soup (or purée in batches in a blender or food processor). Taste the soup and adjust the seasonings, adding more salt and pepper as desired. You can thin out the soup if you wish with the broth you poured off.

4. Heat the soup while you stir together the yogurt and mint. Season to taste with a little salt and white pepper. Ladle the soup into heated serving bowls. Garnish each serving with a dollop of Minted Yogurt and a mint sprig and serve.

Minestrone

MAKES 4 SERVINGS

Wolfgang's EASY TIPS

➤ If you are cooking this on top of the stove, you could substitute canned white beans for the dried to save time. Drain the canned beans, rinse them, and add them with the pasta. However, the dried beans do contribute a lot of flavor to the broth.

➤ You can add color and variety to the soup by adding blanched green beans or sweet peas (blanched fresh or thawed frozen) for their bright color. Add them along with the pasta.

➤ The soup will keep for three or four days in the refrigerator.

I consider Italy's minestrone one of the world's great soups. I love to embellish it at serving time by adding a spoonful of pesto, a drizzle of fragrant extra-virgin olive oil, or a sprinkling of high-quality imported Parmesan cheese to each bowl. In this version, I give you the option of using a pressure cooker. This will not only reduce the cooking time to 30 minutes, but because pressure cookers cook at such high temperatures, the flavors in the pressure cooker version are more intense. Either way, you will love this robust vegetable soup.

½   cup dried great Northern white beans or navy beans, picked through, rinsed, soaked overnight in water to cover by 2 inches, and drained

3   to 4 cups water (more as needed for thinning the soup)

2   tablespoons extra-virgin olive oil, plus additional if desired for drizzling

1   large onion, chopped

2   ounces pancetta, chopped (optional)

2   large garlic cloves, minced

1   (28-ounce) can diced tomatoes in juice

½   cup diced carrots

2   celery stalks, thinly sliced

¼   cup chopped fresh spinach or parsley

2   small potatoes (about 6 ounces), cut in small cubes

1   medium zucchini, halved lengthwise and cut into ½-inch pieces

3   sprigs fresh thyme

Kosher salt and freshly ground pepper

½   cup small dried pasta shells or elbow macaroni

For serving:

½   cup freshly grated Parmesan

½   cup prepared pesto sauce

Extra-virgin olive oil

Using the stove:

1. Drain the beans and combine with 3 cups of water in a 2-quart saucepan. Bring to a boil, reduce the heat, cover, and simmer 1 hour.

2. Heat the oil in a large, heavy soup pot over medium heat. Add the onion and optional pancetta and cook, stirring, until the onion is tender and golden, about 5 minutes. Add the garlic and cook, stirring, for another minute more until fragrant.

3. Add the tomatoes with their liquid, the beans and their broth, the carrots, celery, spinach or parsley, potatoes, zucchini, thyme, and salt and pepper to taste. Bring to a boil, reduce the heat, cover, and simmer 1 hour. Taste and adjust the seasonings. The beans should be tender and the broth fragrant.

4. About 10 minutes before serving, add the pasta to the soup. If the mixture is too thick, add another cup of water (or more). Simmer until the pasta is just tender to the bite. Adjust seasonings and serve, sprinkling each serving with freshly grated Parmesan, a spoonful of pesto, or a drizzle of extra-virgin olive oil.

Using a pressure cooker:

1. Heat a pressure cooker at medium heat and add the oil, onion, and optional pancetta. Cook, stirring frequently, until the onion turns golden, about 5 minutes. Stir in the garlic and cook for about 30 seconds to a minute more until fragrant.

2. Stir in the tomatoes, 3 cups water, the drained beans, carrots, celery, spinach or parsley, potatoes, zucchini, thyme sprigs and salt and pepper to taste. Secure the pressure cooker lid and when high pressure has been achieved, reduce the heat to low and set the timer for 30 minutes.

3. After 30 minutes, turn off the heat and release the pressure, following the manufacturer's instructions. Taste the soup (carefully—it will be very hot) and adjust the seasoning if necessary. If the soup is quite thick, add another cup of water. Stir in the pasta, bring back to a simmer without the lid on, and simmer 5 to 8 minutes, or just until the pasta is tender. Serve hot. Adjust seasonings and serve, sprinkling each serving with freshly grated Parmesan, a spoonful of pesto, or a drizzle of extra-virgin olive oil.

Robust Minestrone with Lentils and Rice

This hearty combination of grains and lentils could become a casual meal in its own right if you just add some crusty bread. While this version is vegetarian, you could substitute chicken broth if you like for the water. I like to use a pressure cooker to speed up the preparation. But it's equally simple when very gently cooked in a slow cooker for about eight hours at the lowest setting, or on top of the stove for an hour.

2	tablespoons extra-virgin olive oil		2	celery stalks, chopped
3	medium leeks, white parts only, halved lengthwise, thoroughly rinsed and chopped		7	cups cold water, vegetable stock, or chicken stock
			⅛	cup uncooked brown rice
6	garlic cloves, chopped		⅓	cup dried dark green Puy-style lentils
2	medium carrots, peeled and cut into ½-inch pieces		½	teaspoon freshly ground black pepper
1	large bay leaf			Chopped fresh flat-leaf parsley, basil, or chives for garnish
½	teaspoon chopped fresh thyme			
2	teaspoons kosher salt		½	cup freshly grated Parmesan for garnish
1	(14-ounce) can peeled and crushed tomatoes			
1½	cups chopped green or savoy cabbage			

Using the pressure cooker:

1. Heat a large pressure cooker over medium heat. Add the oil and sauté the leeks until they begin to soften and smell fragrant, 1 to 2 minutes. Add the garlic and stir together for a few seconds, then add all of the remaining ingredients except the garnishes. Bring to a boil, secure the lid, and bring the pressure cooker to high pressure. When high pressure has been reached, turn the heat to low and set a timer for 20 minutes.

2. When the cooking time is up, turn off the heat and release the pressure, following the manufacturer's instructions. The wild and brown rice and the lentils should be tender. Continue simmering with the lid off until the soup is thick but still fairly fluid, about 10 minutes more. Adjust the seasonings to taste and serve garnished with chopped fresh parsley, basil, or chives and a spoonful of grated Parmesan.

Using the stove:

1. Heat the oil in a large, heavy soup pot over medium heat and add the leeks. Cook, stirring, until tender, 3 to 5 minutes, and add the garlic. Stir together for 30 seconds to a minute until fragrant and add the remaining ingredients except the garnishes. Bring to a boil, reduce the heat, cover, and simmer 1 hour.

2. Adjust the seasonings to taste and serve garnished with chopped fresh parsley, basil, or chives and a spoonful of grated Parmesan.

Clockwise from top: My Favorite Spring Pea Soup, Minestrone, Spiced Carrot and Orange Soup, and Gazpacho.

My Favorite Spring Pea Soup

MAKES 6 SERVINGS

Although I think of this gorgeous, sweet green soup as a spring soup to be made during that small window when English peas hit our farmers' markets, you can, in fact, make it at any time of year with frozen peas, which also have a wonderful sweet flavor.

2½ pounds (7 cups) shelled fresh English peas or defrosted frozen peas	2 cups heavy whipping cream
1 tablespoon olive oil	2 teaspoons kosher salt
3 tablespoons butter	¼ teaspoon white pepper
1 cup finely chopped white onions	2 tablespoons honey
1 quart chicken stock	2 teaspoons lemon juice

1. Set aside ⅓ cup of peas for garnish. Heat a nonreactive pot over medium heat and add the olive oil and butter. When the butter is foaming, add the onion, turn the heat to low, and cook slowly until the onion is translucent and very tender, 5 to 10 minutes. (Don't allow the onion to brown; it will discolor the soup.)

2. Add the stock, cream, salt, pepper, and honey and bring to a boil. Boil for 5 minutes. Turn the heat to high, add the peas, and boil rapidly for 2 minutes, or until the peas are tender.

3. Remove from the heat and purée with either an immersion blender or carefully in batches in a blender until smooth. Strain the purée into a large bowl. Add the lemon juice, adjust the seasonings, and garnish with baby peas before serving.

NOTE: *Do not let the soup sit on the stovetop for too long; it will slowly discolor. If you do not plan on serving it right away, place the pot in an ice bath to cool down as fast as possible to retain the beautiful green color. Reheat and add the lemon juice just before serving, or serve cold.*

Pressure Cooker Chicken Soup
with Parsnips, Celery, and Leeks

MAKES 6 SERVINGS

Chicken soup is my favorite soup to make in a pressure cooker. The results are incredibly fragrant.

1½	**pounds skinless, boneless chicken breasts, cut into ½-inch dice**
1	**medium onion, chopped**
¼	**pound parsnips, peeled and diced**
1	**celery stalk, diced**
1	**large leek, white and light green part only, cleaned and chopped**
6	**cups chicken broth**
1½	**teaspoons kosher salt (more to taste)**
	Freshly ground black pepper
1	**teaspoon finely chopped lemon zest**
1	**cup raw baby spinach leaves (optional)**
2	**eggs, beaten**
1	**cup cooked rice or small pasta, such as orecchiete or macaroni (optional)**
1	**lemon, thinly sliced for garnish**
	Chopped flat-leaf parsley for garnish

1. Place the chicken breasts, onion, parsnips, celery, leek, chicken broth, salt, pepper to taste, and lemon zest in a pressure cooker and turn to high heat. Secure the lid and bring the pressure cooker to high pressure. Reduce the heat to low and set a timer for 12 minutes.

2. When cooking is complete, turn off the heat and release the pressure, following the manufacturer's instructions. Remove the lid. Add the spinach, if using, and drizzle in the beaten eggs, stirring while adding. When the spinach has wilted and the eggs have set, taste and adjust the seasonings. Stir in the rice or pasta if using. Ladle the soup into bowls and garnish each bowl with chopped parsley and a slice of lemon.

Wolfgang's EASY TIPS

➤ You can make this soup on top of the stove, of course. The flavors will be slightly less intense. To make on the stove, combine the diced chicken breasts and the broth and bring to a simmer. Skim off any foam, then add the vegetables, salt, and pepper. Simmer, covered, for 30 minutes. Taste and adjust seasonings. Proceed with step 2. Stir in the spinach. Serve hot, garnished with parsley and a thin slice of lemon.

Cream of Root Vegetable Soup with Sour Cream

MAKES 6 SERVINGS

Root vegetables and their close cousins, potatoes, are the foundation of some of the heartiest, most satisfying soups, the type my mother would routinely make for supper when I was growing up in Austria. All of these vegetables are commonly available in supermarkets, and when you combine them you get a soup with a deliciously complex flavor and a beautiful golden orange color, wonderful either hot or cold. Each vegetable contributes some sweetness to the broth, especially the parsnips—a food that doesn't get enough attention in this country. The soup is incredibly simple to throw together, and if you use a pressure cooker, it will be ready in fifteen minutes.

6	cups water or chicken broth
3	medium carrots, peeled and chopped
2	medium parsnips, peeled and chopped
2	celery stalks, chopped
1	large russet potato, peeled and chopped
1	large turnip, peeled and chopped
1	large leek, white part only, thoroughly rinsed, sliced
½	large rutabaga, peeled and chopped
2	tablespoons chopped flat-leaf parsley
2	teaspoons kosher salt (more to taste)
½	teaspoon white pepper
1	pinch ground coriander
2	tablespoons whipping cream
1	tablespoon unsalted butter
½	cup sour cream
	Minced dill or thinly sliced green onions for garnish

1. **Using the pressure cooker:** Put the water or chicken broth in a pressure cooker and, with the lid off, preheat it on medium-high heat until the liquid begins to simmer. Add all of the vegetables, the parsley, salt, pepper, and coriander. Secure the pressure cooker lid. When high pressure has been reached, reduce the heat to low and set a timer for 12 minutes. When 12 minutes are up, turn off or remove from the heat and release the pressure, following the manufacturer's instructions.

   Using a soup pot: Combine the water or stock, all of the vegetables, the parsley, salt, pepper, and coriander, and bring to a boil over medium-high heat. Reduce the heat, cover, and simmer 45 minutes, until the vegetables are tender and the broth fragrant. Remove from the heat.

2. Remove the lid from the pressure cooker or uncover the pot. With an immersion blender, purée the soup to the desired consistency, as coarse or smooth as you like (you can also do this in a blender or food processor, in batches, or through a food mill). Stir in the cream and butter and adjust the seasonings to taste. Serve immediately or, if you like, transfer the soup to a heatproof bowl, let it cool at room temperature for about half an hour, stirring occasionally, and then cover it with plastic wrap and chill in the refrigerator.

3. Ladle the hot or chilled soup into serving bowls and add a dollop of sour cream and a sprinkling of dill or green onions to each serving. The soup is also delicious served with oven-baked herbed croutons.

Rich Mussel Soup

MAKES 4 TO 6 SERVINGS

Wolfgang's EASY TIPS

➤ Buy your mussels from the best fishmonger you can find. They should smell as clean and briny as the ocean, without even a suspicion of fishiness or ammonia. When you get them home, transfer them at once from their packaging to a bowl, cover with a damp towel, and refrigerate.

➤ Clean the mussels by rinsing them several times with cold water and pulling out their beards. Tap any shells that are gaping open. They should close immediately, indicating that the mussels are still alive. If they do not, throw them out. Throw out any that are cracked, and any that are unusually heavy, indicating that they are packed with sand. Fill a bowl with water and add a tablespoon of salt. Soak the mussels for 15 minutes, drain, rinse thoroughly, and repeat.

➤ Cook the mussels the same day you buy them.

➤ You can serve the soup either as an appetizer or a main course. Serve with grilled country bread rubbed with garlic and drizzled with olive oil.

This luxurious soup was inspired by the first mussel soup I tasted about thirty years ago at Restaurant Paul Bocuse near Lyon. His mussel soup was a revelation. A simple chowder, it featured fresh shellfish that were steamed in their shells with vegetables, fish stock, and white wine, then shucked and bathed in cream with richly perfumed golden saffron and other spices and herbs. The combination of sweet, plump mussels, rich cream, and aromatic seasonings powerfully conveyed to me Bocuse's then-revolutionary message: The best cooking highlights the natural tastes, scents, textures, and colors of fine seasonal ingredients.

2½	pounds fresh mussels in their shells		1	cup dry white wine
½	pound carrots, peeled		1	tablespoon unsalted butter
½	pound leeks, trimmed, thoroughly washed		½	teaspoon saffron threads
½	pound celery, trimmed		½	teaspoon dried thyme
2	shallots, chopped		2	cups heavy cream
2	garlic cloves, peeled and crushed			Kosher salt and freshly ground pepper
2	cups water			Pinch of cayenne
				Juice of ½ small lemon

1. Clean the mussels as instructed in the tips, discarding any that seem overly light, meaning they're probably dead, or any that feel very heavy, meaning they're full of sand. Set the clean mussels aside.

2. Coarsely chop half each of the carrots, leeks, and celery, setting the remainder aside. Place the shallots, garlic, and the chopped vegetables in a large saucepan and add the mussels, water, and the wine. Bring to a boil over medium-high heat, cover, and cook for about 5 minutes, or until the shells have opened. Remove the mussels from the pot with tongs and place in a separate bowl. Discard any that have not opened. Strain the contents of the pan through a cheesecloth-lined strainer set over a large heatproof bowl. Reserve the liquid and discard the solids. Shuck the mussels and discard the shells. Briefly rinse the mussels to rid them of any lingering sand. Place in a bowl and cover. Refrigerate if not serving right away.

3. Cut the remaining vegetables into uniform ¼-inch dice. Melt the butter over low heat in a heavy 6-quart soup pot or Dutch oven. Add the diced vegetables, saffron, and thyme, cover partially, and cook gently, stirring often, for about 10 minutes, until tender and fragrant. Add the cream and raise the heat to medium-high. Bring to a boil and cook, stirring frequently, until the cream reduces and thickens slightly, about 7 minutes. Stir in the strained cooking liquid, raise the heat, and continue boiling until the mixture has reduced slightly, 3 to 5 minutes more. Add salt and pepper to taste. Turn off the heat if not serving right away.

4. Shortly before serving bring the soup back to a simmer and stir in the shucked mussels. Heat through. Taste and adjust salt and pepper, and stir in a dash of cayenne and a teaspoon or two of lemon juice. Ladle immediately into heated bowls and serve.

NOTE: *For an even more intense flavor, you can substitute fish stock for the water when you cook the mussels. Use the recipe on page 53.*

VARIATION: *If you don't want a rich mussel soup, simply steam the mussels and serve them in their shells with the broth. Use the recipe above, but only use half the carrots, leeks, and celery and omit the cream, saffron, and cayenne. Follow the recipe through step 2, but do not shuck the mussels. Strain the liquid and whisk in 2 tablespoons butter. When the butter has melted, distribute the broth among serving bowls and spoon in the mussels. Sprinkle with parsley and serve.*

Gazpacho with Avocado Garnish

MAKES 6 TO 8 SERVINGS

Wolfgang's EASY TIPS

➤ Choose tomatoes that have good color, feel solid and firm but not hard, and are heavy for their size and blemish-free. Good tomatoes should taste sweet and tart at the same time.

➤ Store tomatoes at room temperature. Never put them in the refrigerator, as their sugars will cease to develop and their flavor will be muted.

➤ A nice way to present this soup is in hollowed out giant beefsteak tomatoes.

If you can get vine-ripened tomatoes, which seem to be available year-round, you can bring a bit of summer sunshine into your kitchen even in the middle of winter with this zesty cold soup. If you make it at the height of tomato season, all the better. The gazpacho is like a liquid salad, refreshing as a first course or perfect as a light lunch with crusty bread.

For the gazpacho:

2   pounds sun-ripened tomatoes, cored and chopped

2   celery stalks, chopped

1   small red bell pepper, cored, seeded, and chopped

1   large English cucumber, peeled, halved lengthwise, seeded, and chopped

1½ cups good-quality canned tomato juice or V-8

½   cup vegetable broth or water

½   cup extra-virgin olive oil

¼   cup sherry vinegar

½   cup packed fresh flat-leaf parsley leaves

1   to 2 tablespoons sugar (or to taste)

2   tablespoons tomato paste

½   teaspoon sweet paprika

¼   teaspoon cayenne

2   to 3 teaspoons kosher salt (or to taste)

½   teaspoon freshly ground black pepper

For the avocado garnish:

1   large, ripe but firm Hass avocado, peeled, pitted, and cut into ¼-inch dice

¼   small red onion, peeled and cut into ¼-inch dice

1   tablespoon fresh lime juice

Salt and freshly ground black pepper

For serving (optional):

6   to 8 beefsteak tomatoes

8   sprigs flat-leaf parsley

1. In a large, nonreactive bowl, stir together the tomatoes, celery stalks, red bell pepper, cucumber, tomato juice, vegetable broth or water, olive oil, sherry vinegar, parsley leaves, 1 tablespoon sugar, tomato paste, paprika, cayenne, 2 teaspoons salt, and black pepper. Cover with plastic wrap and refrigerate for 2 hours.

2. In batches, transfer the chilled gazpacho mixture to a food processor fitted with the stainless steel blade and pulse the machine until the soup is coarsely puréed. Transfer the batches, as ready, to another nonreactive bowl. Stir the mixture to blend the batches. Taste it and add salt and pepper to taste and a little more sugar, if necessary, to highlight the sweetness of the tomatoes. Cover with plastic wrap and refrigerate until well chilled, several hours more.

3. Prepare the avocado garnish. In a small bowl, gently stir together the avocado, red onion, and lime juice. Season to taste with salt and pepper. Cover with plastic wrap and refrigerate.

4. If serving in hollowed out beefsteak tomatoes, slice the tops off the beefsteak tomatoes. With a teaspoon or tablespoon, scoop out the seeds and the cores, taking care not to break through the tomatoes' bottoms or outer walls. Place the hollowed-out tomatoes upside down on a platter to drain and refrigerate them until ready to serve.

5. At serving time, place a beefsteak tomato bowl on each of eight serving plates. Ladle the gazpacho into each tomato (or into bowls), top with a generous tablespoonful of the avocado mixture, and garnish with a parsley sprig. Serve immediately.

Warm Spinach Salad

MAKES 6 SERVINGS

Wolfgang's EASY TIPS

➤ For an even heartier salad, add sliced mushrooms and hard-boiled eggs before spooning on the dressing.

➤ Play around with vinegar combinations. For a more pungent dressing, use more wine or sherry vinegar and less balsamic. For a sweet dressing, use all balsamic.

The warm spinach salad has long since turned from an innovative dish into a classic, but I still love it. This version, with the classic bacon and more modern chopped sun-dried tomatoes, caramelized onions, and creamy goat cheese, is one of the prettiest I know. The sweet and tangy deep-red dressing complements the dark green baby spinach leaves.

8	strips lean bacon, cut into ½-inch dice
1	large sweet onion such as Vidalia, Maui, or Walla Walla, peeled and thinly sliced crosswise in rings
1	teaspoon minced fresh garlic
1	tablespoon red wine vinegar or sherry vinegar
3	tablespoons balsamic vinegar

	Kosher salt and freshly ground pepper
½	cup drained oil-packed sun-dried tomatoes, chopped
½	cup extra-virgin olive oil
1	prepacked bag ready-to-serve fresh baby spinach leaves, about 10 ounces
1	log fresh creamy goat cheese, about 6 ounces, cut into ½-inch-thick slices

1. Heat a large nonstick skillet over medium heat and add the bacon pieces. Cook, stirring frequently, until browned and crisp, about 5 minutes. With a slotted spoon, remove the bacon from the skillet and transfer to paper towels to drain.

2. Pour off most of the bacon fat, leaving a thin coating in the skillet. Add the onion slices, separating them into rings, and sauté them over medium heat until they begin to turn a caramel brown color, 5 to 10 minutes. Add the garlic and sauté until it turns translucent, 1 to 2 minutes more. Stir in both the vinegars, add salt and pepper to taste, and stir and scrape with a wooden spoon to deglaze the pan.

3. Add the sun-dried tomatoes and olive oil to the skillet and continue to cook, stirring continuously, just until the ingredients are heated through and blended. Turn off the heat.

4. Arrange the spinach in a bed on a serving platter or individual salad plates. Arrange the goat cheese on top of the spinach and sprinkle with the bacon pieces. With a fork, remove the onion rings from the skillet and arrange them all over the salad. Finally, spoon the warm dressing from the skillet over the salad.

Crab Louie on Belgian Endive

MAKES 4 SERVINGS

This is one of my favorite hors d'oeuvres to serve with Champagne. It's a popular New Year's Eve dish at our house and at the restaurant. On the West Coast, Dungeness crab is at its best in December, so that's what I use. But any good, fresh lump crabmeat will do.

½	pound lump crabmeat	2	tablespoons olive oil
3	tablespoons Thousand Island (page 219) or Russian dressing (page 220)		Kosher salt and freshly ground pepper
			Pinch of sugar
2	tablespoons minced chives	1	teaspoon minced flat-leaf parsley
1	vine-ripened tomato, diced and well drained	24	endive leaves
2	tablespoons red onion	1	whole avocado, diced

1. Pick over the crabmeat to remove any pieces of shell and place in a mixing bowl. Fold in the dressing and chives.

2. In another bowl stir together the tomato, red onion, olive oil, salt and pepper to taste, sugar, and parsley.

3. Place six endive leaves in a flower pattern on each of four serving plates. Place a small mound of the crab mixture in the center. Top the crab with the diced avocado and place a spoonful of the tomato mixture on top.

Wolfgang's EASY TIPS

➤ You can find Belgian endives at upscale markets with good produce sections. Don't confuse them with the curly leafed endive salad, which the French call frisée.

➤ You can use bottled dressing, but your own will be better.

Chicken Salad with Avocados and Mint-Soy Vinaigrette

MAKES 4 SERVINGS

In the spring of 1974, MGM Studios invited me to cater a party for the opening night of the Cannes Film Festival in honor of their film *That's Entertainment!* They wanted a Hollywood-style banquet for 400 people. I decided to start my menu with a signature California ingredient, the avocado. Before leaving for France, I bought 200 from a local farmer. "Don't give me ripe ones," I told him. "I'm serving them a week from now." Unfortunately, the avocados he gave me didn't ripen in time for the event. Luckily, I was able to find other avocados at the Nice Market. I used them for this chicken salad, which features another great example of California produce—romaine lettuce.

For the salad:

2	whole chicken breasts, bone in, skins removed (1½ to 2 pounds)
1	medium onion, quartered
1	garlic clove, crushed
1	bay leaf
½	teaspoon kosher salt
1	romaine heart, or 1 romaine lettuce, outer leaves removed
2	celery stalks, thinly sliced
1	large or 2 small Hass avocados

For the dressing:

2	tablespoons good quality mayonnaise
¼	cup seasoned rice wine vinegar
2	tablespoons finely chopped fresh mint
1	tablespoon soy sauce
½	teaspoon ground coriander
¼	teaspoon kosher salt
¼	teaspoon freshly ground pepper
½	cup peanut oil or canola oil

1. Poach the chicken breasts. Place in a large, heavy saucepan and cover by about 1 inch with water. Add the onion, garlic, and bay leaf and bring to a simmer over medium-high heat. Add the salt and reduce the heat so that the water simmers gently. Cook, partially covered, for 20 to 25 minutes, or until the juice runs clear when the chicken is pierced with the tip of a sharp knife. Remove from the heat and, if time allows, let the chicken cool in the liquid.

2. Remove the chicken from the pot (strain the light broth and use for another purpose). When it is cool enough to handle, either shred the meat or cut it in small dice. Transfer to a bowl.

3. Wash the lettuce, breaking the larger leaves in half across the middle. You will line the platter with these larger leaves. Cut the bottom halves of the leaves and the smaller leaves crosswise into ½-inch-thick slices (chiffonade) and toss with the chicken. Add the celery and toss together.

4. Cut half of the avocado or avocados into dice and add to the chicken. Cut the remaining avocado into thin slices.

5. Make the dressing. Place the mayonnaise, vinegar, mint, soy sauce, ground coriander, salt, and pepper into a food processor fitted with the steel blade and turn it on. Slowly drizzle in the oil. Turn off the processor and pour the dressing over the chicken mixture. Toss well.

6. Line a serving platter or individual plates with the leaves that did not go into the salad and top with the salad. Fan the remaining avocado slices out on the side for garnish. Serve cold or at room temperature.

Wolfgang's EASY TIPS

➤ You can use other dressings, such as Thousand Island or ranch for this, or a thinned out tartar sauce (page 220).

Asian Steak Salad

MAKES 4 SERVINGS

I love the ginger and orange flavors in this steak salad. You can serve it as a starter, or as a light supper.

Wolfgang's EASY TIPS

➤ If you have steak left over from another dish, omit the marinade and just slice the steak as directed and toss it with the dressing.

For the marinade:

2 tablespoons orange or mandarin marmalade

1 teaspoon minced fresh ginger

1 garlic clove

   Kosher salt

½ cup wine vinegar

¼ cup fresh orange juice

½ cup extra-virgin olive oil

For the ginger vinaigrette:

1 medium shallot, chopped

1 (½-inch) piece fresh ginger, peeled and minced

⅓ cup almond oil or extra-virgin olive oil

1 tablespoon dark sesame oil

½ cup seasoned rice wine vinegar

   Kosher salt and freshly ground pepper

For the salad:

2 (8-ounce) New York steaks

   Kosher salt and freshly ground pepper

2 tablespoons unsalted butter

½ pound shiitake mushrooms

4 cups mixed baby salad greens

1. For the marinade, combine the marmalade, ginger, garlic, salt to taste, vinegar, and orange juice in a saucepan. Reduce over low heat to ½ cup. Remove from the heat and let cool. Stir in the olive oil and set aside.

2. For the ginger vinaigrette, in a bowl mix together the shallot, ginger, almond or olive oil, sesame oil, vinegar, and salt and pepper to taste. Adjust the seasonings as necessary and set aside.

3. For the salad, prepare a medium-hot grill. Brush the steaks with some of the marinade and season them with salt and pepper to taste. Grill the steaks to medium rare and set them aside in a warm spot.

4. Heat the butter in a skillet over medium-high heat. Sauté the mushrooms until just tender, 3 to 5 minutes.

5. Toss the salad greens with the ginger vinaigrette, adding any collected meat juices to the dressing. Season the mushrooms with salt and pepper. Mound the salad greens in the center of four dinner plates. Slice the steak thinly on the diagonal and fan the slices around one side of the greens. Arrange the mushrooms decoratively on the opposite side. Serve immediately.

Five Dressings for Five Salads

Your choice of salad dressing should be determined by the ingredients in your salad. The robust romaine lettuce leaves in a Caesar salad can support a thick, pungent dressing, whereas a salad of mixed baby greens wants a lighter balsamic vinaigrette. The classic Italian combination of tomatoes with mozzarella needs only a drizzle of reduced balsamic vinegar and olive oil, and a lemon vinaigrette is perfect with a butter lettuce salad.

Wolfgang's EASY TIPS

➤ No matter what dressing you use, it will only be as good as its ingredients. Choose only the best extra-virgin olive oil (I like the oils from Italy) and wine vinegars. Balsamic vinegar should be aged.

➤ You will get a wonderful, syrupy, intensely flavored balsamic if you reduce it first.

➤ Most dressings, with the exception of those containing citrus juices, keep well for about a week in the refrigerator.

Caesar Vinaigrette

MAKES ABOUT 2 CUPS

Wolfgang's EASY TIPS

➤ This dressing will keep well for about a week in the refrigerator.

Everybody likes Caesar salad, yet we rarely make it at home. If you keep this dressing on hand in the refrigerator, you'll see how easy it is to put one together.

1	egg	2	anchovy fillets, mashed
3	tablespoons fresh lemon juice	⅔	cup peanut oil
1	to 2 teaspoons minced garlic (or more to taste)	⅓	cup extra-virgin olive oil
½	teaspoon Worcestershire sauce	¼	cup freshly grated Parmesan
1	tablespoon Dijon mustard		Kosher salt and freshly ground pepper

1. Whisk together the egg, lemon juice, garlic, Worcestershire sauce, Dijon mustard, and anchovy fillets in a bowl or a miniprocessor. Slowly whisk in the oils. The dressing should be thick. Stir in the Parmesan and salt and pepper to taste. Use as needed with romaine lettuce salads.

Caesar Salad

MAKES 4 TO 6 SERVINGS

For the croutons:

⅛	cup olive oil	2	cups cubed French or sourdough bread
2	tablespoons freshly grated Parmesan cheese, plus some for topping		

For the salad:

2	tablespoons minced garlic
1	teaspoon chopped fresh thyme

1	large head Romaine lettuce, or 2 heads baby Romaine leaves, separated, washed, and dried
½	cup Caesar Salad Dressing (more as desired)

1. Preheat the oven to 350°F. Make the croutons. Combine the olive oil, Parmesan cheese, garlic, and thyme in a large bowl. Add the bread and toss, coating all the croutons. Arrange the croutons in a single layer on a baking sheet and bake until golden, turning from time to time. Remove from the heat and allow to cool. These will keep for a week in a covered container.

2. For the salad, tear the large leaves of lettuce into smaller pieces. Toss with the croutons and dressing. Sprinkle Parmesan on top if desired and serve.

Balsamic Vinaigrette

MAKES ABOUT 1 CUP

The dressing that we keep on hand at the restaurant to dress mixed green salads is easily made at home.

3	tablespoons balsamic vinegar	¼	teaspoon kosher salt
1	tablespoon sherry wine vinegar	⅛	teaspoon freshly ground pepper
1	tablespoon Dijon mustard	½	cup extra-virgin olive oil
1	small shallot, minced	⅓	cup walnut oil
½	tablespoon chopped fresh herbs, such as thyme, tarragon, chives, or parsley		

1. Whisk together the vinegars, mustard, shallot, herbs, salt, and pepper. Slowly whisk in the oils and continue to whisk until emulsified. Refrigerate in a covered container, and whisk again before using.

Wolfgang's EASY TIPS

➤ This dressing will keep well for about a week in the refrigerator.

Mixed Greens Salad

MAKES 4 SERVINGS

It's easy to find bags of mixed baby salad greens in any supermarket. All they need is a quick rinse and spin in the salad spinner.

1	bag salad greens (about 5 cups)	¼	to ½ cup balsamic vinaigrette (or to taste)

1. Toss the greens with the dressing just before serving.

Balsamic Reduction

MAKES ⅓ TO ½ CUP

Wolfgang's EASY TIPS

➤ This will keep in a cool place for months.

When you reduce balsamic vinegar to a syrupy consistency, a few drops will add tremendous flavor to practically any salad.

1   **cup balsamic vinegar**

1. Bring the vinegar to a boil in a small saucepan over medium heat. Turn the heat to low and reduce to ⅓ to ½ cup. The vinegar will thicken as it cools. Refrigerate in a covered container.

Stacked Tomatoes and Mozzarella with Balsamic Reduction

All you need for this vertical rendition of a classic tomato-mozzarella salad is fresh seasonal tomatoes, a drizzle of reduced balsamic vinegar (see above), and a little extra-virgin olive oil.

For each serving:

1   **medium or large tomato, cut crosswise into ¼-inch-thick slices**
    Salt and freshly ground pepper

2   **ounces fresh mozzarella, cut crosswise into ½-inch slices**

3   **to 4 leaves of basil, slivered**

½   **teaspoon reduced balsamic vinegar**

2   **teaspoons olive oil**

1. Stack the tomato slices and mozzarella, seasoning each slice of tomato with salt and pepper, and ending with a tomato slice. Sprinkle the top with salt, pepper, and basil. Drizzle on the balsamic vinegar and the oil just before serving.

2. Garnish with store-bought breadsticks or make your own.

Citrus Vinaigrette

MAKES 1 ⅛ CUPS

Wolfgang's EASY TIPS

➤ This is best if used within a few days of making it.

Reduced orange juice mixed with balsamic vinegar and olive oil or a mixture of olive and walnut or hazelnut oils makes a fine dressing for soft, mild lettuces like butter lettuce.

1½ cups fresh orange juice	⅛ cup olive oil
1 shallot, minced	⅛ cup walnut or hazelnut oil, or use ⅔ cup olive oil in all
1 teaspoon minced fresh thyme	
2 tablespoons balsamic vinegar	Kosher salt and freshly ground pepper

1. Bring the orange juice to a boil in a medium saucepan. Reduce the heat and simmer until the orange juice has reduced to ⅛ cup. Cool to room temperature and mix together with the shallot, thyme, and balsamic vinegar. Whisk in the oil or oils and season to taste with salt and pepper. Refrigerate until ready to use.

Butter Lettuce Salad with Mandarin Oranges

MAKES 4 SERVINGS

You can find cans of Mandarin orange sections in most supermarkets. The salad is also good with fresh tangerine or mandarin sections.

1 head butter lettuce, leaves separated, washed, and dried	2 or 3 radishes, thinly sliced (optional)
⅓ cup Mandarin orange sections	½ cup citrus vinaigrette
2 teaspoons fresh chives	

1. Tear the leaves into medium pieces and toss with the orange sections, chives, radishes, and vinaigrette. Serve at once.

Bacon Vinaigrette

MAKES ⅓ CUP

This pungent dressing is a classic dressing for the French frisée salad made with curly endive, bacon, croutons, and a poached egg. It's also good with spinach salad, like the one on page 70.

3	slices bacon, chopped		Kosher salt and freshly ground pepper
½	cup white wine vinegar		
1	teaspoon sugar	2	tablespoons olive oil

1. Heat a small sauté pan over medium-high heat and cook the bacon until browned and crisp. Remove all but 2 tablespoons of the fat. Add the vinegar and stir, scraping up any browned bits on the bottom of the pan with a wooden spoon. Boil until the vinegar is reduced by half (watch carefully because this happens quickly), about 2 to 3 minutes. Add the sugar and cook until it has dissolved. Season to taste with salt and pepper. Remove from the heat, stir in the olive oil, and keep warm.

Frisée Salad

MAKES 6 SERVINGS

6	eggs	1½	cups croutons
¼	cup white wine vinegar	1	recipe Bacon Vinaigrette (above)
6	cups frisée lettuce, washed and dried		

1. Poach the eggs. Bring 2½ inches of water to a boil in a large, deep sauté pan. When the water comes to a boil, lower the heat to a bare simmer. Add the vinegar and some salt to the water. Crack 1 egg into a small bowl, making sure the yolk remains unbroken. Gently slip the egg into the simmering water. Repeat with the remaining eggs. Cook to the desired degree of doneness, 3 to 5 minutes. Remove from the water with a slotted spoon. Place on clean kitchen towels to drain. Set aside.

2. Make the dressing shortly before serving your salad. Toss all but 2 tablespoons of it with the frisée and the croutons. Distribute the frisée and croutons among six plates and top each one with a poached egg. Drizzle the remaining dressing over the eggs and serve.

PANINI ON THE INDOOR GRILL

Who would have thought that making sandwiches could be a great culinary adventure? But gone are the days of the sandwich made of two cold pieces of bread with a cold piece of turkey or ham slapped in between. Enter panini, the Italian word for toasted sandwiches. And enter the panini grill, an indoor two-sided grill that can make lunchtime as much fun as a barbecue. Warming foods always brings out flavors, and nobody will ever forget the flavors in these panini.

I have never seen a child or a grownup who doesn't like a simple cheese panini. Adding chicken or meat and other ingredients of choice—roasted peppers, sliced artichoke hearts, sun-dried tomato pesto, vegetables grilled on the same panini maker that will toast your sandwich—can transform the grilled cheese sandwich into a wonderful meal full of unexpected flavors and textures. The ingredients wc have at our disposal today—a variety of different cheeses like fontina, mozzarella, roquefort and goat cheese; great breads, from French bread to focaccia; prepared condiments like pestos, mustards, and tapenade; fresh herbs and baby lettuces—makes for a whole new range of possibilities.

As you cook your way through these recipes, you may be confused to see that some of them instruct you to spread a small amount of mayonnaise or butter on the outside of the bread as well as on the inside. This is intentional. The butter or mayonnaise on the outside of the bread will result in browning the panini into a gorgeous, delicious sandwich.

Grilled Salmon Panini

MAKES 4 SERVINGS

I like to use an electric panini maker or double-sided indoor grill to make these because you can use the appliance to cook the salmon perfectly and quickly before assembling and grilling the actual sandwiches. When you make these, you may find yourself saying, "Who needs a stove?"

4	skinless salmon fillets, 3 to 4 ounces each
1	tablespoon extra-virgin olive oil
1	teaspoon finely chopped fresh dill
½	teaspoon kosher salt
½	teaspoon freshly ground black pepper

1	loaf French bread, cut into 4 pieces, each 5 to 6 inches long (or 8 thick slices of another bread of your choice)
4	tablespoons Russian dressing (page 220)
1	tablespoon drained capers
4	very thin slices red onion
2	cups arugula, watercress, or baby lettuce leaves, washed and dried

1. Preheat a panini maker or double-sided indoor grill. Rub your fingertips over the surfaces of the salmon fillets to feel for the tips of any remaining small bones. Use your fingertips or tweezers to pull out the bones.

2. Rub the salmon fillets on both sides with the olive oil and sprinkle them evenly on both sides with dill, salt, and pepper. Put the fillets in the panini maker or grill, close the lid, and cook until the fish is opaque throughout—when the tip of a small, sharp knife is inserted between its flakes at the thickest part, but it is still moist in the middle, 3 to 4 minutes.

3. If using the French bread, while the salmon is cooking, use a serrated bread knife to cut each piece of bread in half horizontally. Spread both cut sides (or all the slices of bread) with Russian dressing. Sprinkle capers evenly on the bottom pieces.

4. When the salmon is done, transfer a fillet to each bottom piece of bread. Turn off the grill and with damp paper towels, carefully wipe down the cooking surfaces, being careful not to burn your fingers. Reheat the grill. Top the salmon fillets with onion slices and place the top piece of bread on each sandwich. Put the sandwiches back in the hot panini maker or double-sided grill, gently close the lid, and cook them until the bread is nicely browned and crusty, about 2 minutes more. Remove the sandwiches from the grill, remove the top piece of bread from each, and insert a layer of salad greens. Return the top pieces of bread, cut the sandwiches in half on the diagonal, and serve.

Wolfgang's EASY TIPS

➤ The type of bread you use needn't be set in stone. If you want a more delicate bread, substitute the crusty French bread with brioche, a roll, or big slices of country bread.

Grilled Shrimp BLT Panini with Shallot Cream Sauce

MAKES 4 DOUBLE-DECKER CLUBS OR 6 REGULAR SANDWICHES

Wolfgang's EASY TIPS

➤ If you don't have a panini maker, cook the shrimp in a grill pan or sauté pan, toast the bread in a toaster or in the oven, then assemble the sandwiches.

➤ The only thing that is time-consuming here is the sauce; if you don't want to bother, just toss the shrimp with about ½ cup of Russian dressing or mayonnaise. It'll still be a magnificent sandwich, and it will also be less rich.

➤ The sauce can be made, the shrimp grilled, and the bacon cooked several hours ahead.

➤ To peel shrimp, use your thumbs to split them apart between the rows of legs, then strip away the thin shells. Be sure also to devein the shelled shrimp, removing the thin, black or gray vein-like intestinal tract that runs just below the surface on the shrimp's outer curve. Use a small, sharp knife to make a shallow slit in the flesh all along the shrimp's length and then, with your fingers, pull out any vein that is revealed.

This is one of my all-time most popular sandwiches. At Spago we serve it for lunch, sometimes substituting lobster for the shrimp. I published a recipe for it in *Adventures in the Kitchen* (Random House, 1991), but that was before I began working with my indoor hinged panini grill. Now I grill the shrimp on the same grill I use for the panini, and the sandwiches are infused with the most wonderful grilled shrimp aroma.

For the shallot cream sauce:

1	teaspoon vegetable oil
5	large shallots, minced
½	cup white wine
1	tablespoon Champagne vinegar
½	cup heavy cream
½	cup unsalted butter, cut into small pieces
½	medium lemon, juiced
¼	teaspoon kosher salt (or to taste)
¼	teaspoon freshly ground pepper (or to taste)

For the grilled shrimp BLT:

¾	pound medium shrimp, peeled and deveined
2	tablespoons olive or vegetable oil
	Kosher salt and freshly ground black pepper
12	thin slices country or sourdough bread
½	cup mayonnaise
2	cups baby lettuce leaves
½	pound Roma tomatoes, cut into 12 slices
12	rashers bacon, cooked until crisp and drained on paper towels

1. Make the shallot cream sauce: Heat the oil over medium heat in a medium saucepan. Add the shallots and cook, stirring continuously to prevent browning, until they begin to release their juices, about 2 minutes. Add the wine and vinegar, raise the heat to high, stir and scrape with a wooden spoon to dissolve any pan deposits, and boil briefly until the liquid reduces slightly, 1 to 2 minutes. Stir in the cream and continue boiling until the liquid has reduced by half, about 5 minutes. Reduce the heat to low and, little by little, whisk in the butter to form a thick sauce. Pour the sauce through a fine-mesh strainer into a clean pan. Season with lemon juice and salt and pepper to taste. Cover the pan and keep warm if making the sandwiches right away.

2. Cook the shrimp. Preheat a panini maker or double-sided electric grill. Or heat a grill pan over medium-high heat. Toss the cleaned shrimp with the oil and season lightly with salt and pepper. Cook

the shrimp in the panini maker or double-sided grill just until they are cooked through and pink, 1 to 1½ minutes, taking care not to overcook them. Or cook in the grill pan for 1 to 2 minutes on each side. Remove from the heat and allow to cool until you can handle them, then cut each shrimp in half lengthwise and set aside. Turn off the grill and allow to cool slightly, then wipe the cooking surfaces clean with paper towels (taking care not to burn your fingers). Turn the grill back on.

3. Toast all of the slices of bread before assembling the sandwiches. To assemble the sandwiches, spread a little mayonnaise on all of the bread slices and arrange a layer of lettuce leaves on four of them for double-decker sandwiches, six for regular sandwiches. Top the lettuce with a layer of tomato slices and season them lightly with salt and pepper. Arrange 2 bacon slices on top of the tomatoes on each sandwich (3 if you're making the double-decker clubs). Add a second slice of bread for double-decker clubs and top it with a thin spread of mayonnaise and a little lettuce.

4. Heat the shallot cream sauce over medium-low heat. Add the shrimp and stir them in the sauce until warmed through, 3 to 5 minutes. Distribute the shrimp and sauce evenly among the 4 or 6 sandwiches and top them with the remaining lettuce and bread slices.

5. Place the sandwiches in the panini maker or double-sided grill, close the machine, and cook until the outer bread slices turn golden brown, 3 minutes. Cut each sandwich diagonally in half and serve.

Grilled Chicken Breast Panini with Artichoke Hearts and Sun-Dried Tomato Pesto

Today the condiments or sauces section of most well-stocked supermarkets, as well as many gourmet shops, carry containers of sun-dried tomato pesto, ready to add a burst of fragrant flavor to these delicious, Tuscan-style sandwiches. Canned artichoke hearts have a surprisingly good flavor and texture that further enhance the sandwiches. Those ingredients, combined with the goat cheese, grilled chicken, and salad greens, result in a multi-dimensional sandwich that, despite the complexity of its flavors, is very easy to assemble.

6	tablespoons extra-virgin olive oil	1	large loaf Italian bread or ciabatta, halved
2	tablespoons lemon juice	½	cup prepared sun-dried tomato pesto
½	teaspoon chopped fresh thyme		
2	garlic cloves, minced	1	(14-ounce) can artichoke hearts, drained well and thinly sliced
	Pinch kosher salt		
	Pinch coarsely ground black pepper	4	ounces fresh creamy goat cheese, crumbled
4	medium (6 to 8 inches long) skinless, boneless chicken breast halves, trimmed	1	cup mixed baby lettuces

1. In a nonreactive mixing bowl, stir together the olive oil, lemon juice, thyme, garlic, salt, and pepper. Add the chicken breasts, turn them in the mixture to coat them well, cover with plastic wrap, and marinate in the refrigerator for at least 1 hour.

2. Preheat a panini maker or double-sided electric grill. Remove the chicken breasts from the marinade, shaking off excess liquid, and cook them in the panini maker or grill, in batches if necessary to prevent overcrowding, until cooked through, 8 to 12 minutes.

3. Meanwhile, cut the Italian loaf in half lengthwise, then cut each half into pieces. Spread the inside of all four pieces with sun-dried tomato pesto. On each bottom half, evenly arrange the artichoke slices and the goat cheese.

4. When the chicken breasts are done, transfer them to a cutting board. Turn off the grill momentarily and clean the surfaces with paper towels, taking care not to burn your fingers (you won't get all the chicken residue off, but it doesn't matter since it will add flavor to the sandwiches). Plug in the machine again and turn it on. With a sharp knife, cut each breast crosswise and at a 45-degree angle into slices about ½ inch thick. Arrange the slices on top of the goat cheese.

5. Close each sandwich with the top piece of bread. Put the sandwiches in the panini maker or grill and cook them until the bread is nicely toasted, 3 to 5 minutes. Remove the sandwiches from the grill, remove the top slice of bread from each, and top with the salad greens. Return the top slices of bread. With a serrated knife, cut each large sandwich in half and place a large sandwich half on each of four serving plates. Serve immediately.

Grilled Vegetable Panini with Fontina Cheese and Pesto

MAKES 4 SERVINGS

You don't need an outdoor grill, or an expensive built-in indoor gas grill, to get the grilled vegetables that so many restaurants feature on their menus. A countertop panini maker or double-sided electric grill does the trick in minutes. Put together a variety of vegetables, add a little of your favorite vinaigrette dressing, a smear of store-bought pesto, and some good cheese, and you have the filling for an incredible sandwich.

4	thick squares focaccia bread, each 4 to 5 inches across
1	medium eggplant, cut crosswise into ½-inch slices
1	medium sweet yellow onion such as Maui, Vidalia, Walla Walla, or medium red onion, peeled and cut into ¼-inch slices
¼	cup balsamic vinaigrette dressing (page 77)
1	large red bell pepper, white ribs removed, quartered, stemmed, and seeded
½	cup good-quality prepared pesto
1	cup shredded fontina cheese

1. Preheat an electric panini maker or double-sided electric indoor grill. With a bread knife, cut each piece of focaccia in half horizontally to make 2 squares of the same size for the top and bottom of your sandwich.

2. Toss the eggplant and onion slices with the dressing, turning to coat the slices lightly on both sides. Set aside.

3. Put the pepper quarters side by side in the panini maker or grill. Close the machine and cook until tender, 5 to 8 minutes. Remove them and set aside.

4. Grill as many eggplant slices as will fit comfortably side by side in the double-sided grill for 4 to 5 minutes, or until tender. Remove and repeat with any remaining eggplant slices. Then grill the onion slices the same way, about 5 minutes per batch.

5. Spread the cut side of each focaccia piece with some of the pesto. Top half of the slices with 2 tablespoons of shredded fontina cheese. Top with the bell peppers. Then evenly distribute the eggplant slices, onions, and remaining fontina. Place the remaining focaccia pieces, cut side down, on top.

6. Put the sandwiches in the panini maker or double-sided grill. Close the machine and cook until the cheese has melted and the bread is golden brown, 3 to 4 minutes. Remove the sandwiches, cut each in half with a sharp knife, and serve.

Wolfgang's EASY TIPS

➤ The vegetables can be grilled ahead and the panini assembled and grilled just before serving. Keep them at room temperature or chill if holding for several hours.

➤ You can substitute or add other vegetables to the mix. Try zucchini and/or portobello mushrooms.

➤ You can substitute ciabatta for the focaccia.

Grilled Steak Panini

MAKES 4 SERVINGS

Wolfgang's EASY TIPS

➤ Hanger steak, flat-iron steak, and flank steak are wonderful and less expensive replacements for New York steak or filet mignon. Once cooked, cut into ¼-inch thick slices before placing on the bread.

I love making steak sandwiches with leftover sirloin, and here I don't even have to hope for leftovers. Just take a nice filet mignon or tournedo and cut it crosswise into thinner steaks, then grill them in the panini maker. Use a mustardy mayonnaise and always top the steak with something green, either spinach or arugula. Serve with homemade potato chips (page 212) and sliced tomatoes.

½ cup mayonnaise

1 tablespoon grainy Meaux mustard

8   slices country bread

½ **pound beef fillets, cut crosswise into ¾-inch-thick steaks**

Kosher salt and freshly ground black pepper

1 handful of baby spinach leaves or arugula

1. Preheat an indoor grill or panini maker. Mix together ⅛ cup of the mayonnaise and the Meaux mustard. Spread each slice of the bread generously on one side with the mixture. Spread a thin layer of the remaining mayonnaise on the other side of the bread slices and set aside.

2. Season both sides of the fillets with salt and pepper. Grill for about 2 minutes, or until nicely grilled on the outside and rare inside. Remove from the grill and place a fillet on the mustard-mayonnaise side of a slice of bread. Top with another slice (mustard side down). Repeat with the remaining bread.

3. Grill the sandwiches in the indoor grill, being careful not to crowd the grill, until the bread is nicely browned, 3 to 4 minutes. Remove the sandwiches from the grill, remove the top slices of bread, and insert a handful of greens. Return the top slice of bread, slice the sandwiches in half diagonally, and serve.

VARIATION: *Add crumbled gorgonzola or blue cheese to each sandwich.*

Roast Beef Panini with Roquefort and Caramelized Shallots

MAKES 4 SERVINGS

The sweet-savory taste of caramelized shallots makes a great complement to medium-rare roast beef from your deli and tangy Roquefort cheese in these crusty sandwiches.

3	tablespoons unsalted butter
6	large shallots, thinly sliced
2	medium baguettes, each cut in half, each piece halved horizontally lengthwise
2	to 4 tablespoons creamy Dijon-style mustard (optional)
1	pound thinly sliced medium-rare roast beef
1	cup crumbled Roquefort cheese

1. Preheat a panini maker or a double-sided indoor grill. In a small sauté pan over medium heat, melt the butter. Add the shallots, season with salt and pepper to taste, and sauté, stirring frequently, until the shallots turn caramel brown, 5 to 7 minutes. Set aside.

2. Spread the cut side of each piece of bread with Dijon mustard to taste, if desired. Arrange the roast beef slices evenly on the bottom halves and top with the shallots and crumbled Roquefort cheese. Place the top halves on the sandwiches.

3. Place the baguettes in the panini maker and grill for 4 minutes or until the cheese melts. Cut each sandwich in half and serve.

Smoked Turkey Reubens with Havarti Cheese

MAKES 4 SERVINGS

Wolfgang's EASY TIPS

➤ You could also bake these sandwiches in a nonstick pan in a 350°F oven for about 10 minutes, or until the cheese is melted.

Some food historians will tell you that the Reuben sandwich was invented by a restaurateur in New York City; others say it originated with a chef of the same name in Omaha, Nebraska. Whatever the truth may be, this recipe is an original in its own right since it replaces the usual corned beef with smoked turkey, the Swiss cheese with Danish Havarti, and the sauerkraut with coleslaw. You can find all these ingredients, plus the traditional Russian dressing, at any good deli or well-stocked market.

8	slices pumpernickel, rye, or pumpernickel-rye swirl bread
2	tablespoons unsalted butter, at room temperature (optional)
¼	cup bottled or homemade Russian dressing (page 220) or Thousand Island dressing (page 219)
8	slices regular or dill-flavored Havarti cheese, about ½ pound total
1	pound thinly sliced smoked turkey breast
½	cup good-quality coleslaw, well drained

1. Preheat an electric panini maker or double-sided indoor grill. Place the 8 slices of bread on a work surface and spread the top of each slice with butter if desired. Turn half the slices over and spread each with 1 tablespoon of Russian dressing. Top the dressing on each with a slice of cheese, then one-fourth of the turkey. Top the turkey on each with one-fourth of the coleslaw, then another slice of cheese, and a top slice of bread, buttered side up.

2. Place as many sandwiches as will fit comfortably side by side in the panini maker or indoor grill. Close the machine and grill until the cheese has melted and the bread is nicely brown and crusty, 3 to 4 minutes. Repeat with any remaining sandwiches. With a sharp knife, cut each finished sandwich diagonally in half and serve immediately.

Grilled Pastrami and Cheese

We make these sandwiches with our own homemade pastrami at the restaurant. Find a good deli and you can easily make them at home. To make this more like a Reuben, see the recipe on page 94 and substitute pastrami for the smoked turkey.

8	slices crusty rye or country bread	¼	cup prepared or homemade Russian dressing (page 220)
2	tablespoons unsalted butter, softened (optional)	8	thin slices fontina cheese, or 1 cup grated
		1	pound thinly sliced pastrami

1. Preheat an electric panini maker or double-sided indoor grill. Place the 8 slices of bread on a work surface and spread the top of each slice with butter if you wish. Turn half the slices over and spread them with 1 tablespoon of Russian dressing. Top the dressing with half the cheese then with the pastrami. Top the pastrami with the remaining cheese and a top slice of bread, buttered side up.

2. Place as many sandwiches as will fit comfortably side by side in the panini maker or indoor grill. Close the machine and grill until the cheese has melted and the bread is nicely brown and crispy, 3 to 4 minutes. Repeat with any remaining sandwiches. With a sharp knife, cut each finished sandwich diagonally in half and serve immediately.

Wolfgang's EASY TIPS

➤ Buttering the outside of the bread will help it brown nicely in the grill.

Fontina and Broccoli Rabe Panini
with Sun-Dried Tomatoes

MAKES 4 SERVINGS

Wolfgang's EASY TIPS

➤ You can blanch the broccoli rabe up to three days ahead if you squeeze it well and keep it in a covered bowl in the refrigerator.

➤ You could substitute blanched greens or even tender green asparagus, either blanched or grilled, for the rapini and Gruyère for the fontina.

This is a vegetarian's dream sandwich, and dedicated carnivores will love it too. I love the contrasts of flavors and colors—the dark green broccoli rabe set against the creamy cheese and deep red sun-dried tomatoes.

1 bunch broccoli rabe, cleaned and trimmed	3 tablespoons softened butter
8 thick slices crusty country bread or brioche	1 cup grated fontina cheese
	½ cup olive oil–packed sun-dried tomatoes

1. Bring a large pot of generously salted water to a boil and add the broccoli rabe. Cook 3 to 4 minutes, until tender, and transfer to a bowl of ice water. Drain and squeeze dry. Chop coarsely and set aside.

2. Preheat a panini maker or double-sided indoor grill. Place the eight slices of bread on a work surface and spread the top of each slice with butter if desired. Turn half the slices over and spread each with a small amount of butter. Top with the cheese, then one-fourth of the broccoli rabe. Top the broccoli rabe with sun-dried tomatoes and then a slice of bread, buttered side up.

3. Place as many sandwiches as will fit comfortably side by side in the panini maker or indoor grill. Close the machine and grill until the cheese has melted and the bread is nicely brown and crusty, 3 to 4 minutes. Repeat with any remaining sandwiches. With a sharp knife, cut each finished sandwich diagonally in half or quarters and serve immediately.

Grilled Cheese on Brioche

This is about as close as you can get to a traditional grilled cheese sandwich. The bread I use is rich brioche and the cheese is the highest quality fontina or Gruyère I can find.

8	thick slices brioche	2	tablespoons softened butter
1	tablespoon mayonnaise	1½	cups grated fontina or Gruyère cheese

1. Preheat a panini maker or double-sided indoor grill. Place the 8 slices of bread on a work surface and spread the top of each slice with a small amount of mayonnaise. Turn half the slices over and spread each with a small amount of butter. Top with the cheese. Butter the top slices of bread and place over the cheese, mayonnaise side up.

2. Place as many sandwiches as will fit comfortably side by side in the panini maker or indoor grill. Close the machine and grill until the cheese has melted and the bread is nicely brown and crispy, 3 to 4 minutes. Repeat with any remaining sandwiches. With a sharp knife, cut each finished sandwich diagonally in half or into quarters and serve immediately.

Wolfgang's EASY TIPS

➤ Spreading a small amount of mayonnaise on the outside of the bread will make your bread golden brown and crispy.

Barbecued Turkey and Green Chili Quesadillas

MAKES 4 SERVINGS

Wolfgang's EASY TIPS

➤ You can also make these in a skillet on top of the stove or on a griddle. Fry the quesadillas in a little olive oil over medium heat until the bottom sides brown, then carefully slide them out of the pan, flip them over, and return them to cook on the other side until golden.

➤ These make a nice starter as well as a light supper or lunch.

Conventional sandwiches made with bread aren't the only kind that you can cook easily and perfectly in an electric panini maker or double-sided indoor grill. Those appliances also do an excellent job making the Mexican tortilla-and-cheese sandwiches known as quesadillas. This version, which you can put together in minutes, is a great way to use up leftover poultry meat. Its delicious smoky-sweet flavor comes from your favorite brand of bottled barbecue sauce.

8	large flour tortillas
1½	tablespoons mayonnaise
2	cups shredded leftover turkey or chicken meat
½	cup good-quality bottled barbecue sauce
4	green onions, thinly sliced

1	can mild green chile, like jalapeño, roasted and peeled, and thinly sliced
2	cups shredded cheese, such as mozzarella, fontina, cheddar, or a mix
	Guacamole and fresh salsa for serving

1. Preheat a panini maker or a double-sided countertop grill.

2. Arrange the tortillas on a work surface and spread a small amount of the mayonnaise evenly over one side of each tortilla.

3. In a mixing bowl, toss together the turkey or chicken and the barbecue sauce. Turn four of the tortillas mayonnaise side down and spread 1 cup of the shredded cheese evenly over them. Top the cheese with the poultry mixture, then the chopped green onions and chile strips, and then the remaining cheese. Place the remaining four tortillas mayonnaise side up on top.

4. Transfer as many assembled quesadillas to the panini maker or double-sided grill as will fit comfortably side by side. Close the lid and cook until the tortillas are golden brown and the cheese has melted, 2 to 3 minutes. Transfer to a platter, cover with foil, and cook the remaining quesadillas the same way.

5. To serve, place a quesadilla on a cutting board and, with a large, sharp knife, press down across its diameter three times to make six equal wedges. Slide the quesadillas onto a plate or platter and serve immediately with guacamole and a spicy salsa on the side.

PASTA AND PIZZA

Pasta and pizza are in the same chapter here because they come from the same place and are made with similar ingredients. I grew up in southern Austria, a few miles from the Italian border, and pasta was a staple in our diet. My mother and grandmother always made our noodles, rolling out the dough very thin and cutting it by hand. I didn't even know what store-bought pasta looked like! As a kid I loved noodles with sweet fillings, but today I love savory, rustic flavors like the ones in this chapter.

I've given you a recipe at the beginning of this chapter for a basic pasta dough that yields easy-to-handle, delicate noodles. I urge you to try to make your own ravioli and tortellini, at least once. They're really quite easy, and the fillings here are incredible. Once you make the ravioli or tortellini, store it in the freezer if you aren't cooking it right away, and bring it out for special occasions. You'll get praise from the whole neighborhood.

Everybody from kids to adults loves pizza. It's a dish I can't wait to get back to even after I've toured gourmet restaurants in France. In 1982, when we first opened Spago in West Hollywood, everybody thought I was crazy for making pizzas, but my idea was to be creative and use wonderful, unexpected ingredients to turn a pizza into a great culinary experience.

Although we think of Italy as the land of pizza, my influence comes from Provence, which also has a pizza tradition. When I worked at Baumanière in Les Baux de Provence, we used to go to a terrific restaurant in nearby Salon de Provence called Chez Gu. There was nothing but a wood-burning pizza oven and a grill at this tiny place, and we couldn't wait to get back there each week to eat more pizza. The chef's dough had a marvelous yeasty flavor; his secret, he told us, was that he let the dough ferment overnight.

When I first came to California I was frustrated that I couldn't find an authentic wood-burning pizzeria. So when I opened my first restaurant I put in a pizza oven. Today pizza has come full circle; at one of Paul Bocuse's restaurants in France they're serving my signature Spago Smoked Salmon Pizza.

Basic Pasta Dough

⁓

MAKES ABOUT 1½ POUNDS PASTA DOUGH, 6 TO 8 SERVINGS

Even though people rarely make pasta at home today, I love homemade pasta so much, and we make it so often at the restaurant that I can't resist including some recipes for homemade pasta dishes in this book. You may think that pasta dough is challenging, but try this and you'll see how easy it can be, especially if you have a pasta attachment on your stand mixer. This is the same pasta dough I published in *Pizza, Pasta & More!* (Random House, 2000).

3	cups flour	2	to 3 tablespoons water (more as needed)
8	large egg yolks		
1	teaspoon salt		Semolina or all-purpose flour for dusting
1	teaspoon extra-virgin olive oil		

1. In a food processor fitted with the steel blade, combine the flour, egg yolks, salt, olive oil, and 2 tablespoons of the water. Process until the dough begins to hold together, then stop the machine and pinch the dough to test it. If it's too dry, add up to 1 more tablespoon of water and process until it forms a moist ball. Turn out onto a lightly floured work surface and knead by hand into a smooth ball. Wrap in plastic wrap and let rest at room temperature for 30 minutes to 1 hour.

2. To roll out the dough using a pasta roller, cut the dough into four equal pieces. Keep the other pieces covered in plastic while you roll out one piece at a time. Set the rollers at the widest opening. Flatten the first piece of dough into a thick strip no wider than the machine to enable it to pass through the rollers. If necessary, dust the pasta very lightly with flour. Run the pasta through the machine. Fold in thirds, crosswise, and run through the machine again. Repeat this procedure two or more times, until the dough is smooth and somewhat elastic. Set the machine to the next smaller opening and run the dough through the rollers.

3. Continue rolling and stretching the dough, using the smaller opening each time, until the next to the last or the last opening is reached, dusting lightly with flour only as necessary. (The strip of dough will be long. If you don't have enough space on your worktable, halfway through the rolling process cut the strip of dough in half and continue to work with each piece separately, keeping the unused dough covered).

4. Shape and cut the pasta as directed in your recipe. Any excess dough can be stored in the refrigerator for several days or rolled out and dried or frozen.

Wolfgang's EASY TIPS

➤ For a firmer dough, use half semolina, half all-purpose flour.

➤ To dry pasta before cooking, line baking sheets with parchment paper, liberally sprinkle semolina flour on top of the parchment, and lay the noodles on top.

Rigatoni with Ragù Bolognese

MAKES 12 SERVINGS

Ragù Bolognese is one of my favorite pasta sauces. It resembles a thick stew of beef and diced vegetables and makes a perfect companion to rigatoni, the tubular macaroni whose ridges so conveniently capture bits of sauce. The quantities of sauce below yield twice as much as you'll need for six portions. Refrigerate half of it for up to three days, or freeze it for four months. The sauce is better the day after you make it, so try to get it done a day before you wish to serve this dish. I recommend adding the hot red pepper flakes.

For the Bolognese sauce:

2 plus 2 tablespoons extra-virgin olive oil

1 pound lean ground beef

Kosher salt and freshly ground black pepper

1 small shallot, minced (about 2 teaspoons)

2 garlic cloves, minced (about 2 teaspoons)

½ cup dry red wine

5 pounds Roma tomatoes, cored, blanched for 30 seconds in boiling water, peeled, seeded, and finely chopped by hand or by pulsing in a food processor fitted with the stainless steel blade

3 tablespoons tomato paste

1 to 3 teaspoons sugar

A bouquet garni consisting of 4 sprigs parsley, 2 sprigs rosemary, 2 sprigs basil, and 2 bay leaves

1 teaspoon whole black peppercorns, tied in a piece of cheesecloth

1 teaspoon kosher salt

1 teaspoon oregano

1 medium onion, finely diced

1 medium carrot, peeled, trimmed, and finely diced

1 medium celery stalk, finely diced

2 cups homemade or good-quality store-bought chicken broth

Red pepper flakes (optional)

For the rigatoni:

1 tablespoon kosher salt

1 pound dried rigatoni

2 tablespoons unsalted butter

1 plus 1 tablespoons olive oil

¾ cup homemade or good-quality store-bought chicken broth

¾ teaspoon minced fresh oregano or basil

3 tablespoons minced fresh parsley

⅓ cup freshly grated Parmesan cheese

Freshly ground black pepper

Shaved or grated Parmesan for garnish

1. Make the Bolognese sauce. Have a large saucepan or Dutch oven standing by while you heat 2 tablespoons of the olive oil in a large, heavy skillet over medium-high heat. Add the beef and sauté, using a wooden spoon to break up the meat into small pieces, until lightly browned, about 5 minutes. Season lightly to taste with salt and pepper. Add the shallots and garlic and sauté until they soften, 3 to 4 minutes more. Set a strainer over a bowl and transfer the meat to the strainer so that the fat will drip off.

2. Add the wine to the pan and stir and scrape to deglaze. Turn off the heat.

3. Transfer the meat to the heavy saucepan or Dutch oven. Pour in the wine from the pan and place the Dutch oven over medium-high heat. Simmer, stirring often, until the wine has almost completely evaporated, 3 to 4 minutes. Stir in the tomatoes, tomato paste, and 1 teaspoon sugar. Add the bouquet garni and the sachet with the peppercorns, along with 1 teaspoon salt and the oregano. Bring to a boil, stir and reduce the heat, and simmer uncovered for 45 minutes, stirring every 5 minutes.

4. Meanwhile, heat the remaining 2 tablespoons olive oil in a small sauté pan over medium-high heat. Add the onion and carrot and sauté for 1 minute. Add the celery and continue sautéing until translucent, 1 to 2 minutes more. Season lightly with salt and pepper.

5. Remove the bouquet garni and the sachet with the peppercorns from the sauce and stir in the vegetables and broth. Simmer, stirring occasionally, until thick, about 1 hour more. Taste and adjust the seasonings with more salt, pepper, or sugar. For a spicier sauce, add some red pepper flakes. Set half of the sauce aside for the rigatoni, and freeze the remaining half.

6. Cook the rigatoni. Bring a large pot of water to a boil. Add the salt and stir in the rigatoni. Cook the pasta until it is al dente, following the manufacturer's suggested cooking time (usually 8 or 9 minutes).

7. While the pasta is cooking, melt the butter with 1 tablespoon of the olive oil in a large sauté pan over medium heat. Stir in the Bolognese sauce you set aside for the rigatoni, the broth, and the oregano. Bring to a simmer. When the pasta is ready, drain. While it is still slightly dripping, add it to the hot Bolognese sauce and stir to combine. Stir in the parsley, grated Parmesan, the remaining 1 tablespoon olive oil, and salt and pepper to taste. Divide among six heated serving plates or pasta bowls. Garnish with Parmesan shavings and serve.

Pasta with Wild Mushrooms, Corn, and Bell Peppers

MAKES 6 APPETIZER SERVINGS, 4 MAIN COURSE SERVINGS

Wolfgang's EASY TIPS

➤ For a lower-fat version, replace the cream with 1 cup diced canned tomatoes.

➤ You could substitute slivered fresh basil for the parsley.

I love to add sweet, tender corn to pasta dishes in late summer when it's at its best. You could make this pasta at other times of the year substituting peas or diced zucchini for the corn. Fresh shiitake mushrooms have a creamy texture that works beautifully at any time of year. Be careful not to overcook the vegetables since they should remain crisp-tender.

1	teaspoon Kosher salt		Kernels from 1 medium or large ear of corn
¼	pound small broccoli florets (from 1 broccoli crown)	½	cup heavy cream
¼	pound sugar snap peas, trimmed, strings removed		Freshly ground pepper
2	tablespoons extra-virgin olive oil	¾	pound fettuccine or other dried pasta of your choice
½	red, yellow, or orange bell pepper, diced	¾	cup freshly grated Parmesan cheese
¼	pound fresh shiitake, chanterelle, or porcini mushrooms, cleaned, trimmed, and sliced	1	tablespoon chopped fresh flat-leaf parsley

1. Bring a medium saucepan full of water to a boil while you prepare the vegetables. Fill a large bowl three-fourths full with ice and water. When the water comes to a boil, add the salt and the broccoli. Cook just until the color brightens, about 30 seconds to a minute, then transfer to the ice water using a slotted spoon or skimmer. Add the sugar snap peas to the boiling water, cook 30 seconds to a minute, or until they are bright, and transfer them to the cold water. Let the peas sit for a couple of minutes in the cold water, then drain the vegetables and pat them dry with paper towels.

2. Bring a pasta pot full of water to a boil. Meanwhile, heat a 12-inch frying pan or casserole over medium-high heat. When the pan is hot, add the olive oil. As soon as the oil swirls freely in the pan, quickly add the broccoli, sugar snap peas, bell pepper, mushrooms, and corn. Toss or stir the vegetables briskly in the pan for a minute or two to heat them well without browning. Add the heavy cream to the pan and bring it to a simmer. Simmer for a few minutes, just until the vegetables are crisp-tender. Add salt and pepper to taste and remove from the heat. Cover and keep warm.

3. When the pasta water comes to a boil, add a tablespoon of salt and the pasta. Cook al dente, following the directions on the package. Drain and toss with the vegetables in the pan. Add the Parmesan and parsley, toss again, taste and adjust seasonings, and serve.

Angel Hair with Shrimp Fra Diavolo and Heirloom Tomatoes

MAKES 6 APPETIZER SERVINGS, 4 MAIN DISH SERVINGS

This is a quick and easy dish to make since it calls for rapid sautéing of the pasta toppings.

1½	**pounds jumbo shrimp, peeled, tails removed, and deveined (see tip on page 86)**
	Kosher salt and freshly ground pepper
2	**tablespoons extra-virgin olive oil**
3	**garlic cloves, peeled and thinly sliced**
½	**teaspoon crushed red pepper flakes**
2	**pounds sun-ripened tomatoes, preferably heirloom varieties, cut into ½-inch pieces, or 1 (28-ounce) can, drained**
1	**teaspoon chopped fresh oregano, or ¼ teaspoon dried**
12	**ounces dried angel hair pasta**
2	**tablespoons chopped fresh flat-leaf parsley**

1. Bring a large pot or pasta cooker of water to a boil while you prepare the sauce. Heat a 12-inch frying pan or casserole over medium-high heat. Lightly sprinkle the shrimp with salt and pepper. As soon as the pan feels hot when you hold your hand an inch or two above its surface, add the oil and swirl the pan to coat the bottom. Without disturbing them, cook the shrimp for 1 to 2 minutes on one side. With tongs, a fork, or a small spatula, flip the shrimp over. Add the garlic and crushed pepper to the pan. The instant the shrimp start to sizzle and before the garlic has time to brown, add the tomatoes and oregano. Stir and scrape the pan with a wooden spoon to dislodge and incorporate the pan deposits into the sauce, and continue cooking until the shrimp are cooked through and the sauce has thickened, 2 to 3 minutes more. Taste and adjust the seasonings, if necessary, with salt and pepper. Remove the pan from the heat, cover, and keep the sauce warm.

2. When the water comes to a rolling boil, add a tablespoon of salt and the angel hair pasta. Cook until the pasta is al dente, tender but still slightly chewy, following the manufacturer's suggested cooking time, usually 2 to 3 minutes.

3. Ladle out ¼ cup of the pasta cooking water, set it aside, and drain the pasta. Add the drained pasta to the sauce and stir or toss it together using tongs or a pasta fork. Heat through for about 30 seconds so the flavors of the sauce penetrate the pasta. If the mixture seems too dry, stir in some or all of the reserved pasta water.

4. Use the tongs or a pasta fork and a serving spoon to transfer the pasta, shrimp, and sauce to individual warmed serving bowls or plates, heaping each serving in an attractive mound. Garnish with parsley and serve.

Wolfgang's EASY TIPS

➤ For the most attractive and delicious results, I like to use heirloom tomatoes from the farmers' market, colorful and flavorful varieties whose production has been revived in recent years. Feel free to substitute any good sun-ripened tomatoes, and when tomatoes are not in season, use a good brand of canned.

➤ If you want to get ahead on this dish, make the sauce a few hours ahead and reheat.

Tagliatelle with Pancetta, Shrimp, and Roasted Tomatoes

MAKES 4 SERVINGS

Wolfgang's EASY TIPS

➤ To butterfly the shrimp, peel and remove the intestinal tract along the top curve of the shrimp. Using the sharp knife that you used for cleaning the shrimp, cut the shrimp along the same incision about halfway through to the other side. When the shrimp cooks, it will open out and twist.

➤ To roast tomatoes, preheat the broiler and line a baking sheet with foil. Place the tomatoes on the foil and set under the broiler, about an inch from the flame. Check after 2 minutes. If the skin is brown and blistered, turn the tomatoes over using tongs. Broil on the other side for another 2 to 3 minutes, or until the skin is brown and blistered. Remove from the heat and allow to cool in a bowl. Then core the tomatoes and remove the skins.

➤ Other types of pasta, such as linguini and fettuccine, will also go well with the topping.

I always love shrimp with pasta and pizza. Pancetta and roasted tomatoes deepen and enrich the flavors in this dish.

4	tablespoons olive oil	4	roasted tomatoes, peeled, seeded, and cut into large chunks
4	ounces pancetta or bacon, cut into small dice	¾	to 1 pound tagliatelle (or to taste)
1	tablespoon chopped garlic		
12	large shrimp, cleaned (page 86) and butterflied	2	tablespoons freshly grated Parmesan cheese
1	teaspoon chile flakes	2	tablespoons coarsely chopped basil
	Kosher salt and freshly ground black pepper		

1. Heat a large sauté pan over medium-high heat and add the olive oil. When the oil is hot, add the pancetta and sauté until crispy and nice and brown. Add the garlic and cook, stirring, for 30 seconds to a minute, until fragrant. Stir in the shrimp, chile flakes, and salt and pepper, and continue to cook until the shrimp are pink and cooked through, about 5 minutes.

2. Add the tomatoes and simmer slowly for 5 minutes.

3. Bring a large pot of salted water or a pasta pot filled with water to a boil and add the pasta. Cook until slightly al dente. (Dried pasta takes about 10 minutes while fresh pasta cooks in seconds.)

4. When the pasta is cooked, drain well, add to the pan with the shrimp, toss well, and garnish with the grated Parmesan cheese and chopped basil. Serve immediately.

Fettuccine Alfredo with Mascarpone Cream Sauce

MAKES 4 TO 6 SERVINGS

Fettuccine Alfredo can be a stodgy dish, but here the cream is tempered with chicken broth, which makes for a much smoother, lighter-textured sauce. Mascarpone, lightly soured Italian cream cheese, adds a marvelous bite to the mixture.

2	tablespoons extra-virgin olive oil	¾	pound dried fettuccine
2	tablespoons unsalted butter	¼	cup freshly grated Parmesan cheese
⅔	cup heavy cream	1	teaspoon freshly ground black pepper
½	cup chicken broth	1	tablespoon chopped fresh flat-leaf parsley, plus more for garnish
4	ounces mascarpone		
1	to 2 tablespoons kosher salt		

1. Bring a large pot or pasta pot of salted water to a boil while you make the sauce.

2. Heat a large frying pan or flameproof casserole over medium-high heat. When the pan is hot, add the olive oil. When the oil is hot enough to swirl easily around the pan, add the butter. When the butter is only partially melted, quickly add the cream and the chicken broth. Bring to a boil. Spoon in the mascarpone and whisk as it melts and the sauce becomes smooth and creamy. Set aside, cover, and keep warm.

3. When the pasta water comes to a boil, add the salt and the pasta. Cook until the pasta is al dente, following the manufacturer's instructions. Drain the pasta, retaining some of the cooking water, and add to the pan with the hot sauce. Stir in the grated Parmesan, pepper, and 1 tablespoon of parsley and spoon in up to ¼ cup of the hot pasta cooking water to help the pasta and sauce blend together more easily. Toss well and, using a pasta server or tongs, transfer the pasta to individual heated pasta bowls or plates. Garnish with more parsley, if you wish, and serve.

Wolfgang's EASY TIPS

➤ It helps to have a pasta pot with an insert for this dish. Then you can easily transfer the cooked pasta from the water to the pan with the sauce, and if you need more water to thin out the sauce it'll be right next to you in the pasta pot.

➤ You can find mascarpone in Italian delis and many well-stocked supermarkets.

Spaghetti with Tomato Sauce
and Tender Garlic-Parmesan Meatballs

MAKES 8 SERVINGS

Wolfgang's EASY TIPS

➤ You can also use a meat grinder to grind the meat and your mixer to blend the ingredients.

➤ You can also use a pressure cooker for this. Follow the recipe through step 3, but use 1¼ cups stock for the sauce. You can make and brown the meatballs while the sauce is simmering, and you can use the pressure cooker for simmering the sauce so that you don't need to wash an extra pot. Place the browned meatballs in the sauce in the pressure cooker, even if it has not simmered for the full 30 minutes, and bring to pressure over high heat. Reduce the heat to low and set the timer for 15 minutes. Remove from the heat and release the pressure. When all of the pressure has been released, carefully open the lid. Stir, adjust seasonings, and proceed with step 5.

For many Americans, a traditional pasta meal still means spaghetti and meatballs. And why not? It's so easy to make a delicious version of this classic dish if you follow a few simple rules. First, make your tomato sauce from scratch, using good-quality canned plum tomatoes (I like the San Marsano variety, imported from Italy, which you can find in well-stocked markets and Italian delis). The meatballs will be more flavorful, and they'll have a wonderfully moist, tender texture if you grind the meat yourself with a meat grinder or chop it in a food processor and then mix in not only eggs and breadcrumbs to bind the mixture but also roasted garlic, Parmesan cheese, and a dash of vinegar.

For the tomato sauce:

¼ cup extra-virgin olive oil

1 medium onion, chopped

7 garlic cloves, minced

1 small can tomato paste (6 tablespoons)

½ cup beef broth, chicken stock, or good quality store-bought beef or chicken broth (1¼ cups if using a pressure cooker)

2 (28-ounce) cans diced tomatoes in their juice

¼ cup red wine

4 small pepperoni slices, diced

1 teaspoon dried oregano

½ teaspoon dried marjoram or thyme

1 bay leaf

Kosher salt and freshly ground black pepper

For the meatballs:

1½ pounds well-trimmed lean beef such as London broil or top round, cut into uniform 1-inch chunks

½ pound well-trimmed lean pork loin, cut into uniform 1-inch chunks

7 roasted garlic cloves (page 129), peeled

2 large eggs

½ cup breadcrumbs or bread soaked briefly in milk

¼ cup freshly grated Parmesan cheese

1 tablespoon chopped fresh flat-leaf parsley

1 teaspoon white vinegar

½ teaspoon kosher salt

Freshly ground black pepper

2 tablespoons extra-virgin olive oil

1½ pounds dried spaghetti

¼ cup slivered fresh basil leaves for garnish

Freshly grated Parmesan cheese

1. Make the tomato sauce. Heat a large, heavy casserole over medium heat. Add the olive oil and as soon as it swirls easily add the onion and sauté, stirring frequently, until translucent but not yet golden, about 4 minutes. Stir in the garlic and sauté about 30 seconds more. Add the tomato paste and sauté, stirring almost continuously, until it darkens in color slightly, about 3 minutes. Add the stock and stir until the tomato paste dissolves. Stir in all the remaining ingredients, season with salt and pepper to taste, cover, and simmer, stirring occasionally, for 30 minutes.

2. While the sauce is simmering, make the meatballs. Turn on a food processor fitted with a steel blade and drop the meat through the feed tube. With the motor running, drop the chunks of beef and pork through the feed tube. With the motor still running, immediately add the roasted garlic, eggs, breadcrumbs, Parmesan, parsley, vinegar, salt, and pepper to taste. Continue processing, stopping once or twice to scrape down the work bowl, until the mixture is smooth and fine. Transfer the meat mixture from the bowl to a mixing bowl, carefully handling the blade. Moisten your hands with cold water and shape the mixture into uniform meatballs about 2 inches in diameter. Place them on a parchment (or wax) paper–lined platter or tray. Cover and chill if not cooking right away.

3. Heat a large skillet over medium-high heat. Add the olive oil. When the oil is hot enough to swirl, place the shaped meatballs in the pan and sauté, moving them around gently with a wooden spoon until they are uniformly browned, about 10 minutes. With a slotted spoon, transfer the meatballs to paper towels to drain. Set aside.

4. When the sauce has simmered for 30 minutes, remove and discard the bay leaf. Taste the sauce and adjust salt. Stir the browned meatballs into the sauce, reduce the heat to low, and continue simmering, stirring gently from time to time, until the sauce is thick and the meatballs are cooked through, about 1 hour.

5. Bring a large pot or a pasta cooker filled with water to a boil. Add a tablespoon of salt. Following the manufacturer's suggested cooking time, add the spaghetti to the boiling water and cook the pasta until it is al dente, tender but still slightly chewy. Drain the pasta and return it to the pot still slightly dripping. Spoon some of the sauce into the pot and toss the pasta to coat it well. Then, using a pasta server or tongs, transfer the pasta to a large serving bowl or individual pasta bowls or plates. Spoon the sauce and meatballs on top and garnish with fresh basil. Serve immediately, passing Parmesan cheese for guests to add to taste.

Straw and Hay Pasta with Fresh Peas and Prosciutto

MAKES 4 SERVINGS

I can't think of a better thing to do with fresh peas during their short spring season than use them in this beautiful, rich pasta dish. Straw and Hay Pasta refers to the combinations of green (straw) and yellow (hay) fettuccine. The fresh peas, cream, and prosciutto are classic accompaniments. I like to spice the sauce up a little with red pepper flakes.

1	tablespoon kosher salt	1	cup shelled fresh peas (1 pound in the shell), blanched unless very small (see first tip)
1	tablespoon extra-virgin olive oil		
1	tablespoon unsalted butter		
½	cup finely minced onion	6	ounces fresh egg fettuccine or angel hair pasta
4	ounces thinly sliced prosciutto, cut into thin julienne strips	6	ounces fresh spinach fettuccine or angel hair pasta
1	cup heavy cream	½	cup freshly grated Parmesan cheese
	Kosher salt and freshly ground black pepper		
	Pinch of red pepper (optional)		

1. Fill a large stockpot or pasta pot with water and add the salt. Place the pot over high heat and bring the water to a rapid boil.

2. Meanwhile, heat a large sauté pan over medium heat. Add the olive oil and then the butter. When the butter has melted, add the onion and sauté, stirring continuously, until it turns translucent but has not yet begun to brown, about 1 minute. Scatter in the prosciutto strips and cook 1 more minute, stirring continuously to keep the strips separate. Add the cream and bring to a simmer.

3. Continue simmering, stirring frequently with a wooden spoon, until the sauce is just thick enough to lightly coat the back of the spoon, 1 to 2 minutes. Taste the sauce and adjust the seasoning with a little salt, if necessary, and black pepper. Add a pinch of red pepper flakes if desired. Stir in the peas, remove the pan from the heat, and set it aside.

4. Add the egg and spinach fettuccine or angel hair to the boiling water and cook until the pasta is al dente, tender but still slightly chewy. This should take only a few minutes. Return the sauce to medium heat. Drain the pasta and immediately add it to the sauce. Toss well to coat the pasta thoroughly.

5. Serve immediately in heated shallow pasta bowls, sprinkling each serving with Parmesan cheese and a generous grinding of black pepper.

Wolfgang's EASY TIPS

➤ The recipe does not instruct you to cook the peas. However, if they are not very small spring peas, blanch them first for 2 minutes in salted boiling water, then transfer them to a bowl of cold water and drain.

➤ You can make this dish at other times of year with frozen peas. Thaw frozen peas by covering them with boiling water. Let them sit for about 5 minutes, then drain.

➤ Fresh egg and spinach pastas can be found in Italian delis and in the freezer or refrigerated section of some supermarkets.

Pappardelle with Braised Duck Legs

MAKES 6 SERVINGS

This is a one-dish meal that requires nothing more than a green salad. I like to serve the robust dish family style from a buffet or the center of the table, where guests can serve themselves as much or as little as they want. But you can also serve the pasta and duck on individual plates.

Wolfgang's EASY TIPS

➤ If you don't want to make your own pasta, feel free to serve this wonderful topping with store-bought fettuccine, or pappardelle if you can find it in an Italian grocery store.

➤ This long-simmering sauce is a perfect candidate for the pressure cooker. Results are rich and intense. See instructions below.

➤ Use a robust red wine, such as a Côtes du Rhone for this.

➤ Whole chicken thighs and legs can be substituted for the duck.

This is a one-dish meal that requires nothing more than a green salad. I like to serve the robust dish family style from a buffet or the center of the table, where guests can serve themselves as much or as little as they want. But you can also serve the pasta and duck on individual plates.

1	recipe Basic Pasta Dough (page 101)	3	tablespoons tomato paste
3	to 4 duck legs	2	plus ½ cups homemade or good-quality store-bought chicken stock
	Kosher salt and freshly ground black pepper		
2	tablespoons olive oil	3	sage leaves
1	medium carrot, cut into ½-inch cubes	5	thyme sprigs
1	small onion, chopped		Semolina flour for dusting
1	celery stalk, cut into ½-inch cubes	2	tablespoons butter
1½	cups red wine, such as a Côtes du Rhone	⅓	cup freshly grated Parmesan
		2	tablespoons chopped fresh flat-leaf parsley

1. While the dough is resting, prepare the duck legs. Preheat the oven to 350°F. Cut each duck leg crosswise across the bone into three pieces and season with salt and pepper to taste. Heat the olive oil over high heat in a large, heavy skillet and sear the duck on all sides until nice and brown, about 10 minutes. Transfer the duck to a heavy casserole and pour off all but a thin film of the fat from the pan. Add the carrot, onion, and celery to the pan, and cook, stirring, until lightly browned, 5 to 10 minutes. Add the red wine to the pan and bring to a boil. Stir and scrape the pan to deglaze the pan deposits and pour into the casserole, along with the vegetables. Add the tomato paste, 2 cups of the chicken stock, and the sage, thyme, and salt and pepper to taste. Bring to a simmer, cover, and place in the oven. Cook 1½ hours, or until the duck is very tender. Remove the casserole from the oven and set aside.

Using a pressure cooker: Follow step 1 as directed, substituting a pressure cooker for the casserole. After all of the ingredients have been added to the pressure cooker, cover, and bring to high pressure. When high pressure has been reached, turn the heat to low and set the timer for 13 minutes. After 13 minutes, turn off the pressure cooker and release the steam using the quick release.

When all of the pressure has been released, carefully remove the lid. Taste and adjust seasonings.

2. Make the pappardelle. Cut the dough into four equal pieces and work with one portion at a time, keeping the others covered with plastic wrap. Roll out the pasta following the directions on page 101. Using a serrated pasta cutter, cut the pasta into 12-inch-long sheets, and then into 1-inch-wide noodles.

3. Line baking sheets with parchment and sprinkle the parchment with semolina flour. Lay the noodles on the sheets to dry for at least 20 minutes while bringing a large pot of salted water to a boil. Meanwhile, in a large sauté pan combine the remaining ½ cup chicken stock and the butter. Bring to a boil. When the butter has melted into the stock, turn off the heat. Taste and season with salt and pepper and keep warm.

4. When the salted water comes to a boil, add the pappardelle and cook just for a few minutes, until the pasta is al dente. Drain the pasta and add to the chicken stock mixture. Place the duck legs on top of or around the pasta. Top with the freshly grated Parmesan, sprinkle with parsley, and serve.

Tortellini with Ricotta, Sage, and Pepper Butter

MAKES 4 SERVINGS

Tortellini looks complicated, but they're no more difficult to make than ravioli. You simply make small ravioli, then pinch two of the corners together to form the tortellini. I love this simple filling of ricotta and goat cheese accented with sage and thyme. It couldn't be easier. Try to find high quality fresh ricotta at an Italian deli.

For the tortellini:

½	recipe Basic Pasta Dough (page 101)
½	cup ricotta cheese
¼	cup Parmesan
¼	cup mascarpone
1	egg yolk
¼	teaspoon kosher salt
	Pinch of pepper
½	cup goat cheese
½	teaspoon sugar
½	teaspoon ground nutmeg

1	teaspoon chopped fresh sage (about 4 leaves)
1	teaspoon chopped fresh thyme
1	egg, beaten
1	tablespoon water
	Semolina flour for dusting

For the sage and pepper butter:

6	tablespoons (¾ stick) unsalted butter
	Pinch of salt
	Freshly ground black pepper
1	fresh sage leaf, plus additional leaves for garnish

1. Make the pasta dough as directed on page 101. While it is resting, make the filling. Combine the ricotta, Parmesan, mascarpone, egg yolk, salt, pepper, goat cheese, sugar, and nutmeg in a food processor and pulse until well combined. Scrape into a bowl and stir in the sage and thyme. Cover and refrigerate.

2. Make the tortellini. Cut the dough into four equal pieces. Keep the other pieces covered in plastic while you roll out one piece at a time through the rollers of a pasta machine into long, wide strips, following the directions on page 101.

3. Combine the beaten egg and water for the egg wash. Brush a strip of dough with the egg wash. Place about 1 teaspoon of filling for each tortellini, placing the mounds about 2 inches apart. Fold the top half of the dough over to cover the mounds of filling. Push the mounds toward the folded edge of the dough and press down around each mound to secure the filling, making sure that there are no air pockets in any mounds. With a 2-inch round cookie cutter, cut the pasta into half-moon shapes to make ravioli (see page 119). Then pinch the two opposing corners of each ravioli

➤ To prevent the tortellini from sticking to your work surface if not cooking right away, as soon as they are made freeze them on pieces of parchment that you have dusted generously with semolina flour. Transfer the pasta directly from the freezer to boiling water.

➤ You can find scalloped cookie cutters in kitchen supply stores. A regular round cookie cutter is a fine substitute if you don't have a scalloped cutter.

Filling and Shaping Tortellini

1.

2.

3.

4.

5.

6.

together to get the tortellini shape. Dust a parchment-lined tray generously with semolina and arrange the tortellini on the tray, dusting them with more semolina. Repeat with the remaining dough, egg wash, and filling. If you have more pasta than filling, cut the remaining pasta into strips and dry it.

4. For the sage and pepper butter, bring a large pot of salted water to a boil. Meanwhile, melt the butter in a small sauté pan over medium heat. Add a pinch of salt and pepper and the sage. Cook the butter until golden brown. Keep it warm while you cook the tortellini.

5. Add the tortellini to the boiling water. Boil gently for about 5 minutes. Transfer the pasta to four warm plates. Grate fresh Parmesan cheese on top and sprinkle generously with black pepper. Spoon the hot butter over the tortellini. Decorate with sage leaves and serve at once.

Half-Moon Ravioli with Wild Mushroom Filling

MAKES 4 SERVINGS

These large ravioli are filled with an intense, flavorful filling that reminds me of the forest. The sauce—equally flavorful—can be used for any kind of pasta. I use it with the garganelli on page 120. Wild mushrooms are available in many supermarkets, whole food stores, and farmers' markets. I like to use a combination; try shiitakes, chanterelles, crimini, and black trumpets.

½   **recipe Basic Pasta Dough (page 101)**

For the filling:

¼   **cup extra-virgin olive oil**

2   **cups finely chopped wild mushrooms**

2   **tablespoons chopped shallots**

1   **teaspoon chopped garlic**

    Kosher salt and freshly ground black pepper

2   **teaspoons chopped fresh thyme**

1   **teaspoon chopped fresh flat-leaf parsley**

2   **cups heavy cream**

2   **ounces soft goat cheese**

3   **ounces mascarpone**

1   **tablespoon grated Parmesan**

For the sauce:

1   **tablespoon olive oil**

4   **ounces wild mushrooms, sliced if large**

1   **tablespoon shallots**

½   **tablespoon chopped garlic**

1   **cup chicken stock, as needed**

1   **tablespoon butter**

    Kosher salt and freshly ground pepper

1   **egg, beaten**

1   **tablespoon water**

2   **tablespoons unsalted butter**

    Freshly grated Parmesan

1. Make the pasta dough as directed on page 101. While the dough is resting, make the filling. Heat a large sauté pan over medium-high heat and add the olive oil. When it is hot, add the mushrooms and sauté until they begin to soften, 3 to 5 minutes. Add the shallots, garlic, salt and pepper to taste, and herbs, and continue to sauté until the mixture is tender and fragrant, about 5 more minutes. Add the heavy cream and bring to a boil. Cook, stirring from time to time, until the mixture is thick and beginning to stick to the pan. Transfer the mixture to a bowl and allow to cool. Stir in the goat cheese, mascarpone, and Parmesan. Taste and adjust seasonings.

Wolfgang's EASY TIPS

➤ If you are not cooking the ravioli right away, to prevent them from sticking to your work surface, as soon as they are made freeze them on pieces of parchment that you have dusted generously with semolina flour. Transfer them directly from the freezer to boiling water.

➤ You can use an assortment of wild mushrooms for this. The filling can be made a day ahead of time. It will thicken up nicely in the refrigerator.

➤ I like to garnish this dish with chanterelles and shiitakes. Dice the mushrooms into small cubes and sauté them with garlic and shallots; sprinkle with a few leaves of chopped parsley. Place the garnish in the center of the plate and surround it with the ravioli.

2. Make the sauce. Heat the olive oil in a medium saucepan over medium-high heat and add the mushrooms, shallots, and garlic. Sauté for 2 minutes, stirring. Add ½ cup of the chicken stock and the butter and bring to a boil. Boil for 3 minutes. Remove from the heat and transfer to a blender or a food processor fitted with the steel blade. Purée, adding more chicken stock as needed to thin the sauce. Return to the pan and if the sauce is too thin, bring to a boil and reduce slightly. Season with salt and pepper to taste. Keep warm.

3. Make the ravioli. Cut the dough into four equal pieces and work with one portion at a time, keeping the others covered with plastic wrap. Roll out the dough, following the directions on page 101, into strips that are approximately 20 inches long and 4 inches wide. Make an egg wash by combining the egg and water and brush over the dough. Spoon out 6 scant tablespoon-size portions of filling along the bottom half of the length of the dough, leaving 2 to 2½ inches between portions. Fold the top half of the dough over to cover the mounds of filling. Push the mounds toward the closed edge of the dough and press down around each mound to secure the filling, making sure that you do not have any air pockets in any mounds.

4. With a 2½-inch round cookie cutter, cut the ravioli into half-moon shapes by laying the cookie cutter partially over the dough with the folded edge across its equator. Dust a parchment-lined tray generously with semolina and arrange the ravioli on the tray, dusting them with more semolina. Repeat with the remaining dough, egg wash, and filling. Place the ravioli in the freezer if you are not cooking them right away.

5. Shortly before serving, bring a large pot of salted water to a boil. Reduce the heat slightly so the water isn't boiling too hard, and add the ravioli. Boil until the ravioli floats to the top, about 5 minutes.

6. Meanwhile, melt 2 tablespoons butter in a large saucepan or skillet. Add the cooked ravioli and toss gently. Divide the sauce among four plates and arrange the ravioli on top. Sprinkle with freshly grated Parmesan and serve.

Filling and Shaping Half-Moon Ravioli

1.

2.

3.

4.

5.

Garganelli with Mushroom Sauce

MAKES 4 TO 6 SERVINGS

Wolfgang's EASY TIPS

➤ The sauce will keep for a few days in the refrigerator and freezes well.

➤ You can purée the sauce in a blender or food processor if you wish.

Garganelli are handmade, ridged tubes of egg pasta. They're made by rolling the pasta around a pencil or spatula handle over a ridged surface such as a comb. The ridges catch the sauce, and the mushroom sauce is a wonderful choice. Garganelli are the only tubular pasta that are made by hand. Feel free to substitute dried fusilli, penne, or rigatoni. Anything with ridges to catch the sauce will work.

1	recipe Basic Pasta Dough (page 101), or ¾ to 1 pound fusilli, penne, or rigatoni

For the sauce:

2	tablespoons olive oil
½	pound wild mushrooms, sliced if large
2	tablespoons shallots
1	tablespoon chopped garlic
1	cup chicken stock
1	tablespoon butter
¼	cup cream
	Kosher salt and freshly ground pepper
	Freshly grated Parmesan for sprinkling

1. Make the pasta dough according to the directions on page 101. While it is resting, make the sauce. Heat the olive oil in a medium saucepan over medium-high heat and add the mushrooms, shallots, and garlic. Sauté for 2 minutes, stirring constantly. Add the chicken stock, butter, and cream, and bring to a boil. Boil for 3 minutes. Remove from the heat. Add a little more chicken stock or cream if the sauce is too thick. Season with salt and pepper to taste. If you wish, purée the sauce in a blender or food processor. Keep warm.

2. Make the garganelli. Cut the dough into four equal pieces and work with one portion at a time, keeping the others covered with plastic wrap. Following the directions on page 101, roll out the dough into long, wide strips, then cut into 1½-inch squares. Turn a square so that the point is facing you. Place a pencil or a small round spoon or spatula handle horizontally on the bottom of the diamond and roll it up in the pasta. Press the pencil down on a ridged surface, such as a comb. Slide the pencil out and repeat with the rest of the pasta. Allow the garganelli to dry for 30 minutes before cooking.

3. Bring a large pot of salted water to a boil and add the garganelli. Cook until it is al dente, which should take only a few minutes. Alternatively, cook fusilli or penne for about 8 minutes, or until it is al dente. Drain and toss with the sauce. Sprinkle with grated Parmesan and serve at once.

Making Garganelli

1.

2.

3.

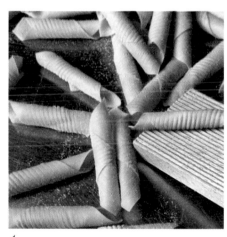

4.

Angel Hair Pasta with Broccoli and Goat Cheese

MAKES 4 TO 6 SERVINGS

Some restaurant favorites are easy and economical, and this is one of them. It makes a great weeknight main course but it's elegant enough for company. The sauce is nothing more than concentrated chicken broth, goat cheese, and butter tossed with bright, tiny broccoli florets cut from the larger crowns.

1 tablespoon plus 1 teaspoon extra-virgin olive oil	Freshly ground black pepper
1 tablespoon pine nuts	3 tablespoons unsalted butter
1½ cups chicken stock or good-quality store-bought chicken broth	4 ounces fresh creamy goat cheese, crumbled
½ pound tiny broccoli florets, cut from the crowns	Kosher salt
1 teaspoon chopped fresh thyme, plus 4 to 6 sprigs for garnish	12 ounces spaghettini or other thin dried pasta strands

1. Fill a large pot or pasta pot with water and add 1 teaspoon of olive oil. Bring the water to a boil. Meanwhile, put the pine nuts in a dry sauté pan and toast them over low heat, stirring constantly, until they turn light golden, 2 to 3 minutes. Transfer to a bowl to cool.

2. Bring the stock or broth to a boil in a saucepan over medium-high heat and continue boiling until the liquid has reduced to half its volume, 12 to 15 minutes. Set aside.

3. Heat a sauté pan over medium-high heat. Add the remaining 1 tablespoon of olive oil and the broccoli, and sauté just until bright green and crispy, about 1 minute. Add the reduced stock or broth and bring to a boil. Add the thyme leaves, pepper to taste, butter, and goat cheese. Whisk together until the cheese melts. Taste and add salt if desired. Remove the skillet from the heat or turn the heat to very low, cover the pan, and keep warm.

4. Add a tablespoon of salt to the boiling water. Add the pasta and cook until it is al dente, tender but still slightly chewy, following the suggested cooking time on its package. Drain and add to the pan of sauce. Toss, using tongs or long-handled spoons, to distribute the sauce and broccoli evenly. Adjust the seasonings to taste with salt and pepper. Divide the pasta among warm serving plates. Garnish each serving with a sprig of thyme, sprinkle with toasted pine nuts, and serve.

All-Purpose Pizza Dough
(with some pizza-making suggestions)

MAKES 4 SMALL (8-INCH) PIZZAS OR 2 LARGE (14-INCH) PIZZAS

This is a simple bread dough, which you can mix by hand or in a stand mixer. You can roll it out into small pizzas, which are easy to manipulate, or you can make big ones. As for toppings, I have offered many to choose from here. But don't stop with these! Master the pizza dough, and then you can be as creative as you wish with the toppings. That's the whole idea behind the California pizza. They're fun, and you can be as inventive as you want to be.

2½ **teaspoons (1 packet) active dry yeast**	1 **tablespoon extra-virgin olive oil, plus additional for brushing the pizza crusts**
1 **cup warm water (105°F to 115°F)**	3 **cups all-purpose flour**
1 **teaspoon honey**	1 **teaspoon salt**

1. In the bowl of a stand mixer, or in a large bread bowl, dissolve the yeast in the water. Add the honey and stir together. Let sit 2 or 3 minutes, or until the water is cloudy. Stir in the olive oil.

2. **Using a stand mixer:** Combine the flour and salt and add it to the yeast mixture all at once. Mix it together using the paddle attachment, then change to the dough hook. Knead at low speed for 2 minutes, then turn up to medium speed and knead until the dough comes cleanly away from the sides of the bowl and clusters around the dough hook, about 5 minutes. Hold on to the machine if it bounces around. Turn out onto a clean work surface and knead by hand for 2 or 3 minutes longer. The dough should be smooth and elastic. When you press it with your finger it should slowly spring back, and it should not feel tacky.

Kneading the dough by hand: Mix together the yeast, honey, water, and olive oil as directed in a medium-size or large bowl. Combine the flour and salt. Fold the flour in a cup at a time using a large wooden spoon. As soon as you can scrape the dough out in one piece, scrape it onto a lightly floured work surface and knead it for 10 minutes, adding flour as necessary until the dough is smooth and elastic.

Using a food processor: Mix together the yeast, honey, water, and olive oil in a small bowl or measuring cup. Place the flour and salt in a food processor fitted with the steel blade. Pulse once or twice. Then, with the machine running, pour in the yeast mixture. Process until the dough forms a ball on the blades. Remove the dough from the processor and knead it on a lightly floured surface for a couple of minutes, adding flour as necessary, until it is smooth and elastic.

Wolfgang's EASY TIPS

➤ Pizza dough can be rolled out, covered airtight with plastic and foil, frozen, then transferred directly from the freezer to a hot oven.

➤ You can make pizza dough ahead and let it rise in a covered bowl in the refrigerator. Just punch it down and knead it a few times when you're ready to roll it out.

➤ If you don't have a pizza wheel for cutting the pizzas, use kitchen scissors or a serrated knife.

3. Transfer the dough to a clean, lightly oiled bowl, rounded side down first, then rounded side up. Cover the bowl tightly with plastic wrap and leave it in a warm spot to rise for 30 minutes (you can leave it for up to an hour). When it is ready the dough will stretch as it is gently pulled.

4. Divide the dough into two to four equal balls, depending on how large you want your pizzas to be. Shape each ball by gently pulling down the sides of the dough and tucking each pull under the bottom of the ball, working round and round the ball 4 or 5 times. Then, on a smooth, unfloured surface, roll the ball around under your palm until it feels smooth and firm, about 1 minute. Put the balls on a tray or platter, cover them with pan-sprayed plastic wrap or a damp towel, and leave them to rest for at least 30 minutes. At this point, the dough balls can be covered with plastic wrap and refrigerated for 1 to 2 days. You will need to punch them down again when you are ready to roll out the pizzas.

5. Preheat the oven to 500°F. Place a pizza stone in the oven to heat. In the meantime, press out the dough. Place a ball of dough on a lightly floured surface. While turning the dough, press down on its center with the heel of your hand, gradually spreading it out to a circle 7 to 8 inches in diameter for small circles, 12 to 14 for larger pizzas. Alternatively, use a rolling pin to get an even circle. With your fingers, form a slightly thicker raised rim around the edge of the circle. Brush everything but the rim with a little olive oil, then top the pizza as you like. You can transfer the pizza to a lightly oiled pizza pan if you like, or you can bake it directly on the stone.

6. Depending on your taste, spread the dough with marinara sauce or pesto sauce (about 2 tablespoons for small pizzas, ¼ to ⅓ cup for larger ones). If you don't have sauce, a can of tomatoes, drained, chopped, and seasoned with salt and chopped sautéed garlic, will do. Top with the shredded or grated cheeses of your choice (I like a mixture of mozzarella and fontina). Add thinly sliced vegetables such as Roma tomatoes, pitted olives, red peppers, or red onions; sautéed sliced vegetables such as mushrooms, eggplant, zucchini, or artichoke hearts; thinly sliced cured meats such as pepperoni or prosciutto; or small pieces of lightly cooked chicken or shrimp. Add a light sprinkling of grated Parmesan or crumbled goat cheese or blue cheese and some minced or julienned fresh herbs such as basil or oregano or dried herbs such as thyme, oregano, or herbes de Provence.

Making a Pizza

1.

2.

3.

4.

5.

6.

7.

8.

9.

10.

11.

12.

7. Dust a pizza paddle (also called a baker's peel) with semolina and slip it under the pizza. Slide the pizza onto the baking stone or into the pizza pan (or place the pizza pan on the stone—the heat from the stone will help it achieve a crisp crust). Bake until the cheese topping is bubbling and the rim of the crust is a deep golden brown, about 10 minutes.

8. Use the pizza paddle to slide the pizza out of the oven and onto a cutting board. Use a pizza cutter or a sharp knife to cut the pizza into slices and serve immediately.

Grilled Pizza

MAKES 4 SMALL (8-INCH) PIZZAS

Wolfgang's EASY TIPS

➤ To turn your grill into an outdoor oven, build a very hot fire in the entire grill well. Place a large baking stone directly over the fire on the grates and let it heat for 20 minutes. You will bake the pizza right on the stone, with the grill covered, and it will be done in 5 to 7 minutes.

➤ If you don't have tomato sauce, simply pulse drained tomatoes from a 14-ounce can in a food processor and season with salt to taste and 1 or 2 chopped fresh garlic cloves sautéed in a little olive oil.

➤ Arrange your topping ingredients on a nearby table or tray to help you work quickly.

➤ You can use store-bought pizza dough if you don't want to make your own.

Grilling pizza may sound strange to you, but it's hardly different from baking it in a wood-fired oven like I do in my restaurants. In this case, you turn your grill into an outdoor oven. The results are equally sensational—a crisp crust with a hint of tasty charring and a smoky aroma that seasons every bite. And this is one grilled treat that you don't have to put into a bun to eat.

For grilled pizza, you can use the recipe for All-Purpose Pizza Dough on page 123, or you can use the one below, which makes a sturdier, crisper dough.

For the pizza dough:

1½ teaspoons dried yeast

1 teaspoon honey

1 cup warm water (105°F to 110°F)

2 cups all-purpose flour

1 cup semolina flour

1 teaspoon salt

1 tablespoon extra-virgin olive oil, plus more for brushing the pizza dough

For the toppings:

1 cup homemade or store-bought marinara sauce (page 216) or pesto sauce

2 cups shredded mozzarella cheese or sliced fresh mozzarella (even better)

2 cups shredded fontina cheese

¼ cup freshly grated Parmesan cheese

Minced fresh thyme, oregano, basil, or sage for garnish

Dried herbs such as oregano or herbes de Provence

Other possible toppings:

Dabs of goat cheese

Sliced grilled vegetables

Sliced pepperoni

Crumbled cooked sausage

Thinly sliced prosciutto

1. Make the pizza dough following the directions on pages 123–124; the semolina replaces 1 cup of the flour in the basic recipe.

2. Turn the dough out onto a clean, lightly floured work surface. Knead it by hand, repeatedly pushing it out, folding it back, and rotating it, until the dough feels smooth and elastic, about 3 minutes. Shape the dough into a ball and place it in a lightly oiled bowl, rounded side down first, then rounded side up, cover it with plastic wrap, and leave it at room temperature to rise for 30 minutes.

3. On a lightly floured surface, cut the dough into four equal pieces. Form each into an even ball, pulling down all around the sides and tucking underneath as you rotate the ball several times.

Then, roll the ball under your palm until it feels smooth and firm, about 1 minute. Place the balls on a lightly oiled tray, cover them with plastic wrap, and leave them to rest for at least 30 minutes. If you are not using the dough right away, it can be refrigerated for up to 2 days.

4. In an outdoor grill, prepare a hot fire, setting the grill rack 3 to 4 inches above the heat. Open the bottom grill vents and close the top ones. Place a baking stone on the rack, cover the grill, and let the stone heat for 20 minutes.

5. To make a pizza, dip one side of a dough ball into flour and place it floured side down on a work surface. From its center outward, use your hands or a rolling pin to stretch out the dough as thinly as possible to the desired shape; do not make a rim.

6. Dimple the pizza dough all over with your fingertips so that it will hold the toppings. Lightly brush or rub the top of each pizza with olive oil. Sprinkle a pizza paddle (also called a peel) or rimless baking sheet with semolina or cornmeal. Place one crust at a time on the peel or rimless baking sheet. Top with ¼ cup of tomato sauce, the cheeses, and other toppings you may desire (except for fresh herbs; sprinkle them on after the pizza is done—dried herbs should be sprinkled on before.) Sprinkle the hot stone with semolina or cornmeal. Carefully slide or lift the pizza onto the stone. Cover the grill again. Cook the pizza until the cheese is melted and the crust is golden brown on the edges, 5 to 7 minutes.

7. Using tongs or a spatula, slide the pizza onto a cutting board. Sprinkle it with fresh herbs. Cut the pizza into pieces and serve immediately. Repeat with the remaining dough and toppings.

Roasted Garlic and Wild Mushroom Pizza

MAKES 4 SMALL (8-INCH) OR 2 LARGE (14-INCH) PIZZAS

Wolfgang's EASY TIPS

➤ You can make the pizza crust ahead of time. Roll it out and wrap it tightly with plastic wrap and foil and store it in the freezer or in the refrigerator. Frozen pizza can be transferred directly to the hot oven.

➤ If you can't find fresh oregano, use 1 teaspoon dried or try fresh marjoram or 2 teaspoons chopped fresh sage.

➤ The roasted garlic cloves will keep for several days in the refrigerator. The cooked mushrooms will also keep for a few days.

➤ You can use store-bought pizza dough if you don't want to make your own.

I like to make this pizza with a combination of mushrooms, such as shiitakes, white button, crimini, and black trumpets. But other mushrooms, such as oyster mushrooms and porcinis, will do. You could also substitute cultivated mushrooms for half the wild mushrooms.

1	recipe pizza dough (page 123)	1	tablespoon chopped fresh oregano
2	tablespoons olive oil		Kosher salt and freshly ground pepper
½	cup thinly sliced red onions		
1	pound assorted mushrooms, cleaned and thickly sliced if large	2	cups grated fontina cheese
		2	cups grated mozzarella cheese
12	roasted garlic cloves (see next page)		

1. Make the mushroom topping while the pizza crust is rising. Heat a large sauté pan over medium-high heat and add the olive oil. When it is hot, add the red onions. Sauté until they begin to soften, 2 to 3 minutes, and add the mushrooms. Sauté until the mushrooms are lightly browned, about 5 minutes, and add the garlic and oregano. Continue to cook, stirring, until the mushrooms are tender and fragrant, about 5 more minutes. Season to taste with salt and pepper.

2. Place a pizza stone on the middle rack of the oven and preheat the oven to 500°F.

3. Divide the dough into four equal pieces and press or roll them out as directed in step 4 on page 124. Lightly brush the inner circle of the dough with oil and sprinkle on the fontina and mozzarella cheeses. Sprinkle the sautéed mushrooms over the cheese.

4. Using a lightly dusted baker's peel or a rimless flat baking tray, slide the pizza onto the baking stone and bake until the pizza crust is nicely browned, 10 to 12 minutes. Remember that the oven is very hot and be careful as you put the pizza in and again as you remove it from the oven. Transfer the pizza to a firm surface and cut it into slices with a pizza cutter or a very sharp knife. Serve immediately.

Roasted Garlic Cloves

12 garlic cloves, peeled and trimmed	1 tablespoon olive oil
	½ teaspoon red pepper flakes

1. Preheat the oven to 375°F. Toss the garlic cloves with the olive oil and red pepper flakes in a small baking dish. Place the dish in the oven and roast the garlic, stirring occasionally, until the cloves are lightly browned, 15 to 20 minutes. Watch the garlic as it browns because it takes on a bitter taste if it roasts for too long. Cool the garlic and transfer it to a container and refrigerate, covered, until needed.

Pizza with Barbecued Beef & Onions

MAKES 4 SMALL (8-INCH) PIZZAS

Wolfgang's EASY TIPS

➤ You could add greens such as spinach, Swiss chard, or kale. If you add Swiss chard or kale, blanch these sturdier greens in boiling salted water first. Drain, squeeze dry, chop coarsely, and add with the onions.

➤ Pork or chicken can be substituted for the beef.

➤ You can use store-bought pizza dough if you don't want to make your own.

Once you master making pizza crust, the pizza becomes a great vehicle for leftovers. Here I've tossed leftover meat with barbecue sauce, then added spinach, onions, and cheese for a really fine California pizza.

¾	pound cooked, shredded beef	1	recipe pizza dough (page 123)
	Kosher salt and freshly ground pepper	2	cups grated mozzarella cheese
¼	cup barbecue sauce	2	cups grated fontina cheese
1	tablespoon olive oil, plus additional for brushing the pizza	¼	cup grated Parmesan cheese
1	medium red onion, thinly sliced	1	bunch cilantro, leaves removed and washed
			Red and green jalapeños for garnish

1. Season the meat with salt and pepper to taste. Toss it with the barbecue sauce and set aside. Place a pizza stone on the middle rack of the oven and preheat the oven to 500°F.

2. Heat a medium skillet over medium-high heat and add the olive oil. When it is hot, add the onion and sauté until it becomes translucent, 2 to 3 minutes. Remove the pan from the heat.

3. Shape each pizza as directed in step 4 on page 124. Brush the pizzas with olive oil. Sprinkle the cheeses evenly over each one and top with the onions and meat with the barbecue sauce.

4. Using a lightly floured baker's peel or a rimless flat baking tray, slide the pizza onto the baking stone and bake the pizza until the crust is nicely browned, 10 to 12 minutes. Remember that the oven is very hot and be careful as you transfer the pizza into and out of the oven. Place the pizza on a firm surface, sprinkle it with cilantro, and cut it into slices with a pizza cutter or a very sharp knife. Garnish with slivered jalapeños and serve immediately.

Pizza with Sausage, Fennel & Peppers

Wolfgang's EASY TIPS

➤ The bottled fire-roasted peppers that you can find in many supermarkets are great to have on hand for dishes like this. You can also roast your own. Place a fresh pepper above a flame and, using tongs, turn it until it is uniformly charred. Place the charred pepper in a bag and twist the bag shut. Allow the pepper to cool, then remove the charred skin and the seeds and membranes. You can also roast peppers in a 400°F oven. Place the peppers on a foil-lined baking sheet and roast them for 30 to 40 minutes, turning them every 10 to 15 minutes.

➤ You can use store-bought pizza dough if you don't want to make your own.

I love the combination of fennel and red pepper, whether they're together in a salad, a pasta, or topping a pizza. I've added fennel sausage to the mix here. If you can't find fennel sausage, mild Italian sausage will do just fine.

2 tablespoons olive oil, plus additional for brushing the pizza crusts	½ cup prepared pesto
2 medium fennel bulbs, cut into eighths, cored, and thinly sliced	2 cups grated mozzarella cheese
	2 cups grated fontina cheese
1 teaspoon finely chopped garlic	¼ cup grated Parmesan cheese
1 teaspoon chopped fresh thyme	1 large roasted red pepper (fresh or bottled)
1 recipe pizza dough (page 123)	6 ounces fennel sausage, crumbled or sliced

1. Heat a large skillet over medium-high heat and add the olive oil. When the oil is hot, add the fennel and sauté until it is just tender, about 5 minutes. Remove the pan from the heat. Stir in the garlic and the thyme.

2. Place a pizza stone on the middle rack of the oven and preheat the oven to 500°F.

3. Roll or press out the pizza dough as directed in step 4 on page 124. Brush lightly with olive oil, then brush each pizza with 2 tablespoons of the pesto. Sprinkle the cheeses evenly over the pesto. Top with the fennel, red pepper, and sausage.

4. Using a lightly floured baker's peel or a rimless flat baking tray, slide the pizza onto the baking stone and bake until the pizza crust is nicely browned, 10 to 12 minutes. Remember that the oven is very hot and be careful as you place the pizza in the oven and again when you take it out. Transfer the pizza to a firm surface and cut it into slices with a pizza cutter or a very sharp knife. Serve immediately.

Pizza with Prosciutto and Arugula

MAKES 4 SMALL (8-INCH) PIZZAS

This easy pizza, known in southern Italy as Pizza Rustica, requires hardly any work beyond making the crusts. Make sure your ingredients are of the highest quality. Sprinkle the crusts with cheese, bake them, and then arrange the arugula, prosciutto, and Parmesan on top.

1 recipe pizza dough (page 123)	1 tablespoon balsamic vinegar
2 cups grated fontina cheese	6 ounces prosciutto, cut or torn into strips
2 cups grated mozzarella cheese	
2 cups baby arugula	1 cup shredded Parmesan cheese
2 tablespoons extra-virgin olive oil	

1. Place a pizza stone on the middle rack of the oven and preheat the oven to 500°F.

2. Roll or press out the pizza dough as directed in step 4 on page 124. Brush the dough lightly with olive oil, then sprinkle on the fontina and mozzarella cheeses.

3. Using a lightly floured baker's peel or a rimless flat baking tray, slide the pizza onto the baking stone and bake it until the crust is nicely browned, 10 to 12 minutes. Remember that the oven is very hot and be careful as you place the pizza in the oven and again as you take it out. Toss the arugula with the olive oil and balsamic vinegar. Transfer the pizza to a firm surface and arrange the prosciutto, arugula, and Parmesan on top. Cut the pizza into slices with a pizza cutter or a very sharp knife. Serve immediately.

MAIN DISHES

When I start thinking about a dinner party, I generally begin by choosing the main course, which is always the main event. I consider the seasons, and whether or not any of my guests have dietary restrictions. If it's a large party, I prefer to prepare a roast, like the dramatic Roast Beef Tenderloin with Mushroom Madeira Sauce on page 169; whereas a pan-seared filet mignon (page 177) or tuna steak (page 147) will do just fine for a dinner for two or four.

Variety is the spice of life, so I've included dishes with many different flavors here, as well as different cooking techniques—roasting and braising, grilling and sautéing. You might be surprised to find several recipes in this chapter that call for or give you an option to use a pressure cooker. My mother often used one during the hot summers in Austria to avoid heating up the kitchen with the oven. But I really learned to appreciate it when I worked at Baumanière in Provence. A customer walked in one day and asked us if we could make him a creamy vegetable soup on the spur of the moment. Using the pressure cooker we made a beautiful soup in fifteen minutes. You'll be impressed with the intense flavors that result when you use the pressure cooker, and you'll achieve the tenderest meat in just minutes.

One of the great advantages of modern life is the availability of fresh fish and shellfish. Just be sure to be flexible: if there's no fresh halibut for the recipe you were planning to cook, use sea bass instead, or vice versa. For larger gatherings I prefer firmer, more oily fish like salmon because they're more resistant to cooking, and not quite as delicate as flaky white-fleshed fish. And remember that white wine with fish is not a hard and fast rule. Try a good pinot noir served slightly chilled, and you'll have a whole new food and wine experience.

I purposely did not include fancy recipes with ingredients you have to fly to Paris to get in this chapter. Making a delicious roasted squab might be easy to do in a restaurant because we know the farmer who raised it, but for the home cook the squab will be difficult to procure. On the other hand, it's easy to find a quality free-range chicken. I get as many compliments for my pan-roasted chicken (page 158) as I do for anything I cook, and it's not because I shave truffles on top. It's because it comes out of the oven with a dark brown skin outside and perfectly moist meat inside. I don't even need a sauce; with a little Dijon mustard and French fries on the side, this is as good as it gets.

Roasted Salmon Fillets
with Red Wine Sauce and Mashed Potatoes

MAKES 4 SERVINGS

This is based on a recipe that I created more than twenty-five years ago. I wanted a fish dish that would go well with red wine. Like many classically trained chefs, I had been taught that red wine was for meat and white wine for fish. While this might be true some of the time, it isn't a hard and fast rule. Fish varieties typically described as "meaty," such as salmon, tuna, and swordfish, all have robust, oily flesh that stands up to red wine. The red wine you choose should not be a bold cabernet sauvignon, but a fruitier, more delicate wine. Pinot noir is ideal. Other varietals that work well are cabernet franc and merlot. I find that Syrahs also tend to overpower most fish. Finally, you can do several simple things during cooking to help form a bridge between the flavors of the fish and the wine. Many of the reds I've mentioned are often described as having an "earthy" flavor, so I'll accompany the fish with a purée of root vegetables; or a gratin of potatoes layered with onions in the style of Lyon, France; or some cabbage braised with bacon. Here I use simple creamy mashed potatoes.

Wolfgang's EASY TIPS

➤ Look for fresh wild salmon (as opposed to farmed) for superior flavor and texture.

➤ When making mashed potatoes, after you drain the potatoes return them to the hot pan, cover tightly, and allow them to steam for 5 minutes. Doing this allows the potatoes to dry out so they'll mash to a beautiful texture and soak up the butter and cream more readily.

➤ Mashed potatoes can be made ahead, cooled, and reheated in the bowl above a pot of simmering water or in a microwave.

For the fish and the potatoes:

4	plus 2 tablespoons (¾ stick) unsalted butter
4	salmon fillets, 6 ounces each
	Kosher salt
1	tablespoon coarsely ground black pepper
1	tablespoon minced fresh ginger
1	tablespoon extra-virgin olive oil
1¼	pounds baking potatoes, peeled and cut into 2-inch chunks
¼	cup heavy cream
	Freshly ground white pepper
	Pinch of freshly ground nutmeg

For the sauce:

¼	pound (1 stick) unsalted butter, divided
3	shallots, minced
2	garlic cloves, minced
1	plum tomato, peeled, seeded, and chopped
2	cups red wine, such as pinot noir or merlot
1	tablespoon balsamic vinegar
1	tablespoon good-quality bottled barbecue sauce
	Freshly ground black pepper

1. Melt 2 tablespoons of the butter. Set the remaining butter aside and cut into small pieces. Brush the salmon fillets on both sides with some of the melted butter. Sprinkle on both sides with salt to taste, black pepper, and ginger, gently pressing the seasonings into the fillets. With the olive oil, brush the bottom of a baking dish large enough to hold the fillets. Place them in the dish and drizzle with the remaining melted butter. Cover the dish with plastic wrap and refrigerate briefly while you start making the mashed potatoes and sauce.

2. Make the mashed potatoes. Put the potatoes in a saucepan filled with enough lightly salted cold water to cover them well. Bring to a boil over high heat, then simmer briskly until the potatoes are fork tender, 15 to 20 minutes. Meanwhile, heat the cream in a small saucepan over low heat. Drain the potatoes well, return to the pan, cover tightly, and let sit for 5 to 10 minutes. Pass them through a food mill set over the saucepan, or put them back in the pan and mash with a potato masher until smooth. Add the warm cream and the butter and stir over low heat with a wooden spoon until thoroughly blended. Season to taste with more salt, white pepper, and nutmeg. Cover and keep warm (or you can reheat them in a microwave just before serving).

3. Make the sauce. Preheat the oven to 500°F. In a medium saucepan over medium heat, heat half of the butter until foamy. Add the shallots and garlic and sauté briefly, just until glossy and aromatic. Stir in the tomato and sauté 2 minutes more. Stir in the wine, raise the heat slightly, bring to a boil, and simmer briskly until reduced to about ½ cup, 10 to 15 minutes. Stir in the vinegar and barbecue sauce. Pour the sauce through a fine-mesh strainer into a clean saucepan and, over low heat, whisk in the remaining butter a little bit at a time, whisking until all of the butter is incorporated into the sauce after each addition. Season to taste with a little salt and pepper. Cover and keep warm while you roast the salmon.

4. Uncover the baking dish and place in the preheated oven. Roast until the salmon is cooked through but still moist and slightly shiny pink in the center when its flakes are separated with the tip of a small, sharp knife, about 10 minutes.

5. To serve, mound the potatoes in the centers of four heated serving plates. With a spatula, place a roasted salmon fillet on top of the potatoes. Spoon the sauce over the salmon and around the potatoes. Garnish with scallions and serve.

Grilled Shrimp and Lemon Wedges on Rosemary Skewers

MAKES 4 SERVINGS

I make these lemony shrimp outside on the grill in summer and on my two-sided indoor grill in winter. The shrimp are marinated in a mixture of lemon juice, olive oil, and garlic before being skewered on rosemary sprigs along with lemon wedges. The grilled lemon infuses the shrimp and the combination is terrific. If you can't find sturdy rosemary sprigs, use wooden skewers, soaking them for 30 minutes before skewering the shrimp and lemon wedges. Serve this shrimp with rice or roasted potatoes.

3 tablespoons freshly squeezed lemon juice	1½ pounds large shrimp, peeled and deveined
3 tablespoons extra-virgin olive oil	2 lemons, cut into 8 wedges, seeds removed
1 teaspoon grated lemon zest	8 sturdy fresh rosemary sprigs, each 6 to 8 inches long
2 or 3 fresh basil leaves, cut into fine julienne strips	Kosher salt and freshly ground black pepper
2 garlic cloves, minced	

1. In a large, nonreactive bowl, whisk together the lemon juice, olive oil, lemon zest, basil, and garlic. Add the shrimp, stir to coat them evenly, cover with plastic wrap, and refrigerate for at least 1 hour and no more than 3 hours.

2. Preheat an outdoor grill, an indoor double-sided grill, or the broiler. With the tip of a small, sharp knife, carefully remove any visible seeds from the lemon wedges.

3. Strip the leaves from each rosemary sprig, leaving just a tuft at one end. With the knife or gardening shears, trim the opposite end of each branch to a point.

4. Remove the shrimp from the marinade and skewer them on the rosemary sprigs, passing the point of each branch through both the head and tail end of each shrimp and alternating the shrimp with lemon wedges on the skewers.

5. When the grill or broiler is ready, season the shrimp on both sides with salt and pepper to taste. Place the skewers on the grill rack directly over the fire or under the broiler, and cook until they turn bright pink all over, 1 to 2 minutes per side, turning the skewers once with long-handled tongs. If using an indoor double-sided grill, grill for 2 minutes only.

Serve immediately, encouraging guests to slide the shrimp and lemon wedges carefully off their skewers and squeeze the warm lemon wedges over the shrimp.

Wolfgang's EASY TIPS

➤ For an Asian flavor, marinate the shrimp in a combination of fresh ginger, garlic, lime, and toasted sesame oil.

➤ Success with shrimp starts when you shop for them. Make sure they're firm and have a fresh, clean scent. Avoid any that look or feel gritty or mushy, are yellowing, have black spots on their shells, or smell unpleasant in any way.

➤ To peel shrimp, use your thumbs to split them apart between the rows of legs, then strip away the thin shells. Be sure also to devein the shelled shrimp, removing the thin, black or gray vein-like intestinal tract that runs just below the surface on the shrimp's outer curve. Use a small, sharp knife to make a shallow slit in the flesh all along the shrimp's length and then, with your fingers, pull out any vein that is revealed.

➤ Always use high heat and cook the shrimp quickly, just until they turn pink and are done all the way through, no longer. Since shrimp vary greatly in size, so will your cooking time.

Sautéed Shrimp with Chardonnay-Dijon Cream Sauce

MAKES 4 SERVINGS

I first served this elegant dish as an appetizer back in the late 1970s when I was the chef at Ma Maison in Hollywood. It was so popular then that people still ask me to cook it for them today at Spago. Everybody loves the combination of the sweet, plump, moist shrimp and the creamy mustard. If they knew how easy it is, they might stay home and cook it for themselves! Even a beginner can succeed with this dish. You can serve the shrimp as a starter, or with rice or pasta as a main dish.

1 pound medium or extra-large shrimp, peeled and deveined	1 tablespoon Dijon mustard or whole grain mustard
Kosher salt and freshly ground white pepper	Chopped fresh flat-leaf parsley for garnish
2 tablespoons extra-virgin olive oil	Rice or pasta for serving as a main dish
1 cup Chardonnay or dry sherry	
½ cup heavy cream	

1. Pat the shrimp dry, put them on a plate, and sprinkle lightly with salt and white pepper to taste. Heat a large, heavy sauté pan over medium-high heat. As soon as the pan feels hot when you hold your hand an inch or two above its surface, add the oil. When the oil is hot enough to swirl easily in the pan, carefully add the shrimp, placing them evenly in the pan. Without disturbing them, cook the shrimp for 2 minutes on one side. With tongs, a fork, or a small spatula, flip the shrimp over and cook them until they are uniformly pink and beginning to curl, about 2 minutes more. Transfer the shrimp from the pan to a platter and cover with aluminum foil to keep them warm.

2. Raise the heat under the pan to high. Add the wine and, with a wooden spoon, stir and scrape to dissolve the pan deposits. Let the liquid simmer until it has reduced in volume by half, 4 to 7 minutes. Reduce the heat and stir in the cream. Reduce slightly and stir in the mustard. Continue simmering until the sauce is thick enough to coat the back of a spoon, about 5 minutes more. Taste the sauce and adjust the seasoning if necessary.

3. Add the shrimp and parsley to the sauce and simmer briefly to heat up the shrimp. Serve with rice or pasta, or on its own as a starter.

Pan-Seared Ahi Tuna with Wasabi Cream Sauce

If you love to eat sushi, you already know wasabi, the fiery little dab of spicy paste made from dried and powdered green Japanese horseradish. Here, I tame wasabi, but only slightly, by blending it into a California-style Chardonnay-cream sauce to make a true classic of Pacific Rim fusion. It goes beautifully with quickly-seared, peppercorn encrusted fillets of fresh ahi tuna.

1½	tablespoons black, white, or mixed whole peppercorns	½	teaspoon kosher salt (or to taste)
¾	teaspoon whole coriander seeds	2	tablespoons unsalted butter, cut into pieces
2	pounds fresh ahi tuna fillets	2	to 3 teaspoons wasabi powder (or more to taste) stirred into a paste in 1 or 2 teaspoons of water; or 2 to 3 teaspoons wasabi paste
1	cup Chardonnay		
1	cup heavy cream		
1	teaspoon fresh lemon juice		
		1	tablespoon olive oil

1. Crack the peppercorns and coriander seeds and spread on a plate. Press the tuna steaks into them firmly on both sides to coat them with the spice mixture. Set the tuna steaks aside.

2. Make the sauce. Bring the wine to a boil in a medium saucepan over high heat and continue boiling until it has reduced by half its volume, 5 to 10 minutes. Stir in the cream and continue boiling until the sauce is thick enough to coat the back of a spoon. Stir in the lemon juice and kosher salt. Using a whisk, beat in the butter a piece at a time until the sauce is thick and glossy. Whisk in the wasabi paste and continue stirring until it is thoroughly combined with the sauce. Taste the sauce and, if necessary, add a little more salt or wasabi.

3. Heat the olive oil in a nonstick skillet over medium-high heat. When the pan is hot, add the tuna fillets and cook them until done rare to medium-rare as you like, 1 minute or a little longer on each side. Remove from the heat and cut crosswise into ⅓- to ½-inch-thick slices.

4. Spoon the sauce attractively onto individual heated serving plates or a platter. Arrange the slices of tuna overlapping on top of the sauce in the center of the plate. Serve immediately.

VARIATION: *Make the Sautéed Squash Ribbons on page 209. Place the cooked squash in a mound in the middle of each plate or on the platter. Spoon the sauce around the squash. Arrange the fish around the squash.*

Wolfgang's EASY TIPS

➤ The sauce can be made hours ahead and left on top of the stove. Reheat gently before serving.

➤ To coarsely crack the peppercorns and coriander seeds, place them in a heavy-duty plastic freezer bag and place the bag on your work surface. Gently pound them with a rolling pin or the bottom of a heavy skillet until they break into large or medium pieces.

➤ You can find small containers of wasabi powder in Japanese markets or in the Asian foods section of well-stocked supermarkets. If you can find wasabi paste, this is preferable to the powdered kind.

Provençal Salmon with Tomato Basil Sauce

MAKES 6 SERVINGS

This summer salmon recipe allows you to prepare the sauce a day ahead so that all you have to do at the last minute is broil the fish. The light sauce, with its sunny Provençal flavors, proves how delicious healthy food can be. Serve with rice, noodles, or steamed potatoes and a green salad.

Wolfgang's EASY TIPS

➤ To peel and seed the tomatoes, bring a saucepan full of water to a full rolling boil over high heat, and fill a bowl with ice and water. With a sharp knife, cut out the core of each tomato and, at the opposite end, score a shallow X in the skin. One at a time, using tongs or a slotted spoon, carefully lower the tomatoes into the boiling water and leave them just until their skins begin to wrinkle, about 30 seconds; then transfer them to the ice water to cool. Peel off the skins from the tomatoes, starting at the X. Cut each tomato crosswise in half and scoop or squeeze out and discard the seeds.

For the sauce:

4	large, firm, ripe tomatoes, peeled, seeded, and finely chopped
2	shallots, minced
1	bunch fresh basil leaves, chopped (about ⅔ cup)
	Grated zest of ½ lemon
½	cup extra-virgin olive oil
2	tablespoons sherry wine vinegar
1	tablespoon minced fresh chives
1	tablespoon minced fresh tarragon
	Kosher salt and freshly ground black pepper
	Cayenne

For the salmon:

	Extra-virgin olive oil
6	fresh salmon fillets, about 6 ounces each
	Kosher salt and freshly ground black pepper
6	small sprigs fresh basil for garnish

1. Make the sauce several hours or the night before. In a nonreactive mixing bowl, stir together the chopped tomatoes, shallots, basil, lemon zest, olive oil, vinegar, chives, and tarragon. Season to taste with salt, pepper, and cayenne. Cover the bowl and leave at room temperature to marinate for several hours or overnight (if your kitchen is very hot, refrigerate).

2. About ½ hour before serving time, preheat the oven to 400°F. Cover a baking sheet with foil and lightly oil the foil with olive oil. When the oven is hot, switch it to its broiler function. Brush the salmon fillets with olive oil, season them with salt and pepper, and arrange them on a baking sheet. Place the salmon under the broiler about two inches from the flame and cook until the top is very lightly browned and the flesh is still slightly pink in the center, 7 to 8 minutes. Meanwhile, taste the sauce and, if necessary, adjust the seasonings to taste.

3. Spoon a generous amount of the sauce onto the middle of each of six heated serving plates. Place the salmon fillets on top of the sauce. Top each fillet with a spoonful of sauce and a basil sprig. Serve immediately, passing any remaining sauce separately.

Veracruz-Style Red Snapper Fillets with Tomatoes, Capers, and Olives

MAKES 6 SERVINGS

Wolfgang's EASY TIPS

➤ It may be difficult for you to find thick snapper fillets as described below. Just buy the thickest and freshest you can find, and adjust the cooking time in the recipe. As soon as you can separate the flakes of fish with a fork and see that the flesh is firm and opaque at its center, the fish is done.

➤ A good-quality sauté pan or frying pan helps the preparation go smoothly and quickly.

➤ The sauce can be made hours or even a day before cooking the fish and serving. It gets even better overnight.

➤ You can present this dish on individual serving plates or on a large, warmed platter.

In the sleepy pueblo of Boca del Rio just south of Veracruz on Mexico's Gulf Coast they make a definitive version of this fresh seafood dish known in Spanish as *huachinango a la veracruzana.* Rather than messing around with a whole fish, and then filleting it as you serve it, I've simplified the classic recipe by starting with widely available red snapper fillets. Serve the fish with steamed white rice or a pilaf to soak up all the good juices.

3	plus 2 tablespoons extra-virgin olive oil
6	garlic cloves, peeled and thinly sliced
4	green onions, thinly sliced
1	jalapeño pepper, halved, stemmed, seeded, deveined, and minced
1	cup pitted green olives, sliced
¼	cup drained capers
3	cups diced canned tomatoes
	Kosher salt and freshly ground black pepper
6	fresh snapper fillets, about 8 ounces each and 1 inch thick
2	tablespoons fish broth or chicken broth
4	tablespoons chopped fresh cilantro or flat-leaf parsley for garnish

1. Heat a large skillet or sauté pan over medium-high heat. Add 3 tablespoons of the olive oil and scatter in the garlic slices. As soon as they start to sizzle, add the green onions, jalapeño, olives, and capers. As soon as they begin to sizzle, add the tomatoes and a pinch each of salt and pepper. Stir well and let the mixture simmer until the tomatoes cook down slightly and smell very fragrant, 10 to 15 minutes. Taste and adjust seasonings.

2. Meanwhile, pat the snapper fillets dry with paper towels. Season them on both sides with salt and pepper to taste. Over medium-high heat, heat another large skillet and add the remaining 2 tablespoons olive oil. As soon as the oil is hot enough to swirl, add the fillets, placing them with their most attractive sides down. When their undersides are golden, after 5 to 7 minutes (3 minutes for thinner fillets), use a spatula to turn them over. Cook for 2 to 5 minutes more, or until the fish is firm and opaque at the center when pierced with the tip of a small knife. Remove the fillets from the skillet to a heated platter and cover with aluminum foil.

3. Pour off the fat and transfer the tomato mixture to the skillet in which you cooked the fish fillets. Add the 2 tablespoons of broth, stir and scrape to dissolve the pan deposits into the sauce and

continue simmering over medium-high heat for 2 to 5 minutes
until the sauce is thick. Add salt and pepper to taste.

4. Transfer a snapper fillet to each warmed serving plate or a large
warm platter and spoon the sauce on top. Garnish with cilantro or
parsley and serve.

VARIATION: *Another way to make this dish is to sear the fish, then finish the cooking in*
the sauce.

Pan-Fried Trout with Lemon and Caper Sauce

MAKES 4 SERVINGS

You no longer have to be a fisherman to enjoy trout, which is a good thing since I'm terrible at fishing. Farmed trout are easy to find in supermarkets and fish markets. It has a delicate flavor, much milder than fish caught in the wild, and demands simple seasonings. This sauce is a classic from Grenoble, France. The sauce of lemon juice and butter is just the right delicate enhancement, with fresh lemon segments providing a sharp counterpoint. Golden croutons not only look beautiful but also add delightful crunchiness. Capers contribute sharp saltiness, and chopped parsley brings fresh flavor and bright color.

2	large or 3 small lemons	4	tablespoons extra-virgin olive oil
¼	pound (1 stick) unsalted butter, divided	2	tablespoons minced shallots
2	(½-inch-thick) slices fresh brioche or white bread, crusts trimmed and discarded, cut into ½-inch cubes	2	tablespoons rinsed and drained capers
8	trout fillets	12	caper berries (about 2 tablespoons), drained and cut lengthwise in halves, or 2 tablespoons more rinsed and drained capers
	Kosher salt and freshly ground white pepper		Finely grated zest of 1 lemon
	All-purpose flour for dusting	¼	cup minced flat-leaf parsley

1. Preheat the oven to 350°F. Prepare the lemons as directed in the tips. Strain off the juice and measure out ½ cup of segments.

2. Make the croutons. Melt half of the butter in a small saucepan over low heat or in a glass bowl in the microwave oven. Toss the bread cubes with the butter and spread them on a small baking sheet or in a baking dish. Put them in the preheated oven and bake until crisp and golden, about 10 minutes. Transfer to a bowl and set aside.

3. Season the trout fillets with salt and white pepper to taste and lightly dust them with flour. Over high heat, heat a sauté pan large enough to hold all the fillets without crowding (or cook the fillets in batches, using half the olive oil for each batch). Add the olive oil. When the oil is hot, add the trout fillets boned side down and sauté until their undersides are golden brown, about 3 minutes. With a metal spatula, carefully turn the fillets over and cook until their other sides are golden brown, 2 to 3 minutes more. Carefully transfer two fillets to each of four heated serving plates. Scatter the croutons over and around the fillets.

4. Add the remaining butter to the pan. When it has melted add the shallots. Sauté over high heat until the butter turns golden brown. Add the lemon juice and stir and scrape with a wooden spoon to deglaze the pan deposits. Add the lemon pieces, capers, caper berries, lemon zest, and parsley, and heat through, about 1 minute more. Spoon this sauce over and around the trout fillets and serve.

Easy Paella

MAKES 4 SERVINGS

Wolfgang's EASY TIPS

➤ You could also add scallops, chunks of fish, slices of squid, or crab to the rice. Or you could do a chicken and sausage paella with chunks of breast meat and thick slices of Spanish sausage or chorizo.

➤ You can make a quick, light fish broth by simmering the shrimp shells for 30 minutes while you prepare the other ingredients. Strain through a cheesecloth-lined strainer and use for the paella, alone or in combination with chicken stock.

➤ Don't overcrowd the pan. This is a rice dish and you want to make sure that the proportion of rice to proteins is high.

I've made this paella on top of the stove, in the traditional way, and I've also made it in a pressure cooker, which works surprisingly well. Either way, it's a beautiful dish, and this one is very easy to put together.

2	tablespoons olive oil
1	medium onion, chopped
1	medium or large red bell pepper, diced
2	large garlic cloves, minced
2½	cups long grain rice
3½	cups fish broth or chicken broth (or a combination)
¾	cup white wine
2	teaspoons kosher salt, less if broth is salted
12	large shrimp, peeled and deveined
12	small clams, thoroughly scrubbed and rinsed
12	black mussels, thoroughly scrubbed and rinsed
½	cup tender young peas, fresh or frozen
2	tablespoons chopped fresh flat-leaf parsley, plus more for garnish

Generous ½ to ¾ teaspoon saffron threads (to taste), crushed with your fingers

Pinch of freshly ground black pepper

Pinch of cayenne

1. Heat the oil over medium heat in a large, heavy skillet, or over low heat in a pressure cooker with the lid off, and add the onion and red pepper. Cook, stirring, until the onion begins to look translucent, about 3 minutes. Stir in the garlic and the rice and continue to stir together for about 1 minute until the rice is coated with oil.

2. Add the broth and wine and bring to a full boil over medium-high heat. Add all the other ingredients, reduce the heat, and simmer 15 to 20 minutes until all of the liquid has evaporated and the rice is tender and beginning to stick to the pan. Turn off the heat and allow to sit undisturbed for 10 minutes.

Using the pressure cooker: Add the broth and wine and bring to a boil over high heat. Add all of the ingredients, immediately secure the lid, bring to pressure, reduce the heat to low, and set a timer for 5 minutes. As soon as the cooking time is up, turn off the heat or remove the pressure cooker from the stovetop. Set it aside and let the pressure reduce naturally, without using the quick release. When the float valve indicates that the pressure has been released (7 to 10 minutes), release the quick-release valve (a

small amount of remaining pressure will be released), and carefully remove the lid.

3. Stir the mixture briefly to distribute the ingredients evenly. Serve in shallow serving bowls or plates, garnished with parsley.

Whole Roasted Garlic Chicken
with Chardonnay Butter Sauce

MAKES 4 SERVINGS

Every cook needs a good roasted chicken recipe. This is much like the roasted chicken we sometimes make at Spago. What gives it its marvelous flavor is the garlic that is placed under the skin before roasting.

3	**garlic cloves, thinly sliced**
2	**tablespoons chopped fresh flat-leaf parsley, plus more for garnish**
2	**tablespoons extra-virgin olive oil**
	Kosher salt and freshly ground black pepper
1	**whole frying chicken, about 4 pounds**
½	**cup Chardonnay**
2	**tablespoons lemon juice**
3	**tablespoons unsalted butter, cut into pieces**
1	**tablespoon chopped fresh tarragon, plus additional for garnish**
	Lemon wedges for garnish

1. Preheat the oven to 450°F. Oil a flameproof roasting pan large enough to accommodate the chicken. In a small bowl, toss together the sliced garlic and parsley. Ease your fingers between the skin and meat over each side of the breast and evenly distribute the garlic-parsley mixture under the skin. Rub the chicken with olive oil and sprinkle all over with salt and pepper.

2. Place the chicken in the roasting pan breast side down. Place in the oven and set the timer for 15 minutes. After 15 minutes, turn the heat down to 350°F. Turn the chicken on its side and roast for 15 minutes. Flip onto its other side and roast for another 15 minutes. Flip the chicken over so the breast is up and roast until the skin is nicely browned and the juices run clear when the chicken is pierced at the thickest part of the thigh with the tip of a knife, or until a thermometer inserted into the thigh reads 165°F, 30 to 40 minutes.

3. Remove the chicken from the oven and transfer it from the pan to a serving platter. Pour excess fat from the pan. Put the pan over high heat, add the wine, and stir and scrape with a wooden spoon to deglaze the pan deposits. Stir in the lemon juice. Bring the liquid to a boil and continue boiling until its volume reduces by half, 2 to 3 minutes. One piece at a time, whisk in the butter. Stir in the tarragon and transfer to a blender. Blend until the sauce has a nice green color. Taste and add a little salt and pepper if desired.

Quartering a Roasted Chicken

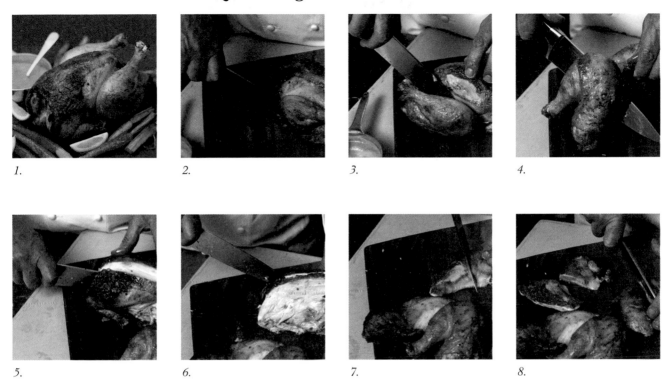

1.

2.

3.

4.

5.

6.

7.

8.

4. Spoon the sauce onto warmed serving plates. With a large, sharp knife or cleaver, cut the chicken into serving pieces and transfer them to the plates. Garnish with tarragon and accompany with lemon wedges for each person to squeeze over the chicken to taste.

Pan-Roasted Chicken
with Lemon and Whole-Grain Mustard

MAKES 2 TO 4 SERVINGS

This is my secret for success with a small roasted chicken. Its skin will be mahogany brown and crackling, while all of its meat, white and dark alike, will be moist and flavorful. The chicken's anatomy, with the tender, low-fat breast meat so prominently exposed to the oven's dry heat, makes it difficult to perfect oven-roasted chicken, since it's easy to overcook the light meat. Flattening the chicken by removing the backbone—butchers call this "butterflying"—is an easy and convenient way to get around the problem. Butterflying changes the anatomy of the chicken so that it cooks more evenly. If you have a service-oriented butcher, he will know what you mean when you ask him to butterfly the bird (if he doesn't, ask him to cut out the backbone and flatten it while keeping it intact). If you always buy your chicken at the supermarket where there seems to be no butcher in sight, it's easy to do it yourself. All you need is a pair of poultry shears (see second tip).

1 whole frying chicken, 3 to 4 pounds, butterflied (see tips)	Juice of 2 large lemons (6 to 8 tablespoons)
1 sprig fresh flat-leaf parsley, 2 fresh basil leaves, or 1 small sprig rosemary	2 tablespoons whole-grain mustard
Kosher salt and freshly ground white pepper	4 tablespoons unsalted butter, cut into several pieces
2 tablespoons extra-virgin olive oil	¼ cup minced fresh flat-leaf parsley or finely shredded fresh basil
1 cup chicken stock or good-quality canned chicken broth	

1. Preheat the oven to 450°F. Prepare the chicken. From the neck opening, gently ease your fingertips between the skin and the meat to loosen the skin all over the breast, taking care not to tear the skin. Insert the parsley sprig, basil leaves, or rosemary sprig under the skin. Season the chicken generously on both sides with salt and pepper.

2. Heat an ovenproof skillet large enough to hold the chicken over high heat. Add the olive oil and swirl it in the skillet. As soon as you begin to see slight wisps of smoke, carefully place the chicken skin side down in the skillet. Sear the chicken, undisturbed, while reducing the heat little by little to medium, until its skin has turned golden brown and crisp, 5 to 7 minutes. With tongs, carefully turn the chicken skin side up.

3. Put the skillet with the chicken into the preheated oven and cook until the chicken is deep golden brown and the juices run clear when the thickest part of the thigh meat is pierced with a thin skewer, 10 to 15 minutes more, depending on its size. When the chicken is done, remove it from the skillet with tongs and transfer it to a cutting board.

4. Pour off all but a thin glaze of fat from the skillet. Return the skillet to high heat, add the chicken stock or broth and the lemon juice, stir and scrape with a wooden spoon to deglaze the pan deposits, and boil the liquid until it has reduced by half its volume, 3 to 4 minutes. Turn down the heat, add the mustard, and, stirring briskly with a wire whisk, add the butter a piece at a time to make a creamy sauce. Make sure each piece has been incorporated completely before adding the next. Season the sauce to taste with salt and pepper and stir in half of the parsley or basil.

5. To serve, spoon the sauce into the centers of two to four heated serving plates. With a large, sharp knife, cut the chicken into two halves or four equal pieces. Place the chicken on the plates, sprinkle with the remaining parsley or basil, and serve.

Countertop Grilled Chicken Breasts
with Garlic and Parsley

MAKES 2 SERVINGS

The versatility and ease of an electric panini maker or countertop double-sided grill shines in this version of one of my favorite chicken recipes. The countertop grill will give you moist, perfectly cooked, crispy–skinned chicken in half the usual time.

1	whole chicken breast, halved and boned, skin left on	¼	teaspoon freshly ground black pepper
8	plump garlic cloves, peeled	2	tablespoons unsalted butter
¼	cup chopped flat-leaf parsley	1	medium lemon, juiced
¼	teaspoon kosher salt		

1. Preheat an electric panini maker or double-sided countertop grill. Ease your fingers between the chicken's skin and meat. Bring a small saucepan of water to a boil. Add the peeled garlic cloves and boil them for 1 minute. Drain well and rinse with cold water. Cut the garlic cloves lengthwise into paper-thin slices. Put the garlic in a small bowl with the parsley, salt, and pepper, and toss well. Stuff half of the garlic mixture under the skin of the chicken breasts, then lightly salt both sides.

2. Place the chicken skin side up in the panini maker or countertop grill. Close the lid and cook the chicken until its skin is deep golden brown and the meat is cooked through, about 12 minutes. Test by piercing the meat with a thin skewer and checking to see that the juices run clear.

3. While the chicken is cooking, melt the butter in a small sauté pan over medium-high heat. Add the remaining garlic-parsley mixture and sauté until the garlic starts to turn golden, 3 to 4 minutes. Add the lemon juice and stir and scrape with a wooden spoon to dissolve the pan deposits. Taste the sauce and, if necessary, adjust the seasoning with a little more salt and pepper.

4. Transfer the chicken breasts to two heated plates, spoon the sauce over and around the chicken, and serve.

Buttermilk-Marinated Pan-Fried Chicken Breasts

MAKES 4 SERVINGS

Buttermilk adds a wonderful tangy flavor to fried chicken, and it also tenderizes the meat. The chicken breasts are browned in a pan and finished in the oven, resulting in a crispy dish that is less greasy than traditional fried chicken. I like to use Japanese panko in my breading mixture. Serve with lemon wedges for each person to squeeze over the chicken to taste. Enjoy the leftovers cold on their own, in sandwiches, or diced and tossed with salad greens and your favorite dressing.

4	skinless, boneless chicken breast halves, rinsed well and patted dry
½	plus ½ teaspoon kosher salt
½	cup buttermilk
1	cup panko or breadcrumbs
1	teaspoon minced garlic
1	teaspoon chopped fresh oregano
1	teaspoon finely chopped fresh flat-leaf parsley
1	teaspoon freshly ground black pepper
	Vegetable oil as needed for frying
	Lemon wedges for garnish

1. Put the chicken breasts in a mixing bowl. Sprinkle them evenly with ½ teaspoon of the salt. Add the buttermilk, turn the chicken breasts to coat them evenly, cover the bowl with plastic wrap, and marinate in the refrigerator for 30 minutes or longer.

2. Preheat the oven to 350°F. Heat a large sauté pan over medium-high heat. If your sauté pan is not an ovenproof one, have a baking pan large enough to accommodate all of the chicken breasts ready next to the sauté pan. Meanwhile, toss together the panko or breadcrumbs, garlic, oregano, parsley, black pepper, and the remaining ½ teaspoon salt in a shallow bowl or baking pan. One by one, turn the buttermilk-marinated chicken breasts in the mixture to coat them evenly.

3. Add 4 tablespoons oil to the hot pan, or enough to coat the pan in an even layer about ½ inch thick. When it swirls easily, add the chicken breasts, rounded side down. Cook in batches if the pan is not large enough to hold all 4 chicken breasts without crowding. Turn the heat down slightly and cook on each side until golden brown, 3 to 4 minutes per side. Drain very briefly on paper towels, transfer to the baking dish, and place in the oven. Finish cooking the chicken breasts in the oven, 7 to 10 minutes.

4. Transfer the chicken breasts to a platter or individual serving plates, garnish with lemon wedges, and serve.

Stir-Fried Chicken Breast
with Red Bell Peppers and Snow Peas

MAKES 4 SERVINGS

Wolfgang's EASY TIPS

➤ Vary the mixture of vegetables with your own favorites, such as broccoli and sugar-snap peas, carrots and turnips.

➤ Cut the vegetables into small, even pieces and blanch them for a few seconds in boiling water, then shock them in ice water and drain before stir-frying. Harder vegetables such as turnips and winter squash can be blanched for a little longer.

The curved surface of a classic Chinese wok conducts heat evenly and facilitates the stirring action that makes it so quick and easy to cook small, uniformly sized pieces of food, typified by this simple, colorful, delicious combination. You can also use a wide, heavy sauté pan for this dish.

½	pound snow peas, trimmed	1	(5-ounce) can sliced water chestnuts, drained
2	tablespoons peanut oil	1	teaspoon grated fresh ginger
1	pound skinless, boneless chicken breasts, cut crosswise into ½-inch-thick strips	2	tablespoons bottled teriyaki or hoisin sauce
	Kosher salt and freshly ground black pepper	¼	teaspoon hot red pepper flakes (optional)
1	teaspoon sugar	1	tablespoon Asian-style toasted sesame oil
3	garlic cloves, minced		
2	strips orange zest, each about 3 inches long	2	tablespoons chopped fresh cilantro
1	large onion, halved and thinly sliced	4	cups steamed white rice
1	large red bell pepper, quartered, stemmed, seeded, and cut crosswise into thin strips		

1. Bring a medium-size saucepan full of water to a boil. Fill a large bowl with ice cubes and water. When the pot of water reaches a boil, add a teaspoon of salt. Add the snow peas and cook 15 seconds, then remove from the boiling water using a skimmer or slotted spoon and transfer to the ice water. Allow the peas to sit in the ice water for a few minutes, then drain.

2. Heat a wok or a large skillet over high heat. Add the peanut oil. As soon as it is hot enough to swirl easily around the wok, season the chicken strips with salt and pepper to taste, add them to the wok, and cook, stirring continuously, for about 2 minutes.

3. Add the sugar, garlic, orange zest, onion, bell pepper, water chestnuts, and ginger, and continue to stir-fry for 3 minutes more.

4. Add the snow peas, teriyaki or hoisin sauce, optional hot red pepper flakes, and sesame oil. Continue to stir and toss the ingredients until they are evenly coated with the sauce and the snow peas are hot and tender-crisp, 2 to 3 minutes more. Sprinkle on the cilantro and serve hot over steamed rice.

Crabmeat and Chicken Potpie

MAKES 4 SERVINGS

A humble chicken potpie becomes stylish when crabmeat is added to the mix. It's great for an informal dinner party because you can make the filling ahead of time. When your guests arrive just top it with rounds of store-bought frozen puff pastry, brush it with egg wash, and put it in the oven.

½	pound lump crabmeat
1½	pounds skinless, boneless chicken, cut into 1-inch chunks
	Kosher salt and freshly ground black pepper
2	plus 1 tablespoons all-purpose flour
2	plus 2 tablespoons vegetable oil
2	plus 2 tablespoons unsalted butter
½	pound red-skin potatoes, cut into ½-inch pieces
½	pound carrots, peeled and cut into ½-inch pieces
1	medium yellow onion, peeled and diced
2	garlic cloves, minced
	Pinch of crushed red pepper flakes
1	sprig thyme
1	bay leaf
1	cup white wine
2	cups chicken stock or good-quality canned chicken broth
1	cup heavy cream plus 1 tablespoon for brushing
¼	cup dry sherry
½	cup shelled or frozen peas
½	pound (1 sheet) frozen puff pastry, defrosted following package instructions
1	egg

1. Carefully pick through the crabmeat and discard any pieces of shell or cartilage. Transfer to a bowl, cover, and refrigerate until needed.

2. Season the chicken pieces with salt and pepper, and toss in a mixing bowl with 2 tablespoons of the flour until evenly coated. In a large skillet over high heat, heat 2 tablespoons of the oil. Add the chicken pieces, reduce the heat slightly, and sauté, turning them occasionally until light golden and cooked through, 5 to 10 minutes. Using a slotted spoon, transfer the chicken to a plate and set aside. Add the remaining 2 tablespoons oil and 2 tablespoons of the butter to the pan, then add the potatoes, carrots, and onion and sauté until they begin to look glossy and bright, 2 to 3 minutes. Reduce the heat to medium, stir in the garlic, red pepper flakes, thyme, and bay leaf, and sauté just until the vegetables begin to color slightly, 2 to 3 minutes more.

3. Add the wine, turn up the heat, stir and scrape with a wooden spoon to deglaze the pan deposits. Simmer until the liquid reduces by about half, 3 to 5 minutes. Add the chicken stock and 1 cup of cream. Bring the liquid to a boil, reduce the heat slightly, and simmer briskly until the liquid reduces by about half again and is thick and creamy, about 15 minutes. Remove the sprig of thyme and the bay leaf.

4. Stir in the reserved chicken pieces and the sherry. Stir together the remaining 2 tablespoons butter and remaining 1 tablespoon flour and stir this paste into the mixture. Season the sauce to taste with salt and pepper. Gently stir in the reserved crabmeat and the peas. Transfer to four large individual ovenproof 2-cup soup bowls, four ramekins of the same size, or a 2-quart baking dish. Cover with plastic wrap and refrigerate until the filling is cold, at least 1 hour.

5. Preheat the oven to 400°F. Make sure the puff pastry is no thicker than ¼ inch. With the tip of a sharp knife, cut the pastry into four circles that will overhang the rims of the serving bowls or ramekins by about ½ inch; for a single large baking dish, cut four circles that will overlap the top by 1 inch, or use one large sheet.

6. In a small bowl beat together the egg and the remaining 1 tablespoon of cream to make an egg wash. Brush the outsides of the rims of the ramekins. Place the bowls, ramekins, or baking dish on a baking tray and place the puff pastry circles on top, draping them over the sides of the dishes. Pierce the tops with the tip of a paring knife. Brush with the egg wash and press the pastry gently against the sides of the dishes. Carefully transfer the baking sheet to the oven and bake until the filling is bubbling hot and the pastry is a deep golden brown, 25 to 35 minutes. Serve hot.

Assembling the Chicken Potpie

1.

2.

3.

4.

Roast Beef Tenderloin with Mushroom Madeira Sauce

MAKES 8 SERVINGS

This makes a marvelous holiday meal. Serving roast beef is, to me, like dressing up in a black tie. It elevates the meal's entire tone. A beef main course also lets you serve a great red wine such as a cabernet sauvignon, Rhône, or Barolo. One of my favorite roasts is the tenderloin, the same piece of meat that is cut crosswise into filets mignons. Though far from a bargain, it's well worth the cost. And you don't have to search for the most expensive prime meat, since choice tenderloin is sufficiently well-marbled and tender to work perfectly. Do, however, seek out a piece with the widest possible diameter so there's less risk of overcooking, and use a meat thermometer.

Wolfgang's EASY TIPS

➤ If your butcher hasn't done this, before cooking, you'll need to trim off excess fat and the silverskin, a tough membrane covering part of the meat. Insert a sharp knife just beneath the silverskin and loosen it by cutting parallel to the surface, then pull off.

➤ How big a tenderloin you buy depends on how many guests you'll have and the extent of your menu. For a simple meal with salad to start, vegetable and potato sides, and a light dessert, buy 12 ounces uncooked per person. (The meat loses up to a third of its weight during cooking.) For a more elaborate multicourse menu plan on 8 ounces uncooked per person. Buy more than you think you'll need and transform leftovers into delicious breakfast hash or lunchtime sandwiches. Or cut off part of the tenderloin and use it at a later time, cut into thick filets mignons.

➤ For even cooking, use a heavy roasting pan.

For the meat:

1   (4-pound) whole beef tenderloin roast, preferably the wide end, cut, trimmed, and tied

Kosher salt and freshly ground black pepper

2   tablespoons olive oil

1   large onion, peeled, cut into 1-inch chunks

2   celery stalks, cut into 1-inch chunks

2   medium carrots, peeled, cut into 1-inch chunks

For the sauce:

2   tablespoons olive oil

2   to 4 tablespoons butter (or to taste)

½   pound button mushrooms, or a mixture of button mushrooms and shiitakes, quartered or cut into eighths if large

2   shallots, minced

2   garlic cloves, minced

1   cup Madeira

2   cups homemade chicken stock or good-quality canned chicken broth

¼   cup heavy cream

2   teaspoons Dijon mustard

2   teaspoons bottled barbecue sauce

2   tablespoons chopped flat-leaf parsley or chives for garnish

1. Adjust the oven shelf to the middle position and preheat the oven to 400°F. Meanwhile, if the butcher hasn't done this for you, at 1-inch intervals, tie kitchen string around the tenderloin's diameter to give it a uniform, compact shape. Season all over with salt and pepper to taste.

2. Heat a small, heavy roasting pan or large ovenproof sauté pan on top of the stove over high heat. Add 2 tablespoons of the olive oil. Sear the tenderloin until uniformly well browned, 2 to 3 minutes per side. Remove the tenderloin from the pan.

3. Add the onion, celery, and carrots to the pan, reduce the heat slightly, and sauté, stirring occasionally, until golden, 5 to 7 minutes. Place the tenderloin on top and transfer the pan to the preheated oven. Roast the tenderloin until medium rare, 18 to 20 minutes. An instant-read thermometer inserted into its center should register 130°F. Remove the tenderloin from the pan and place it on a carving board. Cover with aluminum foil and leave the roast to rest in a warm spot while you prepare the sauce.

4. While the meat is roasting, prepare the sauce. Heat a heavy sauté pan or medium saucepan over medium-high heat. Add the olive oil. As soon as it is hot, add 2 tablespoons of the butter, the mushrooms, shallots, and garlic. Sauté, stirring frequently, until the mushrooms are light golden, about 5 minutes. Set aside.

5. Place the roasting pan over medium-high heat. Add the Madeira and stir and scrape with a wooden spoon to dissolve the pan deposits. Raise the heat and boil the Madeira until reduced to about ¼ cup, 5 to 7 minutes. Add the chicken stock and continue to boil until reduced by half, 10 to 12 minutes. Strain the mixture into the pan with the mushrooms (discard the onion, celery, and carrots), stir together, and bring to a simmer. Stir in the heavy cream and continue boiling the sauce until thick enough to coat the back of a spoon, about 3 minutes. Reduce the heat to a gentle simmer and stir in the mustard, barbecue sauce, and, if you wish, another 2 tablespoons butter, a little at a time. Stir until well blended and satiny. Carefully pour in any meat juices that have collected from the resting tenderloin and stir. Season to taste with salt and pepper.

6. With the tip of a sharp knife, carefully snip off the strings from the roast. Cut the meat across the grain into slices ¼ to ½ inch thick. Arrange them on the heated platter or individual serving plates, garnish with parsley or chives, and pass the sauce in a heated bowl or sauceboat for guests to help themselves.

Peppered Filets Mignons with Sherry and Raisins

MAKES 6 SERVINGS

Steak au poivre, as the French call beefsteaks crusted with cracked peppercorns, has become a staple of classic cuisine. But don't let the French words make you think that there is anything difficult about this dish. In fact, it is a rapid, very easy sauté, which I've made even more impressive with a simple sauce that complements the flavors of the beef and pepper with a hint of sherry and the tangy sweetness of raisins.

2	tablespoons whole black peppercorns	1	cup dry sherry
2	tablespoons whole white peppercorns	1	cup beef stock or good-quality canned beef or chicken broth, or ½ cup hoisin sauce
6	filet mignon steaks, about 6 ounces each, trimmed of excess fat	½	cup seedless golden or brown raisins
	Kosher salt	3	tablespoons unsalted butter, cut into small pieces
2	tablespoons mild-flavored oil such as canola or safflower oil		

1. Crack the peppercorns as directed in the tips. Put the cracked peppercorns on a plate. One by one, sprinkle both sides of each filet evenly with salt to taste, and then press each side into the peppercorns to coat it.

2. Over high heat, heat a heavy skillet or sauté pan large enough to hold the steaks comfortably (cook the steaks in batches if your pan is not big enough). Add the oil and as soon as you see the slightest wisps of smoke carefully add the steaks. Cook the steaks undisturbed for 4 minutes, then carefully turn them over and cook 4 minutes more for medium-rare. For well-done steaks reduce the heat to medium low and cook a few more minutes on both sides. Transfer the steaks to a heated platter and cover with aluminum foil to keep them warm while you make the sauce.

3. Pour off the excess fat from the skillet and return it to high heat. Add the sherry, stir and scrape with a wooden spoon to deglaze the pan deposits, and boil until it reduces to about half its original volume, 4 to 5 minutes. Add the stock and raisins and continue boiling until the liquid reduces by half again, 4 to 5 minutes more (if using hoisin sauce, simply stir it in). A piece at a time, whisk in the butter to form a thick, glossy sauce. Adjust the seasoning to taste with a little salt.

4. Transfer the steaks to individual serving plates. Stir the juices that have collected on the platter into the sauce. Spoon the sauce over and around the steaks and serve.

Wolfgang's EASY TIPS

➤ To crack the peppercorns, put them in a resealable heavy plastic food-storage bag. Place the bag on a flat work surface and, with the bottom of a heavy saucepan or skillet, tap them lightly to crack them into large pieces.

➤ If you want your steaks well done, lower the heat in the pan so that the outsides of the steaks don't burn.

➤ Serve with mashed potatoes or rice to soak up the delicious juices.

Roast Prime Rib of Beef with Garlic-Herb Crust

MAKES 6 TO 8 SERVINGS

Few main courses make a bigger impression than a magnificent prime rib of beef. Yet the effort that goes into this meal is minimal. In this version the roast is crusted with a mixture of garlic and fresh herbs, which makes it all the more aromatic. I begin my roast beef at high heat (450°F) and after twenty-five minutes turn the heat very low. This ensures a crusty exterior that has great flavor because the meat caramelizes when it cooks at high heat, but a rare, juicy center. If steakhouse prime rib is what you've tasted in the past, this one will be a revelation.

Wolfgang's EASY TIPS

➤ Let the roast come to room temperature before roasting. This should take about an hour.

➤ To ensure a rare or medium-rare roast, it pays to invest in a digital thermometer, easy to find at kitchen supply and hardware stores. Look for the type with the heatproof wire that attaches to a timer. Set it to the desired temperature, and an alarm will go off when the meat is ready.

➤ It's very important to allow the meat to sit for at least 30 minutes after roasting so that the juices can run back into the meat.

➤ You can make this dish with a boneless prime rib. Place the meat on a rack. The roasting time will decrease.

1	(4 to 5-pound) bone-in prime rib of beef, at room temperature
8	garlic cloves, minced
4	tablespoons minced fresh rosemary
2	teaspoons dried thyme
4	tablespoons freshly ground black pepper
2	tablespoons kosher salt

1. Preheat the oven to 450°F with the rack in the center (if your roast won't fit with the rack in the center, use the lower rack). Place the roast ribs down on a rack in a large, heavy roasting pan. In a small bowl, stir together the garlic, rosemary, thyme, pepper, and salt. Spread the herb mixture all over the surface of the meat, pressing it firmly into the meat. Insert a roasting thermometer into the meat, making sure that its tip reaches the very center of the roast without touching bone.

2. Place the roasting pan on the oven's center rack (if possible). Cook the roast for 25 minutes, then lower the oven setting to 250°F and continue roasting until the thermometer reads 120°F for rare or 125°F for medium rare, 1½ to 2 hours. Remove the roast from the oven, transfer it to a platter, cover it with aluminum foil, and allow it to rest in a warm spot for 30 minutes. Tip any juices that accumulate on the platter into a sauceboat.

3. Uncover the prime rib and carve it across the grain into thick or thin slices, like you and your guests prefer. Pass the meat juices at the table for guests to help themselves.

Pan-Seared Beef Filets in Port-Dijon-Cream Sauce

This rich, classic, yet utterly simple pan sauce will turn any steak into a dinner party dish. It goes equally well with beef, chicken, and lamb, so substitute a skinless, boneless chicken breast or lamb chops for the filet mignon whenever you wish. I love the combination of the mellow, sweet port, the Dijon mustard with its smooth bite, and the rich cream.

4	(6-ounce) filets mignons, trimmed of excess fat	½	cup heavy cream
	Kosher salt and freshly ground pepper	1	tablespoon Dijon mustard
2	tablespoons extra-virgin olive oil	2	tablespoons unsalted butter, cut into pieces
½	cup port wine	1	tablespoon chopped fresh flat-leaf parsley or chives

1. Sprinkle both sides of each steak evenly with salt and pepper to taste.

2. Over high heat, heat a heavy skillet or sauté pan large enough to hold the steaks comfortably. Add the oil and as soon as you see the slightest wisps of smoke carefully add the steaks. Cook the steaks undisturbed for 4 minutes on both sides for medium rare. For well done steaks, reduce the heat to medium low and cook for a few more minutes on each side. Transfer the steaks to a heated platter and cover with aluminum foil to keep them warm while you make the sauce.

3. Pour off excess fat from the skillet and return it to high heat. Add the port and stir and scrape with a wooden spoon to deglaze the pan deposits. Turn the heat down so that the liquid in the pan is not boiling, and stir in the cream. Simmer the mixture briskly until it is thick enough to coat the back of the spoon, 3 to 4 minutes more. Whisk in the mustard and, a piece at a time, the butter. Adjust the seasoning to taste with a little salt and pepper, if necessary.

4. Transfer the steaks to individual serving plates. Stir the juices that have collected on the platter into the sauce. Spoon the sauce over and around the steaks, garnish with parsley or chives, and serve immediately.

Wolfgang's EASY TIPS

➤ A good, heavy sauté pan or skillet will cook the beef perfectly and help you finish the sauce in just minutes.

➤ For well-done steaks reduce the heat so that the outsides don't burn, and cook a little longer.

➤ Always add the mustard at the end of cooking so that it doesn't curdle.

➤ Keep the accompanying dishes simple—bright green vegetables or orange carrots or squash, baked or roasted potatoes, or wilted spinach go nicely. So does a good green salad.

Wine-Braised Brisket of Beef
with Caramelized Pearl Onions and Dried Apricots

MAKES 8 SERVINGS

➤ If you can't find a 5-pound brisket at your supermarket, cook two smaller pieces.

➤ While the meat braises, keep the heat gentle since boiling tightens rather than relaxes the meat's fibers. Check the liquid in the cooking vessel and if it's bubbling more than slightly, turn down the heat. The results should be so tender that you can pull the meat apart with a fork.

➤ To prepare the pearl onions, bring a saucepan of water to a boil. Add the pearl onions and blanch them for 30 seconds. Drain and immediately immerse them in a bowl of ice and water. Cut the very ends off at the stem ends, peel the onions, and leave them whole.

➤ For neater slices, you could let the brisket cool before cutting it across the grain. Reheat the slices in the sauce. That makes brisket an ideal dish to prepare ahead. Just cook and slice it the day before, and reheat it in the oven in its sauce for about half an hour at 300°F before serving.

Braising is a great way to coax tenderness from tough cuts of meat. The term applies when the main ingredient is a relatively large cut and the amount of liquid is relatively small. The moist, gentle heat gradually breaks down the meat to melting softness while releasing the big flavor that hardworking muscles develop. Beef brisket is one of my favorite candidates for braising. The cut comes from just under the first five ribs, behind the foreshank. Large and stringy, brisket is usually sold cut into halves, one relatively square and the other tapering to a point. Both are delicious, but the point cut, as it is known, has more flavor because it is slightly fattier. Here I braise the meat in a combination of beef broth and red wine, with aromatic root vegetables and dried apricots, a popular Eastern European flourish.

5	pounds beef brisket
2	tablespoons kosher salt
1	tablespoon freshly ground black pepper
1	bottle red wine
	All-purpose flour
2	plus 2 plus 2 tablespoons vegetable oil
10	garlic cloves, peeled and smashed
6	large shallots, peeled and thinly sliced
2	medium carrots, peeled, cut into 1-inch chunks

2	celery stalks, cut into 1-inch chunks
1	medium leek, white part only, cut into 1-inch chunks
1	cup dried apricots
6	sprigs fresh flat-leaf parsley
2	sprigs fresh thyme
2	bay leaves
2	tablespoons tomato paste
2	quarts plus ¼ cup homemade beef stock or good-quality canned beef broth
1	cup pearl onions
	Minced parsley for garnish

1. Season the brisket evenly on both sides with salt and pepper. Cover and refrigerate for 2 hours. Meanwhile, in a medium saucepan, bring the wine to a boil and continue boiling until it reduces to half its original volume, 15 to 20 minutes.

2. Preheat the oven to 350°F. Evenly sprinkle the brisket all over with flour, shaking off excess. Heat a heavy Dutch oven over high heat. Add 2 tablespoons of the oil. When it is almost smoking, turn the heat to medium high, carefully add the brisket, and sear until well browned, about 5 minutes per side. Transfer the brisket to a platter. Pour off the fat from the Dutch oven and add another

2 tablespoons of oil. Add the garlic, shallots, carrots, celery, and leek, and sauté until glossy and lightly browned, about 5 minutes. Add half of the apricots and all the parsley, thyme, bay leaves, and tomato paste, and continue to cook 1 minute more.

3. Return the browned brisket to the Dutch oven and add the reduced wine and 2 quarts stock or broth. If the brisket is not completely covered with liquid, add enough extra stock, broth, or water to cover. Bring the liquid to a simmer. Cover the pot and carefully place it in the oven. Cook until the brisket is fork tender, 2 to 2½ hours. Meanwhile, blanch and peel the onions as instructed in the tips, leaving them whole. Cut the remaining apricots into ¼-inch strips.

4. In a small sauté pan, heat the remaining 2 tablespoons oil over medium-high heat and sauté the pearl onions until lightly golden, 5 to 7 minutes. Add the apricot strips and pour in the remaining ¼ cup stock or broth, stirring and scraping with a wooden spoon to deglaze the pan deposits. Reduce the heat and simmer gently until tender, about 5 minutes. Cover and keep warm.

5. When the meat is done, carefully transfer it to a heated platter, cover with aluminum foil, and keep warm. Boil the liquid in the Dutch oven until it thickens and reduces to about 1 quart, 15 to 20 minutes. Pour it through a fine-mesh strainer into a bowl, taste, and adjust the seasonings if necessary with more salt and pepper.

6. To serve, use a sharp knife to cut the brisket across the grain into ¼-inch slices. Arrange the slices on heated serving plates or on a heated platter, spoon half the sauce over it, and garnish with the pearl onions and apricots. Sprinkle with minced parsley and pass the remaining sauce on the side.

Beef Goulash

MAKES 6 TO 8 SERVINGS

Every culture has its own traditional hangover prevention dishes. In Austria, goulash soup is what you eat before you go to bed to prevent a hangover after a long night of partying. My mother used to make it whenever there was a big party in our village. Revelers would stay out as late as six in the morning, and then stop at the bakery on the main square for the day's first fresh-baked loaves, which they'd eat at home with their goulash before falling into bed with satisfied stomachs. This recipe is more of a stew than a soup, but the flavors are the same. In Austria we serve it with spaetzle, noodles, rice, dumplings, or potatoes. Kaiser rolls are also a traditional accompaniment.

2 tablespoons vegetable oil

1 pound onions, peeled and finely chopped

1 tablespoon sugar

3 tablespoons sweet paprika

2 teaspoons hot paprika

3 tablespoons tomato paste

1 tablespoon minced garlic

1 tablespoon chopped fresh marjoram

½ teaspoon chopped fresh thyme

2 teaspoons kosher salt (or more to taste)

½ teaspoon freshly ground black pepper

3 pounds boneless beef shank, well-trimmed and cut into 1-inch cubes

3 cups homemade chicken stock or good-quality canned chicken broth

1 cup water

2 tablespoons balsamic vinegar

1 tablespoon caraway seeds, toasted in a dry skillet over medium-low heat until fragrant, 1 to 2 minutes, and coarsely ground

1. Heat a heavy 4-quart stockpot or Dutch oven over high heat. Add the oil. When the oil is hot, add the onions and sugar and sauté, stirring occasionally, until the onions look glossy, about 3 minutes. Reduce the heat to medium and continue to cook, stirring frequently, until the onions are golden, 5 to 10 minutes more.

2. Add the sweet and hot paprika, tomato paste, garlic, marjoram, thyme, salt, and pepper. Sauté, stirring continuously, for 1 minute. Stir in the beef cubes, chicken stock, water, balsamic vinegar, and caraway seeds. Bring the liquid to a boil and then reduce the heat to low to maintain a gentle simmer. Partially cover the pot and simmer, stirring occasionally, for 1½ hours, or until the meat is very tender. Turn off the heat and skim off the liquid fat glistening on the surface. Taste and add more salt and pepper if desired. Serve hot with spaetzle, dumplings, potatoes, rice, or Kaiser rolls.

Ground Beef and Pork Chipotle Chili
with Kidney Beans

MAKES 6 SERVINGS

I like a good chili that has a well-rounded spiciness, strong but not overwhelming. Chipotle chiles, the smoke-dried form of the familiar jalapeño, give just the right rich, spicy flavor to this recipe. You can find small jars of chipotle powder in the seasonings aisle of well-stocked markets, but if it's unavailable, substitute any medium-hot pure red chili powder. However you prepare it, set out bowls of tomato salsa, sour cream, shredded cheddar or jack cheese, chopped sweet onion, and sliced avocado for guests to add to their servings as they like.

¼	cup extra-virgin olive oil
2	pounds ground beef
1	pound ground pork
1	cup chopped onion
3	garlic cloves, minced
2	to 3 tablespoons chipotle chili powder (or to taste)
2	tablespoons pure ground chili powder
2	tablespoons ground cumin
1	teaspoon dried oregano
1	teaspoon paprika
1	(28-ounce) can crushed tomatoes
2	cups beef or chicken stock or good-quality canned broth
1	cup dark beer
3	tablespoons tomato paste
	Kosher salt and freshly ground black pepper
3	tablespoons masa harina
1	(15-ounce) can red kidney beans, drained

For garnish:

Tomato salsa

Sour cream

Shredded cheddar or Jack cheese

Chopped sweet onion

Sliced avocado

Chopped fresh cilantro

1. Heat a large, heavy skillet over medium-high heat and add half the olive oil. When the oil is hot, add the beef and pork and sauté, in batches if necessary, stirring and breaking up the meat into small chunks with a wooden spoon, until it is evenly browned, about 10 minutes. Pour the liquid and fat off from the pan before adding the next batch of meat. With a slotted spoon, transfer the meat from the pan to a bowl.

2. Heat the remaining olive oil in a large, heavy casserole or Dutch oven over medium heat and add the onion, garlic, chipotle powder, chili powder, cumin, oregano, and paprika. Sauté until the onions are tender, about 5 minutes. Stir in the meat and its juices, the crushed tomatoes, stock, beer, and tomato paste. Add

salt and pepper to taste. Bring the mixture to a simmer, cover, and simmer over low heat for 2 to 3 hours until very fragrant and thick. Stir often.

   Using the pressure cooker: Use the pressure cooker for step 2. After adding all of the ingredients, secure the lid on the pressure cooker. Bring the cooker to high pressure, then reduce the heat to low and set a timer for 15 minutes. After 15 minutes, release the pressure from the cooker, following the manufacturer's instructions. Carefully remove the lid.

3. Put the masa harina in a bowl. Ladle in about half a cup of liquid from the pot and stir it into the masa harina with a fork. When the mixture is smooth and free of lumps, stir it back into the chili along with the beans. Simmer, stirring frequently, until the liquid has thickened, about 10 minutes. Season to taste with salt and pepper and ladle the chili into bowls. Pass the garnishes at the table.

Braised Lamb Shanks with Squash and Peas

MAKES 6 SERVINGS

Wolfgang's EASY TIPS

➤ Cook the shanks in an attractive, flameproof Dutch oven or covered casserole that you can use to present the finished dish at your dinner table.

➤ You can begin the dish in the morning or the day before, browning the lamb and cooking the mixture for an hour or so, then finish it close to serving time. Even better, make it a day ahead so you can skim off the fat before reheating and serving.

This makes an elegant, deeply satisfying main course at any time of year. Many hearty lamb dishes like this one include potatoes, however I use pattypan squash, which is much lighter but still absorbs the marvelous gravy. If you can't find the round, scalloped pattypans, use zucchini. You could also make the dish with diced winter squash.

6	lamb shanks, ½ to ¾ pound each	3	cups beef stock or good-quality canned beef broth
1	teaspoon chopped fresh rosemary	1	cup peeled fresh pearl onions (see tips page 178), or frozen pearl onions
	Kosher salt and freshly ground black pepper	¾	pound pattypan squash, cut into ½-inch cubes (1 heaped cup cubes)
2	plus 1 tablespoons extra-virgin olive oil	½	cup frozen tiny peas
1	medium or large onion, chopped		Fresh rosemary sprigs for garnish
2	medium carrots, peeled and chopped	2	tablespoons chopped fresh flat-leaf parsley for garnish
2	teaspoons minced fresh garlic		
½	cup dry red wine		
1	cup drained canned diced tomatoes		

1. Preheat the oven to 350°F. Season the lamb shanks all over with the rosemary and salt and pepper to taste. Heat a Dutch oven over medium-high heat. Add 2 tablespoons of the oil and, when it is hot, the lamb shanks in batches. Sauté, turning them occasionally, until they are browned all over, about 10 minutes. Remove from the heat and transfer the shanks to a plate. Pour off the fat from the Dutch oven and add the remaining 1 tablespoon olive oil to the Dutch oven. Add the onion and carrots and cook, stirring, until tender and beginning to color, about 5 minutes. Add the garlic and stir together for a minute until fragrant.

2. Add the red wine and stir and scrape the bottom of the casserole to deglaze the pan. Return the lamb shanks to the casserole. Add the tomatoes, beef broth, pearl onions, and squash. Add a little salt and pepper, cover, and transfer to the preheated oven. Cook until the meat is so tender that it practically falls off the bone when touched with a fork, 1½ to 2 hours. Add the peas during the last half hour of cooking.

3. With a slotted spoon, transfer the vegetables and lamb shanks to a heated serving platter. Arrange the lamb shanks on top of the vegetables and cover with foil to keep warm. Spoon as much of the fat from the surface of the liquid in the pot as you can.

4. Return the Dutch oven to the stovetop and bring to a boil over medium-high heat. Skim off the fat that rises to its surface. Taste and adjust seasonings. Pour the sauce over the lamb shanks and vegetables, garnish with rosemary sprigs and parsley, and serve.

Marinated Rack of Lamb with Honey-Mint Vinaigrette

MAKES 4 SERVINGS

Wolfgang's EASY TIPS

➤ You can substitute less expensive chops from the tenderloin, loin, or sirloin for the pricey rack of lamb, or make skewers of kebab chunks cut from the shoulder or leg.

➤ Lamb becomes even more flavorful and tender if you marinate it overnight. This Persian-inspired marinade is one of my favorites; it complements lamb's taste with tangy-sweet pomegranate juice. The juice is sold in many well-stocked supermarkets and imported food stores, as well as in farmers' markets. If the juice proves elusive, substitute fresh apple cider. Steamed couscous or basmati rice goes perfectly as a side dish for the juicy meat, and stir-fried vegetables make an impressive garnish.

➤ Before carving the roasted lamb racks, let them rest, covered with foil, for 5 to 10 minutes so the juices can settle back into the meat. After carving, lightly sprinkle each chop with fleur de sel (flakes of French sea salt), kosher salt, or even regular salt to bring out the lamb's full flavor.

As a child we got to eat lamb only on special springtime occasions, like Easter. Maybe that's why I love it so much. And today lamb is available year-round, making it possible to enjoy the incomparably sweet yet robust meat more often. One of my favorite cuts is the rib section, sold whole as the impressive rack of lamb or portioned into one- or two-bone chops. Lately I've discovered excellent imported lamb racks at reasonable prices. A small rack weighing three-quarter to one pound will generously serve one person, though some racks can be twice that size and serve two.

For the marinated lamb:

4	small racks of lamb, ¾ to 1 pound each, or 2 large racks of lamb, 1½ to 2 pounds each, trimmed
2	cups bottled pomegranate juice or fresh apple cider
½	cup soy sauce
2	tablespoons honey
3	cups chopped scallions (about 8 medium scallions)
2	teaspoons crushed red pepper flakes
4	garlic cloves, finely chopped
2	plus 2 tablespoons extra-virgin olive oil

Fleur del sel or kosher salt and freshly ground black pepper

For the honey-mint vinaigrette:

½	cup seasoned rice wine vinegar
½	cup packed fresh mint leaves
¼	cup packed fresh flat-leaf parsley leaves
1	tablespoon honey
½	tablespoon chopped fresh ginger
1	cup peanut oil or vegetable oil
¼	cup golden raisins
	Kosher salt
	Fresh lime juice

1. First, marinate the lamb. In a nonreactive container large enough to hold all the lamb racks side by side, combine the juice, soy sauce, and honey. Stir in the scallions, red pepper flakes, and garlic. Add the lamb racks, bone side up, cover with plastic wrap, and refrigerate overnight. You can also transfer the marinade to a resealable plastic bag and marinate the lamb racks in the bag, turning them from time to time.

2. Preheat the oven to 400°F. Line a baking sheet with foil.

3. Heat a large skillet over high heat. Add 2 tablespoons of the olive oil and reduce the heat slightly. Remove half of the lamb from the marinade, shake off excess liquid, season with salt and pepper to taste, and sear the meat all over until nicely browned, about 5 minutes total. Transfer to the baking sheet. Repeat with the remaining 2 tablespoons of oil and lamb. Discard the marinade.

4. Transfer the baking sheet to the preheated oven and roast until medium rare, 130° to 135°F on an instant-read thermometer inserted into the center of the meat without touching the bone. Small racks will be done in 15 to 20 minutes, larger racks in 20 to 25 minutes. Remove from the oven, cover with aluminum foil, and let the meat rest for 5 to 10 minutes.

5. Meanwhile, prepare the vinaigrette. In a blender or food processor, combine the rice wine vinegar, mint, parsley, honey, and ginger. Blend or process until thoroughly puréed. With the motor running, drizzle in the oil to form a thick emulsion. Transfer to a bowl and stir in the raisins. Season to taste with salt and lime juice.

6. On a carving board with a sharp knife, cut between the bones of each rack, carving single-bone chops from larger racks and double-bone chops from smaller racks. Spoon some vinaigrette onto each plate. Arrange the chops on top and lightly sprinkle each chop with a little fleur del sel or salt. Drizzle more vinaigrette over the lamb and serve hot.

Pan-Seared Pork Chops
with Hoisin Sauce and Dried Cranberries

MAKES 4 SERVINGS

Wolfgang's EASY TIPS

➤ You can substitute barbecue sauce for the hoisin sauce if you wish. It's even easier to find and equally rich, savory, and complex. Look for a brand that has a nicely balanced flavor, not too sweet and not too tangy.

➤ Serve the pork chops with steamed rice or mashed potatoes to help soak up the juices.

➤ You could substitute capers or gherkins for the dried cranberries.

Hoisin sauce is the modern answer to demi-glace, the ingredient that classical European cooks spend hours making to get rich pan sauces. To get demi-glace, they must start by roasting veal bones and aromatic vegetables to a deep brown color. Then they simmer them very slowly for six hours or more to extract all their flavor and color into a brown stock. Finally, they strain that stock and continue boiling it until it reduces down to a deep brown, complex syrup, the demi-glace. Since a home cook doesn't have a brigade of full-time kitchen employees to do all of this, Chinese hoisin sauce, made from fermented wheat or soybeans, makes a great stand-in. It's as thick as jam and as savory as nicely seared meat, even though it contains none. Here I use it to enhance a port wine sauce with dried cranberries, an easy and elegant accompaniment to pork chops.

4	(10 to 12-ounce) boneless or bone-in pork chops	1	cup port
	Kosher salt and freshly ground pepper	¼	cup dried cranberries
1	tablespoon finely chopped fresh rosemary or thyme	1	to 2 tablespoons bottled hoisin sauce or good-quality bottled barbecue sauce
2	tablespoons extra-virgin olive oil	1	teaspoon chopped fresh chives
1	plus 1 tablespoons unsalted butter, cut into small pieces		

1. Preheat the oven to 400°F. Heat a large, heavy-bottom, ovenproof skillet or sauté pan over medium-high heat. Meanwhile, pat the pork chops dry with paper towels and sprinkle them on both sides with salt and pepper to taste and the fresh herbs.

2. Add the oil to the hot skillet and as soon as the oil is hot enough to swirl around easily add 1 tablespoon of the butter and the pork chops, spacing the chops about 1 inch apart. Cook the chops undisturbed until their undersides are golden brown, 2 to 3 minutes. Use tongs to turn them over and sear about 1 minute more. Transfer the pan to the oven and roast until the chops are cooked through but still slightly pink at the center, 12 to 15 minutes.

3. Remove the pan from the oven, transfer the chops to a platter, and cover them with aluminum foil to keep them warm while you make the sauce. Pour off all of the fat from the skillet. Return the skillet to the stovetop over medium-high heat and pour in the

port. With a wooden spoon, stir and scrape to deglaze the pan deposits. Add the dried cranberries and continue simmering the port briskly until it reduces to about half its original volume, about 5 minutes. Stir in 1 tablespoon of the hoisin sauce or barbecue sauce and continue simmering, stirring frequently, until the mixture is thick enough to coat the back of a spoon; taste the sauce and, if you like, stir in a little more hoisin or barbecue sauce. Then whisk in the remaining butter a piece or two at a time until the sauce looks creamy and glossy. Taste the sauce and, if necessary, add a little more salt and pepper.

4. Return the pork chops to the skillet, turn them in the sauce to coat them well, and continue simmering until the chops are heated through, 1 to 2 minutes more. Transfer the chops to heated plates and spoon the sauce over and around them. Garnish with chives and serve immediately.

Asian-Style Pork Hotpot with Squash and Eggplant

MAKES 4 SERVINGS

Wolfgang's EASY TIPS

➤ In most markets or butcher shops, the large primal cut of pork shoulder, which can weigh 12 to 18 pounds with the bone in, is sold divided into two more manageable family-sized pieces: the rectangular upper half, commonly but somewhat confusingly called pork butt (or Boston roast); and the more bony but also delicious portion known as picnic roast. Both are available bone-in or boneless. For quicker cooking and easier serving in the following recipe, ask the butcher to bone either cut for you, then to trim off excess fat and cut it into uniform large chunks 2 x 3 inches each. Some markets will already have large, boneless chunks of shoulder ready for sale.

➤ You could make this same recipe using pork shanks, allowing one whole bone-in shank about 6 inches long per portion. Lamb shoulder or beef shoulder, or even your favorite chicken pieces, bone-in or boneless, skin-on or skinless, also work well.

As a boy I loved coming home from school on an autumn afternoon to the rich aroma of pork shoulder simmering on our kitchen stove. My mother always cooked it with marjoram, thyme, caraway, garlic, a dash of paprika, salt, and pepper, and she served slices of the meltingly tender meat and spoonfuls of its fragrant sauce over buttered noodles or mashed potatoes. Such an everyday meal tasted far better to me than the quick-cooking pork chops or tenderloin that my family reserved for special occasions. When I began to travel the world as a chef, I learned that most cuisines have similar slow-cooked dishes featuring humble cuts of pork. This Asian version is one of my favorites.

2½	pounds well-trimmed boneless pork butt, cut into 2 x 3-inch pieces	2	cups plum wine or other sweet wine such as cream sherry or port
	Kosher salt and freshly ground black pepper	½	cup good-quality light soy sauce
2	plus 2 tablespoons peanut oil or vegetable oil, plus more for cooking the vegetables	¼	cup rice wine vinegar
2	large onions, about 1¼ pounds total weight, peeled and thinly sliced	3	cups water, homemade chicken stock, or good-quality canned chicken broth
	1-inch piece fresh ginger, peeled and minced	¾	pound slender Asian-style eggplants, cut diagonally into 1-inch chunks
6	garlic cloves, peeled and minced	¾	pound winter squash such as butternut, acorn, or kabocha, peeled and cut into 1-inch cubes or diamonds
3	whole star anise		
2	cinnamon sticks	2	green onions, trimmed, cut into 1½-inch pieces, and then cut lengthwise into thin julienne strips
½	teaspoon dried red pepper flakes		
			Steamed white rice for serving

1. Preheat the oven to 350°F. Season the pork with salt and pepper to taste. Heat a large, heavy sauté pan over high heat and add 2 tablespoons of the oil. Add the pork and sauté until evenly golden brown, 5 to 7 minutes Transfer to a plate or bowl.

2. In a heavy casserole or other stovetop-to-oven braising pan over high heat, heat the remaining 2 tablespoons of oil. Add the onions and sauté until golden, 5 to 7 minutes. Add the seared pork, ginger, garlic, star anise, cinnamon sticks, and red pepper flakes.

Continue to sauté until the mixture is aromatic, about 5 minutes more.

3. Pour in the plum wine, soy sauce, and vinegar, and stir and scrape with a wooden spoon to deglaze the pan deposits. Add the water and stock or broth and bring the liquid to a boil. Reduce the heat to a simmer and cook for 10 minutes more. Turn off the heat. Cover the casserole, put it in the preheated oven, and cook until the pork pieces are tender, about 1 hour.

4. Meanwhile, prepare the vegetables. Heat a large sauté pan over high heat. Add a thin film of oil and sauté the eggplant until golden brown, 5 to 7 minutes. Season with salt and pepper. Remove the eggplant from the pan. Add more oil and, still over high heat, sauté the squash until golden brown. Season with salt and pepper. Set the vegetables aside.

5. With a slotted spoon, remove the pork from the casserole. Remove and discard the star anise and cinnamon sticks. If you have time, strain the braising liquid and place it in the freezer for 15 minutes. Then lift the fat from the top. Transfer the onions and braising liquid to a blender or food processor, in batches if necessary to avoid overfilling, and process until puréed. Or purée with a hand blender. Return the puréed mixture to the casserole and, if it is too thick, stir in just enough water to bring it to a creamy consistency. Stir in the pork pieces and vegetables, cover, return to the oven, and cook until the vegetables are tender and the meat is tender enough to cut with a fork, about 20 minutes more. Taste the sauce and adjust the seasonings with salt and pepper. Ladle the pork, vegetables, and sauce into individual heated serving bowls. Garnish with the green onions and serve immediately, passing steamed white rice alongside.

Indoor Grilled Meat Patties with Eggplant and Mushrooms

MAKES 6 TO 8 SERVINGS

Wolfgang's EASY TIPS

➤ For a complete, satisfying main course, serve with Fresh Mushroom Sauce (page 214) and Horseradish or Wasabi Mashed Potatoes (page 208).

➤ If you like, add a finely chopped red bell pepper to the mixture.

➤ To cook in a frying pan, heat a tablespoon of vegetable oil over medium-high heat and cook for 4 minutes on each side.

This is a juicy mixture of ground meat and flavorful vegetables. The patties can be cooked quickly in an electric panini maker or a double-sided countertop grill. A skillet on top of the stove will also do the job quickly.

4	slices globe eggplant, each about ½ inch thick
2	tablespoons extra-virgin olive oil, plus extra for brushing the eggplant
2	medium shallots, minced
½	pound mushrooms, coarsely chopped
	Kosher salt and freshly ground pepper
½	cup heavy cream
2	pounds ground lamb, pork, or veal, or a combination
2	large eggs, lightly beaten
2	tablespoons minced garlic
2	teaspoons ground cumin
1	teaspoon chopped fresh thyme

1. Preheat a panini maker or double-sided countertop grill. Brush the eggplant slices on both sides with olive oil, place them in the grill, close the lid, and cook until tender, 3 to 4 minutes. Turn off the heat, remove the eggplant slices, and let them cool.

2. Heat the 2 tablespoons of olive oil in a small skillet over medium-high heat. Add the shallots and sauté them until they turn pale golden, 3 to 5 minutes. Add the mushrooms, season lightly with salt and pepper, and sauté, stirring frequently, until they have softened, 3 to 4 minutes more. Pour in the cream and cook until it has reduced to form a fairly thick paste with the mushrooms and shallots, with no excess liquid, 5 to 7 minutes more. Remove the skillet from the heat, transfer the mixture to a mixing bowl, and let it cool for about 10 minutes.

3. Chop the cooled eggplant and add it to the mixing bowl along with the ground meat, eggs, garlic, cumin, thyme, and a little salt and pepper. Stir the mixture until the ingredients are thoroughly blended.

4. Reheat the panini maker or double-sided grill, or heat a large skillet over medium-high heat. With moistened hands, form the mixture into large square patties, about 3 x 3 inches and ¾ inch thick. Place as many patties on the cooking surface as will fit comfortably, close the lid, and cook until nicely browned and cooked through, about 4 minutes. Transfer to a heated platter and cover with aluminum foil to keep warm while you cook any remaining batches. Top with mushroom sauce and serve.

Pressure Cooker Barbecued Pulled Pork

MAKES 4 SERVINGS

Cooked in a covered casserole in the oven, this classic Southern-style pork recipe takes a good three to three and a half hours to become so tender you can shred it with a fork. When you slice the meat first and cook it in a pressure cooker, however, you can get absolutely tender, ready-to-eat pork in well under an hour. Using a good-quality store-bought barbecue sauce and packaged barbecue rub makes the recipe even easier.

1½ **pounds pork butt, cut crosswise into ¼-inch thick slices**	1 **tablespoon extra-virgin olive oil**
Kosher salt and freshly ground black pepper	1 **cup good-quality canned chicken broth**
3 **tablespoons commercial barbecue rub**	½ **cup good-quality bottled barbecue sauce**

1. Heat a large, heavy skillet over medium-high heat. Lightly season the pork slices on both sides with salt and pepper to taste, then sprinkle them evenly on both sides with the barbecue rub.

2. Add the olive oil to the skillet. As soon as it is hot, add the pork slices and turn them until evenly browned, 5 to 7 minutes.

3. Transfer the pork to the pressure cooker and add the chicken broth. Secure the pressure cooker lid and bring the pressure to high. When high pressure has been reached, reduce the heat to low and set a timer for 12 minutes.

4. When the time is up, turn off the heat and let the pressure return to normal on its own without using the quick-release. When the pressure has returned to normal, use the quick-release to make sure all the pressure has been released, then carefully remove the lid. Using a fork and a knife, shred the meat.

5. Stir in the barbecue sauce, secure the lid again, and bring the pressure cooker back to high pressure over high heat. Reduce the heat to low and set a timer for 10 minutes more.

6. As soon as the pork is done cooking, use the quick-release valve to release pressure, following the manufacturer's instructions. Stir together the meat and sauce, shredding it more with a fork if you wish. Serve hot.

Wolfgang's EASY TIPS

➤ To serve the pulled pork in the traditional style, pile it on soft sandwich rolls topped with coleslaw. Or be untraditional and make quesadillas using flour tortillas and the quesadilla recipe on page 98.

➤ This dish can be made ahead and reheated. It will taste even better the next day.

Barbecued Pork Ribs with Spicy-Sweet Rub

MAKES 4 SERVINGS

Wolfgang's EASY TIPS

➤ You'll coax the most flavor and tender texture from back ribs by cooking them slowly, covered, over indirect heat—with a fire that occupies only part of the grill's bed and with the ribs placed on the part of the grill rack not directly over the heat. To catch dripping grease that might otherwise cause flare-ups, and to give off steam that helps keep the meat moist, place a drip pan half-filled with water in the fire bed directly under the ribs. Use any large metal or foil pan that you don't mind sacrificing to your permanent grilling tools.

➤ For the best flavor, apply the rub the night before, but leave out the salt, which will draw out too much moisture during prolonged exposure.

➤ You can vary the amount of cayenne in the rub. If you don't want the ribs to be too spicy, reduce the amount; if you want them really spicy, increase it.

➤ You can also bake these ribs in a 350°F oven. Put them in an oiled baking dish, cover with foil, and bake for 1 to 1½ hours.

I first ate ribs as a boy in Austria, where they are typically seasoned with a garlic-caraway rub. Pork back ribs have a sweet flavor that goes well with the smoke of a live fire and with the spicy-sweet seasonings traditionally used in barbecue. As their name suggests, back ribs come from the loin, or back section. They have more meat and are more tender than spareribs, which are cut from the side or belly. Baby back ribs are simply smaller, narrower slabs of back ribs. To season the ribs, I prefer to use a dry rub rather than barbecue sauce. That way, you really taste the meat. During cooking, the rub will capture the pork's juices that might otherwise drip away. Meanwhile, the rub's sugar slowly caramelizes, helping to form a savory-sweet crust that makes the ribs even more appealing.

2	whole racks pork back ribs, 3 to 3½ pounds total weight

For the spicy-sweet rub:

2	tablespoons brown sugar
2	tablespoons onion powder
2	tablespoons garlic powder
2	tablespoons dried thyme
2	tablespoons dried oregano
1	tablespoon mild paprika
1	tablespoon hot paprika
1	teaspoon cayenne (more or less to taste)
2	teaspoons ground coriander
1	teaspoon freshly ground black pepper
1	teaspoon freshly ground white pepper
1	tablespoon kosher salt

1. If you don't have a butcher who can do this, prepare the pork racks. Rinse them under cold running water and thoroughly pat dry. To remove the membrane from each rack, place the rack on a work surface meaty side down. Starting at the bone at one corner, use a small, sharp knife to begin peeling away the membrane. When you have about 1 inch or so of the membrane free, use a paper towel or kitchen towel to grip it firmly; then, pull away from the corner to strip the entire membrane from the rack, using the knife to assist you at any sticking points. Repeat with the other rack. Set the racks aside.

2. Mix together all the ingredients for the spicy-sweet rub except the salt in a small bowl (include the salt only if you plan to cook the ribs in an hour or so). Rub the seasoning mixture evenly over both sides of each rack, pressing it firmly into the meat. If you plan to cook them soon, cover loosely with plastic wrap and leave at room

temperature. Otherwise, tightly wrap each rack of ribs in plastic wrap and refrigerate for up to 24 hours.

3. One hour before grilling, remove the racks from the refrigerator, unwrap them, sprinkle evenly with salt, and leave them loosely covered at room temperature.

4. Build a fire in an outdoor grill for indirect-heat cooking. For a circular grill, carefully push the hot coals to the perimeter of the fire bed; for square or rectangular charcoal grills, push the hot coals into half of the bed; and for a gas grill, preheat the entire grill and then turn off the burners on one side. Carefully place a metal drip pan half-filled with water in the part of the fire bed away from the coals or lit burners and under the part of the cooking grid where the ribs will cook. Set the cooking grid about 6 inches above the heat. Soak a wad of paper towels or a clean cloth with some cooking oil, grip firmly with long-handled grill tongs, and grease the bars of the cooking grid where you'll be placing the ribs.

5. Place the ribs on the cooking grid above the drip pan and close the grill's cover. Cook the ribs until they are so tender that a bone wiggles easily when twisted, 1¼ to 1½ hours, turning the rib racks over every 20 to 30 minutes and, if using charcoal, adding about a dozen new lumps of coal to the fire every 30 minutes. Transfer the ribs from the grill to a cutting board. With a sharp knife or a cleaver, cut each rack either into 2 equal portions or into individual ribs between the bones. Serve hot.

Rack of Pork with Dried Fruit Stuffing

MAKES 4 TO 6 SERVINGS

Wolfgang's EASY TIPS

➤ If you can't get your butcher to butterfly the pork rack, it's easy to do yourself. First, run the knife down between the meat and the bones from the top almost to the bottom, leaving the meat attached at the bottom. The meat should fall from the bone in one big piece. Next make an incision across the middle of the big piece of meat, and open it up like a book.

➤ You can experiment with different combinations of dried fruit, such as dates, figs, or raisins.

This is a dramatic way to serve pork chops. A French pork rack is a rack of chops that have not been cut apart. The meat can be partially separated from the bone and opened up or butterflied so that the entire rack can be topped with a stuffing, then rolled up and tied. Dried fruit always makes a marvelous accompaniment with pork, and this stuffing, accented with lots of caramelized onions, ginger, cinnamon, and star anise, is no exception.

8	ounces prunes, chopped	¼	cup extra-virgin olive oil
2	ounces dried apricots, chopped	3	tablespoons unsalted butter
1	tablespoon chopped fresh sage	2	large yellow onions, peeled and sliced
1	tablespoon chopped fresh rosemary	2	tablespoons finely chopped fresh ginger
1	French pork rack containing 6 to 8 chops, 2½ to 3½ pounds, butterflied	½	cinnamon stick
		1	whole star anise
		¼	cup maple syrup
	Kosher salt and freshly ground black pepper	2	cups apple cider

1. Toss together the chopped prunes and apricots with half the sage and rosemary in a bowl.

2. Season both sides of the pork with salt and pepper to taste. Spread the chopped prune and apricot mixture in an even layer over the inside of the pork rack. Moisten your fingers and press the filling down into the meat, then roll up the meat tightly against the bones. Using kitchen twine, tie the pork rack between each of the bones. Season the outside with salt, pepper, and the remaining herbs.

3. Preheat the oven to 350°F. Heat the olive oil in a large, heavy skillet over high heat. Sear the pork rack on all sides until evenly browned, 5 to 7 minutes. Remove the pork and set aside. Pour off the fat from the pan.

4. Reduce the heat under the skillet to medium and add the butter. When it has melted, add the onions, ginger, cinnamon stick, and star anise. Sauté, stirring frequently, until the onions are golden brown, about 10 minutes. Stir in the maple syrup and continue sautéing, stirring continuously, until the mixture has a deep

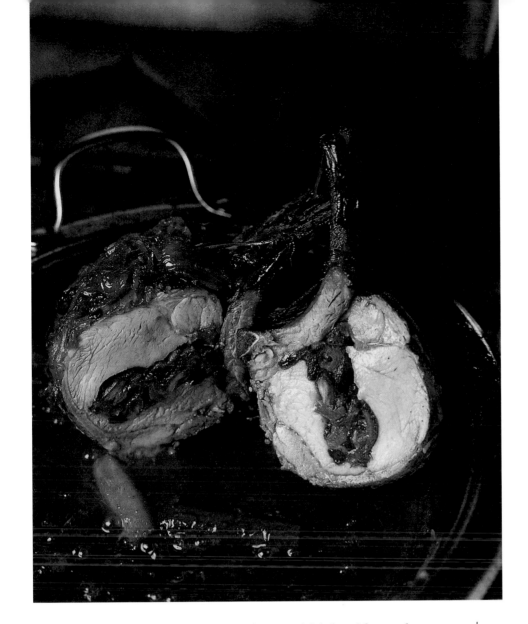

caramel color, about 5 minutes longer. Add the cider to the pan. Stir and scrape the pan with a wooden spoon to deglaze the pan deposits. Cook until the liquid has reduced by half, 5 to 10 minutes. Remove and discard the cinnamon stick and star anise. Taste and adjust seasonings.

5. Transfer the pork to a roasting pan or baking dish and cover it with half the onion mixture. Roast the pork until the roasting thermometer inserted into its thickest part not touching the bone registers 160°F, 1 to 1½ hours. Cover it with the remaining onion mixture halfway through roasting.

6. When the pork is done, remove it from the oven, cover the dish with foil, and let the pork rest for 10 minutes so the meat juices settle. With a sharp knife, carve the pork between the bones into chops. Serve on heated plates, spooning the onions and pan juices over and around the pork.

Roasted Pork Loin with Granny Smith Apples

MAKES 6 TO 8 SERVINGS

Roasting tart apples with a handsome top loin of pork makes a beautiful presentation and a special meal.

½	cup apple juice
¼	cup balsamic vinegar
½	cup good-quality bottled barbecue sauce
2	tablespoons Dijon mustard
4	garlic cloves, crushed
1	teaspoon chopped fresh marjoram leaves
1	(3 to-5-pound) whole boneless pork top loin

	Kosher salt
1	teaspoon freshly ground black pepper
4	Granny Smith apples, cored and halved (or 8 crabapples, cored)
	Fresh marjoram sprigs for garnish

1. In a mixing bowl, whisk together the apple juice, balsamic vinegar, barbecue sauce, and mustard. Stir in the garlic and marjoram. Put the pork in a large, heavy-duty, sealable plastic food-storage bag. Pour in the apple juice mixture. Seal the bag, taking care not to leave any air. Place the bag, sealed edge up, in a large mixing bowl to catch any accidental leaks and refrigerate for at least 1 hour, or as long as overnight.

2. Preheat the oven to 400°F. Remove the pork from the marinade, reserving the marinade, and pat dry. Sprinkle the pork generously all over with salt and black pepper and place it on a rack in a roasting pan.

3. Roast the pork for 15 minutes. Baste the roast with the reserved marinade, and reduce the heat to 325°F. Place the apples in the roasting pan around the pork loin. Continue roasting, basting every 15 minutes for the first half hour only, until the center of the meat registers 150°F on an instant-read thermometer, 1 to 1½ hours more. Transfer the pork and the apples to a carving platter and garnish with sprigs of marjoram. Keep warm.

4. Pour the juices from the roasting pan into a small saucepan. If necessary, add a little water to the roasting pan to deglaze any deposits that remain on its bottom; add this liquid to the saucepan. Skim off any fat floating on the surface of the liquid. Bring to a boil and simmer until it has a syrupy consistency, 3 to 5 minutes. Transfer the sauce to a sauceboat.

5. Carve the pork roast across the grain into ½-inch-thick slices. Arrange overlapping slices of pork and a whole crabapple or an apple half on each serving plate and spoon some of the sauce over the meat.

SIDE DISHES AND SAUCES

Side dishes are just as much a part of the meal as the main course and should never be considered an afterthought. Think of the side dish as an ideal partner for the main course. It could be as simple as a green vegetable cooked al dente and seasoned with a few herbs or browned breadcrumbs (page 204) or rich mashed potatoes spiced with the Japanese horseradish called wasabi (page 208). Or it could be more elaborate, like the fragrant eggplant gratin with basil and tomato on page 210. In these pages you'll find just a few simple recipes that are among my favorites.

I've also included some hot and cold dressings and sauces that will go well with a variety of dishes here. Try the Sun-dried Cherry Pinot Noir Sauce this year for a change with your Thanksgiving turkey. Or serve the Fresh Mushroom Sauce on page 214 the next time you roast a chicken or make hamburgers. The small amount of effort that goes into a sauce can transform an everyday meal into a dinner party feast. And if you've never tasted homemade mayonnaise and homemade mayonnaise-based dressings like Thousand Island (page 219) and Russian dressing (page 220), your life is about to change. You may never buy another bottled salad dressing again.

Wild Rice and Arborio Risotto with Sautéed Apple

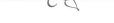

MAKES 4 TO 6 SERVINGS

My first encounter with wild rice had an elegance that perfectly matched the grain's slender shape and subtle flavor. I was working in the kitchen at the famous Maxim's restaurant in Paris, and one night we offered a special main course of sautéed salmon in Champagne sauce, accompanied by wild rice pilaf. The contrasts between the tender, rich-tasting pink fish, its ethereal butter sauce, and the deep-brown, chewy, nutty-tasting grains were sublime. I've loved wild rice ever since, and I have enjoyed experimenting with it in all kinds of dishes, from little savory wild rice pancakes topped with smoked salmon to Chinese-style stir-fried wild rice to airy soufflés flecked with the grain; it adapts well to so many different preparations. Here precooked wild rice adds another dimension to a creamy risotto.

Wolfgang's EASY TIPS

➤ When you shop for wild rice, look for it packaged in clear plastic that lets you check to make sure the grains are clean and largely unbroken. Once you open the bag, store the rice in an airtight container in the pantry.

➤ Prepare wild rice separately from other grains, since it requires more water than common rice and takes longer to cook. Generally, you'll need up to three times as much liquid as the volume of wild rice you're cooking. Simmer the grains gently, covered, for about three-quarters of an hour, until they appear to have burst open and are tender but still chewy. Then drain off any excess liquid by pouring the wild rice into a strainer. In the recipe that follows, you can add any liquid you pour off to the stock you use for the risotto.

➤ You can cook the wild rice and the sautéed apple long before you make the risotto and reheat gently before adding to the risotto.

➤ I like risotto to be liquid enough so that if you tip the plate it slides over the plate into a large flat layer.

For the wild rice:

1   cup wild rice

2   tablespoons unsalted butter

1   shallot, minced

3   garlic cloves, minced

3   cups chicken or vegetable stock or broth, heated

¾   teaspoon kosher salt (less if the stock is salted)

     Freshly ground black pepper

For the sautéed cinnamon apple:

2   tablespoons unsalted butter

1   apple, peeled, cored, and cut into ¼-inch dice

2   tablespoons sugar

1   (3-inch) cinnamon stick

     Kosher salt and freshly ground black pepper

For the risotto:

3   cups chicken or vegetable stock or broth

2   tablespoons unsalted butter

2   tablespoons extra-virgin olive oil

1   shallot, minced

⅔   cup Arborio or Carnaroli rice

⅓   cup dry white wine

     Kosher salt and freshly ground black pepper

¼   cup freshly grated Parmesan cheese

1. Prepare the wild rice. Put the rice in a fine-mesh sieve, rinse under cold running water, and drain. In a heavy saucepan over medium heat, melt the butter. Add the shallot and sauté until translucent, 3 to 4 minutes. Add the garlic and sauté for another 30 seconds, until fragrant. Add the wild rice and stir to coat it evenly with the butter. Pour in 2½ cups of the hot stock or broth, add salt and pepper, and bring to a boil. Reduce the heat to maintain a bare simmer, cover the pan, and cook until the wild rice is tender but still chewy, 45 to 50 minutes, stirring occasionally and adding more stock as necessary if the liquid in the pan is absorbed before the rice is done. Drain off any stock remaining in the pot and add it to the stock you will use for the risotto. Fluff the rice with a fork, cover the pan, and set aside. Keep warm.

2. Make the sautéed cinnamon apple. Melt the butter in a small sauté pan over medium heat. Add the diced apple, the sugar, and the cinnamon stick and sauté until the apple is glossy and tender, 3 to 5 minutes. Season lightly to taste with salt and pepper. Remove the cinnamon stick. Cover and set aside.

3. Make the risotto. In a saucepan, bring the stock or broth to a boil and reduce the heat to keep it barely simmering. Heat the butter and olive oil together over medium heat in a large heavy skillet or saucepan, add the shallot, and sauté until translucent, 3 to 4 minutes. Add the Arborio rice and stir to coat it evenly with the butter. Stir in the wine and simmer until the pan is almost dry, 2 to 3 minutes. Using a ladle, add 1 ladleful of simmering stock or broth to the rice. Cook the rice, stirring continuously with a wooden spoon, until the liquid has been almost completely absorbed. Add another ladleful and repeat the process until you have used up most or all of the liquid and the rice is tender but still chewy and surrounded by a creamy and slightly runny sauce, 20 to 25 minutes. Taste and add salt and pepper as desired. Stir in the reserved cooked wild rice.

4. If necessary, reheat the apples gently. Stir half of them into the risotto mixture. Taste and adjust the seasonings. Spoon the risotto mixture onto warm plates, sprinkle on the Parmesan, top with the remaining apples, and serve immediately.

Making Risotto

1.

2.

3.

4.

5.

6.

7.

Asparagus with Brown Buttered Breadcrumds

MAKES 4 SERVINGS

Wolfgang's EASY TIPS

➤ Cooking vegetables briefly in boiling water, then cooling them quickly by plunging them into ice water, or "shocking," is a great technique for bringing out the bright colors of a vegetable and bringing both its taste and its texture close to their peak before the final few moments of cooking. After shocking, the vegetable can be patted dry, covered, and refrigerated until the time comes to complete its preparation just before serving.

➤ Look for thick spears of asparagus, which are easy to cook perfectly al dente, tender but still slightly crisp. Use a vegetable peeler to remove the tough skin by holding the spear by its bumpy tip and peeling away from you, starting just below the tip. Lay a newspaper down on your work surface for easy cleanup. This sounds like a lot of work, but you'll be able to peel a pound of thick asparagus spears in about 5 minutes. Line up the peeled asparagus with their tips even and trim off the stem ends to get spears about 8 inches long.

I love this classic Austrian-style recipe for asparagus, my favorite spring vegetable. I blanch the asparagus for just a few minutes in boiling water, then immediately transfer the spears to a bowl of ice water. When I'm ready to serve, I turn the asparagus spears in a pan of butter just until they are heated through, and then top them with buttery browned breadcrumbs. Blanching the asparagus and then shocking them in ice water allows you to get the lion's share of the work done hours before you serve whenever it's convenient for you.

1	pound asparagus, peeled and trimmed (see tip—thin spears need not be peeled)	½	cup unseasoned breadcrumbs
			Kosher salt and freshly ground black pepper
2	plus 2 tablespoons unsalted butter	1	tablespoon minced fresh flat-leaf parsley

1. Fill a saucepan or straight-sided frying pan large enough to hold all the asparagus with generously salted water and bring to a boil over high heat. Meanwhile, fill a bowl large enough to hold all the asparagus about three-fourths full with ice cubes and water.

2. Add the asparagus to the boiling water and cook the stems until tender but still slightly crisp, 3 to 4 minutes, testing by removing a spear with tongs, cutting off a small piece from the stem end, and carefully tasting it.

3. With tongs or a large skimmer, remove the asparagus from the boiling water and immediately immerse the stems in the bowl of ice water. Leave them there for several minutes, until completely chilled. Drain the asparagus well and, if you aren't going to complete the recipe right away, refrigerate them in a covered container.

4. Before serving, in a sauté pan large enough to hold the asparagus, melt 2 tablespoons of the butter over medium heat. Add the asparagus and sauté, turning it with tongs, until the spears have heated through, 3 to 5 minutes. Transfer the asparagus to heated serving plates.

5. Add the remaining butter to the pan and cook over medium-high heat until it begins to turn golden, 1 to 2 minutes. Stir in the breadcrumbs and continue cooking until the mixture begins to turn a deep golden brown. Season to taste with salt and pepper and spoon the buttery breadcrumbs over the asparagus. Garnish with parsley and serve immediately.

Two Potato Purées

MAKES 6 TO 8 SERVINGS

(page 208)

Wolfgang's EASY TIPS

➤ Roasting the sweet potatoes caramelizes some of their natural sugars for a richer, more complex flavor that is highlighted with brown sugar, sweet spices, and butter and cream.

➤ Make the mashed white potatoes while you are roasting the sweet potatoes.

These two holiday classics are marvelous side by side, and there's no reason to wait for the holidays to make them. Separately or together, the purées go well with pork chops or roast pork loin, steaks or roast beef, lamp chops, and, of course, chicken.

1	recipe mashed potatoes (page 208), without the horseradish or wasabi	¼	teaspoon ground cinnamon
½	cup hazelnuts		Pinch of ground nutmeg
2	pounds whole jewel or garnet sweet potatoes, scrubbed		Pinch of ground ginger
½	cup heavy cream		Kosher salt and freshly ground white pepper
¼	pound (1 stick) unsalted butter, cut into small chunks	1	teaspoon chopped fresh thyme or marjoram (optional)
2	tablespoons brown sugar	1	tablespoon minced flat-leaf parsley or chives

1. Make the mashed potatoes and set aside.

2. Preheat the oven to 350°F. Spread the hazelnuts on a baking sheet and bake until golden brown, 10 to 12 minutes. Immediately empty the nuts into a folded kitchen towel; fold the towel over them and rub the hazelnuts inside to remove their skins. Pick out the nuts and set aside to cool. Discard the skins. When the nuts have cooled, coarsely chop them with a sharp knife or in a food processor fitted with the metal blade. Set aside.

3. Raise the oven temperature to 400°F. Cover a baking sheet with foil. Pierce the sweet potatoes in a few places with the tip of a sharp knife and place them on the baking sheet. Bake until very soft when pierced with a thin skewer or knife tip, 45 minutes to 1 hour. Remove from the heat and allow to cool until you can handle them.

4. Steady each cooked sweet potato with a folded kitchen towel and cut in half lengthwise, taking care to keep your hands clear of steam. Holding each half in the folded towel, scoop the pulp out of the skin into the food mill. Discard the skin. Purée through a food mill fitted with a fine blade, or in a food processor. With a whisk (or in the food processor), stir in the hot cream, 4 tablespoons of the butter and the brown sugar, cinnamon, nutmeg, and ginger. Beat until thoroughly combined. Season to

Clockwise from the top: potato purée, sweet potato purée, horseradish or wasabi potato purée.

taste with salt and white pepper. Cover the bowl and keep the sweet potatoes warm over a pan of simmering water if serving right away.

5. Just before serving, reheat the potatoes, either in a bowl above simmering water or in the microwave. Put the remaining 4 tablespoons butter in a small saucepan over medium heat. Melt the butter and then swirl the pan continuously over the heat until the butter turns nut-brown and fragrant. Remove from the heat and stir in the hazelnuts and optional thyme or marjoram.

6. Transfer the sweet potatoes to a serving dish and drizzle the hazelnut butter over them. Transfer the mashed Yukon Gold potatoes to another serving dish and garnish with parsley or chives. Serve immediately.

Wolfgang's EASY TIPS

➤ Sweet potatoes will not become gummy in a food processor. If you don't use the processor, use a food mill or ricer so that the potatoes' fibers are strained out.

Horseradish or Wasabi Mashed Potatoes

MAKES 6 SERVINGS

Wolfgang's EASY TIPS

➤ My favorite potatoes for mashed potatoes are Yukon Golds or similar fairly starchy, yellow-fleshed varieties that are easily found in farmers' markets. Baking potatoes also work well.

➤ Cook the white potatoes in lots of salted boiling water, being careful not to cook too long, then drain well and let steam in the hot pan with its cover on to rid the potatoes of any extra moisture. This will prevent your mashed potatoes from being watery.

➤ Never use a food processor for mashed white potatoes because the mixture will be gummy. A standing mixer fitted with the paddle attachment works well, as does a food mill or potato ricer.

➤ Use a stand mixer with the paddle attachment. Or have one to whip the potatoes through a food mill or potato ricer, or mash them with a handheld potato masher.

➤ Wasabi powder and paste are available at Asian markets and at gourmet ingredients stores. I prefer the paste. Before stirring the powder into the mashed potatoes, dissolve it in a couple of teaspoons of water.

I like my mashed potatoes with lots of butter and cream, and one of my favorite ways to season them is with horseradish or the Japanese horseradish called wasabi. They are just a little bit pungent this way.

2½ pounds baking potatoes, peeled and cut into even 1½- to 2-inch chunks	Pinch of freshly ground white pepper
1 teaspoon kosher salt, plus more for seasoning the whipped potatoes	Pinch of freshly grated nutmeg
⅔ cup milk or heavy cream, or a combination	2 to 3 teaspoons prepared horseradish or wasabi powder stirred to a paste in 2 teaspoons water, or use prepared wasabi paste
6 to 8 tablespoons unsalted butter, cut into small pieces	

1. Put the potatoes in a saucepan filled with enough cold water to cover them well. Add the salt. Bring the water to a boil over high heat, then reduce the heat to medium and simmer briskly until the potatoes are fork tender, 15 to 20 minutes.

2. Meanwhile, combine the milk or cream and butter in a small saucepan. Heat them over low heat until the butter has melted.

3. Drain the potatoes well and return to the pot. Cover tightly and let sit undisturbed for 5 minutes. Transfer to the bowl of a stand mixer fitted with the paddle attachment. Beat at medium-low speed while you gradually add the hot cream-butter mixture, a generous amount of salt, and the white pepper and nutmeg. Beat the mixture until it is smooth, light, and fluffy, 3 to 5 minutes. Beat in the horseradish or wasabi, taste, and adjust seasonings. Add more horseradish or wasabi if you want a more pungent flavor.

4. If you are serving right away, bring a few inches of water to a boil in a saucepan large enough to support the stand mixer's bowl on its rim. When the potatoes are whipped, reduce the heat to very low, place the mixer bowl of potatoes on top of the pan, and cover the bowl with aluminum foil to keep the potatoes warm. Alternatively, transfer the potatoes to a microwave-safe bowl and reheat before serving in the microwave. Do not heat for too long or they will be watery.

Sautéed Squash Ribbons

MAKES 4 TO 6 SERVINGS

This is a wonderful way to serve summer squash. The ribbons look beautiful and are especially effective as a vehicle for a sauce. If you don't eat pasta, try this as a substitute with marinara sauce. Since zucchini is a year-round vegetable in supermarkets, you can make this dish whenever you want to. Use your imagination to dress it up with diced fresh tomatoes in summer or edible flowers or minced fresh herbs. I use the ribbons as a marvelous accompaniment to Pan-Seared Ahi Tuna with Wasabi Cream Sauce (page 147).

(page 147)

Wolfgang's EASY TIPS

➤ A vegetable peeler is the best tool to use to get the strips.

➤ Don't cook the squash for too long or too far ahead or it will lose its appealing texture.

2	pounds zucchini, or a mixture of zucchini and yellow squash
1	to 2 tablespoons butter or olive oil, as desired
	Kosher salt and freshly ground pepper
2	tablespoons chopped fresh chervil
2	tablespoons slivered fresh basil

1. Using a vegetable peeler, cut the squash into long, wide strips. Discard the middle parts with the seeds.

2. Heat the butter or olive oil over medium-high heat in a large, heavy skillet. Add the squash and sauté, stirring often, until just tender and bright, 3 to 5 minutes. Do not overcook. Season to taste with salt and pepper and remove from the heat. Sprinkle with the fresh herbs and serve.

Summer Eggplant Gratin

MAKES 4 TO 6 SERVINGS

Wolfgang's EASY TIPS

➤ To prepare the tomatoes, bring a saucepan of water to a boil. Fill a bowl with ice and water. Cut out the cores of the tomatoes at their stem ends and score a shallow X in their skins at their flower ends. Carefully lower the tomatoes into the boiling water and leave them until their skins wrinkle, about 30 seconds. Remove them with a slotted spoon or wire skimmer and transfer to the bowl of ice water to cool. Peel each tomato and cut in half crosswise and gently squeeze out the seeds. Chop the tomatoes into ¼-pieces.

➤ Instead of peeling the entire eggplant, slice off the stem and flower ends and peel off the skin lengthwise in alternating strips about ½ inch wide.

➤ Smaller eggplants that feel heavy for their size have a mild flavor. However, don't buy eggplants that are too thin, or it will be difficult to overlap them in the dish.

In my early twenties I went to work at L'Oustau de Beaumanière, a three-star restaurant in Provence, where I learned how delicious eggplant could be when cooked for a long time and combined with other Mediterranean ingredients like tomatoes, garlic, and fresh herbs. Then its texture becomes as tender as custard and it develops a rich, fully rounded, earthy flavor. I especially enjoy eggplant when I slice and bake it in a gratin, a style of dish that takes its name from the French word for "crust." The recipe that follows is absolutely simple and delicious and makes a perfect side dish for grilled or roasted meat or poultry, like the Roast Beef Tenderloin on page 169. The gratin tastes wonderful if made a day ahead and reheated. Or try it cold with a splash of vinegar and a sprinkling of chopped fresh basil.

2	plus 1 plus 1 tablespoons olive oil	
1	tablespoon chopped garlic	
½	teaspoon red pepper flakes	
2	pounds firm, sun-ripened tomatoes, peeled, seeded, and cut into ¼-inch pieces or 1 (28-ounce) can, drained, seeded, and chopped	
1	teaspoon sugar	

Salt and freshly ground black pepper

1	tablespoon chopped fresh basil
2	pounds small, slender eggplants, peeled as described in the tip and sliced about ½ inch thick
½	cup shredded Swiss cheese

1. Preheat the oven to 375°F. Butter a shallow oval gratin dish that is about 12 inches long, or a 2-quart baking dish.

2. Heat 1 tablespoon of the olive oil in a large, heavy, nonstick sauté pan over medium-high heat and add the garlic and red pepper flakes. Sauté until glossy, 20 to 30 seconds, and add the tomatoes, sugar, and salt and pepper. Sauté, stirring often, until the tomatoes cook down to a chunky sauce, about 15 minutes. Taste and correct seasonings, stir in the basil, and transfer to a bowl.

3. Clean and wipe dry the sauté pan and add 2 tablespoons of the olive oil. Heat over medium-high heat. When the olive oil is hot, add the eggplant slices in an even layer. Cook on both sides until browned and tender, 3 to 5 minutes per side. Drain on paper towels.

4. On the bottom of the dish, arrange half the eggplant slices, overlapping each other slightly in concentric rings to form a single layer. Sprinkle evenly with salt and pepper. Top with half the

tomatoes. Repeat the layers. Layer on the shredded cheese. Drizzle on the remaining tablespoon of olive oil.

5. Bake for 25 minutes, then turn the oven heat down to 350°F. Bake another 20 minutes, or until the eggplant slices are completely tender when pierced with the tip of a sharp knife and the top is lightly browned. If the cheese begins to brown too much before the eggplant is done, cover the baking dish with foil. Present the baking dish at table on a heatproof pad, scooping individual servings onto each plate.

Homemade Potato Chips

MAKES 12 TO 16 SERVINGS

Wolfgang's EASY TIPS

➤ An automatic deep fryer that maintains the temperature of the oil and has a built-in basket to lift out the food makes frying these chips easy. You could also use a good, deep, heavy pan or skillet.

➤ A mandolin or a less expensive slicer will help you get very thin slices, which will be crisper when deep-fried.

➤ You need not peel the potatoes if they have thin skins. Older potatoes tend to have thick, gnarled skins and should be peeled.

➤ Always season the potato chips as soon as they come out of the oil, so that the seasoning sticks.

These chips make a delicious and casual side dish. Serve them as an hors d'oeuvre with an assortment of seasonings. They're great with burgers or sandwiches or with steak. After you try these you may never want to open a bag of store-bought potato chips again.

4	**pounds baking potatoes or Yukon Golds, scrubbed clean**
	Peanut oil for deep frying
	Kosher salt

Seasoning possibilities:

Freshly ground black pepper

Salt mixed with cayenne

Freshly grated Parmesan

Salt mixed with chopped fresh thyme or rosemary

Thinly sliced or slivered truffles

1. If the potatoes have thick, gnarly skins, as older potatoes do, peel them. Otherwise, just scrub. Cut the potatoes crosswise into very thin slices and put them in a bowl of cold water. Leave them to soak for about 10 minutes, then drain and very carefully pat the slices completely dry with separate layers of paper towels.

2. Put several inches of oil in an automatic deep fryer or a deep, heavy pan or skillet. Set the deep fryer or bring the oil in the pan to 350°F.

3. In batches, deep-fry the potato slices, turning them with a wire strainer if necessary to cook them evenly until they turn light golden brown, 2 to 3 minutes. Lift out the basket or scoop out the potatoes with a deep-fry skimmer and spread them onto paper towels to drain. Sprinkle right away with salt and your choice of seasonings. Bring the oil back up to 350°F before adding the next batch.

4. Arrange the chips attractively in one or more napkin-lined baskets and serve.

Sun-Dried Cherry Pinot Noir Sauce

MAKES ABOUT 3 CUPS

Be sure to choose a good pinot noir for this sauce because the character of the wine makes a big contribution to its heady flavor. I like to serve it with roast turkey or with any other grilled or roasted poultry or meat.

1 cup sun-dried cherries	1 cup pinot noir
½ cup orange juice	1 teaspoon chopped fresh thyme leaves
½ cup port wine	
1 tablespoon extra-virgin olive oil	2 tablespoons hoisin sauce
1 large shallot, minced	1 tablespoon unsalted butter
2 cups chicken stock or good-quality canned chicken broth	Kosher salt and freshly ground black pepper

1. Put the sun-dried cherries in a nonreactive bowl and add the orange juice and port. Cover with plastic wrap and refrigerate until the cherries are plumped up, at least 1 hour or as long as overnight.

2. Heat the olive oil in a medium saucepan over medium heat. Add the shallot and sauté until tender but not yet browned, 3 to 4 minutes. Stir in the chicken stock, pinot noir, and thyme. Raise the heat to medium-high, bring the liquid to a boil, and continue boiling until it reduces by half its volume, about 15 minutes. Stir in the hoisin sauce.

3. Add the plumped cherries and their liquid to the pan. Bring the liquid back to a boil, reduce the heat to maintain a brisk simmer, and continue cooking, stirring occasionally, until the liquid turns slightly syrupy, 7 to 10 minutes.

4. Reduce the heat to low. In 2 or 3 pieces, whisk in the butter. Season to taste with salt and pepper. Cover the pan and keep the sauce warm over very low heat until ready to serve.

Wolfgang's EASY TIPS

➤ Many markets and gourmet specialty stores today carry packages of sun-dried cherries, which look like deep-red raisins and have a wonderful fruity flavor that complements the taste of the wine.

Fresh Mushroom Sauce

MAKES ABOUT 2½ CUPS

Wolfgang's EASY TIPS

➤ If your mushrooms are sandy, wipe them with a damp piece of paper towel, then trim off the bottom of the stem before slicing.

➤ You could substitute chicken broth for the beef broth.

This simple sauce goes wonderfully with Indoor-Grilled Meat Patties (page 192) or any simply sautéed, grilled, or roasted meat or poultry. For the best results, use half wild mushrooms and half button mushrooms. If you want a really rich taste, add two tablespoons hoisin sauce before adding the butter at the end.

2 tablespoons extra-virgin olive oil	1 cup beef stock or good-quality canned beef broth, or chicken stock or broth
¼ pound wild mushrooms, such as chanterelles and shiitakes, cleaned and thinly sliced	2 tablespoons hoisin sauce (optional)
¼ pound button mushrooms, cleaned and thinly sliced	6 tablespoons unsalted butter, cut into 6 pieces
1 tablespoon minced shallots	Kosher salt and freshly ground black pepper
1 tablespoon minced garlic	
½ cup port wine	

1. Heat a saucepan over medium-high heat and add the olive oil. As soon as the oil is hot enough to swirl freely, add the mushrooms, shallots, and garlic. Sauté, stirring continuously, until the mushrooms begin to brown slightly, 3 to 4 minutes.

2. Add the port and boil until it has reduced by half its volume, 4 to 5 minutes. Add the stock or broth, bring it to a boil, and continue boiling until it has reduced by about one-third and the sauce has thickened slightly, 5 to 7 minutes.

3. Reduce the heat to low. Whisk in the hoisin sauce if desired. A piece at a time, whisk in the butter until completely melted. Season to taste with salt and pepper.

Making Fresh Mushroom Sauce

1.

2.

3.

4.

5.

6.

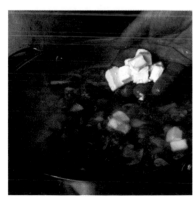

7.

Marinara Sauce

MAKES ABOUT 4 CUPS

Wolfgang's EASY TIPS

➤ When tomatoes are not in season, make this sauce with a good brand of canned tomatoes. Recipe-ready chopped and peeled tomatoes will speed things up considerably.

This is a simple tomato sauce that you can use for pasta, pizza, or any dish that calls for a tomato sauce. Sun-dried tomatoes add another flavor dimension to the sauce.

2 tablespoons extra-virgin olive oil	½ cup chopped sun-dried tomatoes
1 small onion, minced	½ to 1 teaspoon sugar (or to taste)
3 garlic cloves, minced	
1 tablespoon tomato paste	Kosher salt and freshly ground pepper
3 pounds Roma tomatoes or fresh ripe heirloom tomatoes or 2 (28-ounce) cans tomatoes, peeled, seeded, and diced	¼ cup julienned basil

1. Heat the olive oil in a large saucepan or heavy skillet over medium heat. Add the onion and sauté until tender, about 5 minutes. Add the garlic and cook 1 minute longer, or until fragrant. Add the tomato paste, tomatoes, sun-dried tomatoes, sugar, and salt and pepper to taste and cook, stirring often, for 20 minutes, or until the tomatoes have cooked down and the sauce is thick. Taste and add salt and pepper if necessary. Stir in the basil.

VARIATION: *If you want a smoother, less rustic sauce, before stirring in the basil pulse in a food processor or put through the medium blade of a food mill.*

Red Wine-Shallot Sauce

This easy sauce goes wonderfully with roast beef or pan-cooked steaks.

½	plus ½ cup dry red wine	1	shallot, minced
2	cups beef stock or good-quality canned beef broth	5	tablespoons unsalted butter
1	tablespoon tomato paste or hoisin sauce		

1. After roasting or pan-cooking your beef or steak, transfer the meat to a platter, cover with foil, and keep warm. Pour off excess fat from the pan. Add ½ cup of the wine and stir and scrape with a wooden spoon to deglaze the pan deposits. Transfer to a saucepan and stir in the remaining wine, beef stock or broth, tomato paste or hoisin sauce, and shallot. Bring the liquid to a rapid boil and continue boiling until it reduces by half, about 5 minutes. Whisk in the butter 1 tablespoon at a time. Reduce the heat slightly and continue simmering the sauce briskly until it is thick enough to coat the back of a spoon, 3 to 5 minutes more. Transfer to a sauceboat and serve.

Wolfgang's EASY TIPS

➤ You could substitute chicken stock for the beef broth.

Mayonnaise

MAKES ABOUT 1 ½ CUPS

Wolfgang's EASY TIPS

➤ Handheld blenders, mixers, and food processors all work well for mayonnaise. The immersion blender allows you to put everything in the bowl at once, even the oil, and within seconds you have mayonnaise.

➤ You can substitute vegetable oil for some or all of the olive oil if you wish.

Oh, the hours I spent as a young chef making mayonnaise by hand! I developed incredible muscles in my shoulder, forearm, and wrist whisking egg yolks in a large bowl as I slowly drizzled in oil. Today, though, a good hand mixer, hand blender, or food processor makes aching arm muscles a thing of the past. If you don't have a processor with the whisk attachment, use the stainless steel blade. Use this classic sauce, on its own or enhanced with chopped fresh herbs, onions, capers, or other seasonings, as a sandwich spread, mixed with salads, or as an accompaniment to cold seafood or poultry.

2	tablespoons white wine vinegar or Champagne vinegar		Kosher salt and freshly ground pepper
1	large egg	1	cup olive oil
1	teaspoon Dijon mustard		

1. Place the vinegar, egg, mustard, salt, and pepper in a regular bowl or in the bowl of your food processor fitted with the steel blade or whisk attachment. Begin beating the mixture and slowly drizzle in the oil. Continue to beat or run the machine until all of the oil has been added. You will have beautiful mayonnaise in seconds. Transfer to a bowl or jar, cover tightly, and refrigerate until ready to use.

Using an Immersion Blender

1.

2.

3.

4.

Thousand Island Dressing

MAKES 2 CUPS

This dressing, which is close to Russian dressing but has more ketchup, is terrific on Reuben sandwiches and seafood salads.

1   tablespoon white wine vinegar or Champagne vinegar

1   large egg

Kosher salt and freshly ground pepper

1   cup vegetable or olive oil

3   tablespoons store-bought relish

5   tablespoons ketchup

1   teaspoon Worcestershire sauce

2   tablespoons minced red onion

1   tablespoon chopped flat-leaf parsley

1. Place the vinegar, egg, and salt and pepper to taste in a bowl or the bowl of your food processor fitted with the steel blade or whisk attachment. Begin beating the mixture and slowly drizzle in the oil. Continue to beat or run the machine until all of the oil has been added. When you have a thick mayonnaise, stop beating and stir or whisk in the remaining ingredients. Blend well and refrigerate in a jar or covered bowl until ready to use. It will keep for a week.

Wolfgang's EASY TIPS

➤ This is another mayonnaise-based dressing and can be made in seconds with a hand blender or mixer or in a food processor fitted with a whisk or steel blade. Once you have a thick mayonnaise, you can stir or whisk in the remaining ingredients.

➤ If you use commercial mayonnaise, omit the first four ingredients and substitute 1½ cups mayonnaise.

My Russian Dressing

MAKES 1 ¼ CUPS

This is Russian dressing with a few additions, like parsley and cornichons, barbecue sauce and chives. I like to serve it with turkey or beef burgers, and it's great on almost any kind of sandwich.

¾	cup mayonnaise, homemade (page 218) or commercial	½	tablespoon chopped chives
			Juice of ½ lemon
¼	cup ketchup	2	tablespoons store-bought barbecue sauce
1	tablespoon chopped cornichons or sweet pickles		
½	tablespoon chopped flat-leaf parsley	2	tablespoons chopped red onion

1. Stir together all the ingredients. Keep in a jar or covered bowl in the refrigerator until ready to use. It will keep for a week.

Tartar Sauce

MAKES 1 ½ CUPS

This is just mayonnaise with briny, savory additions. Serve it with fish or with cold meats.

1	recipe Mayonnaise (page 218)	1	tablespoon chopped fresh tarragon
1	tablespoon chopped cornichons	1	tablespoon chopped fresh chives
1	tablespoon drained, rinsed capers	½	teaspoon sugar

1. Make the mayonnaise as directed. Stir in the remaining ingredients. Store in a jar or covered bowl in the refrigerator until ready to use.

Wolfgang's EASY TIPS

➤ Cornichons are small French pickles. If you can't find them in your supermarket with the other pickles, try a gourmet market.

DESSERTS

I save the best for last. I'm always thinking about dessert, even while I'm eating my dinner. I've been this way since I was a kid, and my pastry chef knows that she always has to make extra marjolaine (page 258) and lemon bars (page 262) when I'm around. But you don't have to be a pastry chef to make great tasting desserts. You'll see as you cook your way through this chapter how simple it is to make a wonderful chocolate mousse, crème brûlée, or even baked Alaska. Desserts should be as multidimensional as other courses. Just as I rarely season my appetizer or main dish with salt alone, desserts shouldn't rely only on sugar. Spices, nuts, and chocolate all add flavor. And fresh fruit speaks for itself.

Although you can get many fruits and berries year-round, there's nothing better than eating fruit at the height of its season. At the restaurant our dessert menu changes with the seasons. We make cherry cobbler with the wonderful cherries we find at the farmers' market in late spring, and peach melba with raspberry sauce in summer. On the other hand, not all desserts rely on seasonal fruits. You can make the Pineapple Upside-Down Cake on page 248 at any time of year, because in Hawaii it's always summer. The same goes for any of the cookies.

Often the occasion dictates what the grand finale of your meal should be. A birthday dinner calls for a sachertorte (page 260) or a marjolaine so you can light a few candles. But a zesty lemon bar with a few fresh berries will do just fine after a light lunch. If you're making a meal with Asian influences, try the Banana Spring Rolls on page 229. And for an old-fashioned American chicken dinner, there's nothing better than my Granny Smith Apple Pie with Cheddar Cheese Crust.

Old-Fashioned Ginger Spice Cookies

When I was a kid, I loved to help my mother bake, especially during the holidays. I have wonderful memories of the treasures that came out of the kitchen in our little Austrian farmhouse: spicy honey-nut Lebkuchen, the chewy dried fruit bread called Kletzenbrot, buttery Weihnachtsbaekerei, and crowds of gingerbread men. My mother always got started early with her baking; cookies like these ginger spice cookies allow that. They get even better with time, and the butter and molasses in them keep them moist.

2¾	cups all-purpose flour	¼	teaspoon salt
1	teaspoon baking soda	½	cup granulated sugar
½	pound (2 sticks) unsalted butter, cut into 1½-inch pieces	½	cup packed light brown sugar
		1	teaspoon ginger juice (see note)
2	tablespoons ground ginger	1	egg
1	teaspoon ground cinnamon		
½	teaspoon ground cloves	¼	cup blackstrap molasses

1. Sift together the flour and baking soda and set aside.

2. In the bowl of a stand mixer, or in a large bowl with electric beaters, cream the butter at medium speed until light and fluffy, about 1 minute. Add the ground ginger, cinnamon, cloves, and salt, and continue to beat for another 30 seconds to a minute. Add the granulated and brown sugars and beat until smooth, about 1 minute. Beat in the ginger juice and the egg. Scrape down the sides of the bowl and beat in the molasses.

3. At low speed, gradually beat in the flour. When it is just incorporated, stop the machine and scrape down the sides of the bowl.

4. Place handfuls of the dough side by side in a log shape on two pieces of parchment, roll up, and wrap in plastic. Refrigerate for at least 1 hour, preferably overnight.

5. Preheat the oven to 350°F, with the rack in the lower third. Line baking sheets with parchment paper. To shape a cookie, pinch off a piece of dough, about ½ ounce or a tablespoon, and roll it between the palms of your hands to form a ball about 1 inch in diameter. Place on the baking sheet. Place the balls about 2 inches apart. Bake 14 to 16 minutes, reversing the trays front to back halfway through to ensure even baking. When done, the bottoms of the cookies will be lightly browned and the cookies just firm to the touch. Remove from the oven and cool on racks, or slide the parchment off the trays and cool on the parchment.

Wolfgang's EASY TIPS

➤ Cookies will keep for several weeks if you pack them airtight and keep them at room temperature after they cool.

➤ You can make the dough ahead and keep it in the refrigerator for up to a week. Then you can bake whenever you have a free moment.

➤ Cookies make great gifts. To pack them, choose sturdy, attractive metal containers with tight-fitting lids. Line the containers with plastic wrap, foil, or wax paper, and place a crumbled layer of the same material on the bottom as a protective cushion. Place two cookies bottom to bottom and wrap them in more plastic wrap, twisting the ends of the wrapper like a bonbon. Repeat this for as many cookies as you wish to include. Arrange them carefully in the container and add more cushioning as necessary so they won't bounce around.

➤ To make ginger juice, place grated ginger in a fine-mesh strainer and press out the juice into a bowl.

My Mother's Linzer Cookies

MAKES ABOUT 3 DOZEN COOKIES

Wolfgang's EASY TIPS

➤ It helps to have more than one cookie sheet when baking quantities of cookies. That way you can have one ready to go into the oven while the other is baking. I prefer shiny metal sheets to the dark ones because dark metals absorb heat more quickly and can make cookies brown too fast. Always line the cookie sheets with parchment paper. Then you can quickly slide the entire batch on the paper off of the cookie sheet to cool.

➤ After rolling out the dough and before cutting the cookies, place the dough in the freezer for 15 to 30 minutes to facilitate cutting.

My mother would always begin baking in early December and keep it up right through the holidays. But she wasn't working frantically the whole time. She just knew that the earlier you start your holiday baking, the more you'll be free to enjoy the big celebrations. The ingredients in her cookies promote tenderness and retain moisture so that they stand up well to storage for several weeks when properly packed. My mother's Linzer cookies not only stay moist thanks to their ground hazelnuts and raspberry jam, but they actually improve in flavor as their subtle blend of spices matures. They remain one of my favorites.

½	pound whole shelled hazelnuts	½	teaspoon ground cinnamon
1	cup cake flour, plus more for dusting	¼	teaspoon freshly grated nutmeg
½	cup all-purpose flour, plus more for dusting	¼	teaspoon ground cloves
½	pound unsalted butter, at room temperature if using a hand mixer	¼	teaspoon salt
		1	teaspoon grated lemon zest
1	cup granulated sugar	1	cup raspberry jam
1	egg		Powdered sugar for dusting

1. Preheat the oven to 350°F. Spread the hazelnuts in a single layer on a baking sheet and toast them in the oven until golden, 10 to 12 minutes. Empty them into a folded kitchen towel, enclosing them between the folds, and rub them to remove their skins. Transfer the nuts to a food processor fitted with the stainless steel blade and discard the skins. Add the flours. Process until the nuts are finely ground.

2. In a stand mixer fitted with the paddle attachment, or in a large mixing bowl with a handheld electric mixer, beat the butter and granulated sugar together at medium-high speed until light and fluffy. Add the egg, cinnamon, nutmeg, cloves, salt, and lemon zest and continue mixing for 1 minute. Reduce the speed to low and gradually add the nut-flour mixture. Mix just until the mixture comes together into a smooth dough. Scrape the dough onto a sheet of plastic wrap and gently press it into a flat disc about 2 inches thick. Wrap the dough in plastic wrap and refrigerate for at least 2 to 3 hours, or preferably overnight.

3. Remove the dough from the refrigerator and divide it into quarters. Place one piece between two sheets of lightly dusted parchment paper and roll out to an even ⅛-inch thickness. Repeat with the other pieces of dough. Place in the freezer for 15 minutes or longer.

4. Preheat the oven to 350°F with the rack in the lower third. Line baking sheets with parchment paper. Remove the dough from the freezer, one sheet at a time. Carefully peel the top piece of parchment off the dough and, using a round 2-inch fluted- or straight-edged cookie cutter, cut out circles of dough. With a ½-inch diameter circular cookie cutter, cut out holes from the centers of half of the larger circles, giving them shapes resembling rings (the holes will make nice mini-cookies).

5. Carefully transfer the cookies to the baking sheets, placing them about ½ inch apart. If the dough is too soft to transfer easily, return it to the freezer for 15 to 30 minutes. If you need to bake the cookies in batches make sure you let the baking sheets cool before baking each batch. Bake the cookies in the preheated oven until golden brown, 10 to 14 minutes. Slide the parchment onto cooling racks, wait 10 minutes, and then carefully transfer the cookies to the racks to cool completely.

6. Return the cookies to your work surface. Place a scant teaspoon of jam on each cookie without the holes and spread in an even layer. Generously dust the cookies with the holes with powdered sugar, either from a sugar sifter or from a fine-mesh sieve held over the cookies and tapped with your hand, and neatly place them on top of the jam so that the jam pokes out the center.

White and Dark Chocolate Chunk Cookies

MAKES ABOUT 5 DOZEN COOKIES

My pastry chef, Sherry Yard, has taught me a thing or two about chocolate chip cookies. These are a bit more elegant than commercial cookies, because I use the best chocolate I can find. And instead of little chips, the chocolate is cut into chunks, so there's more of it in each cookie.

6	ounces bittersweet chocolate	½	cup granulated sugar
4	ounces white chocolate	⅓	cup packed light brown sugar
1¾	cups all-purpose flour	1	large egg
½	teaspoon baking soda	1	teaspoon vanilla extract
¼	teaspoon salt		
¼	pound (1 stick) unsalted butter, cut into ½-inch pieces		

1. Cut the chocolate into ¼- to ½-inch pieces using a serrated knife. Sift together the flour, baking soda, and salt.

2. In the bowl of a standing mixer fitted with the paddle attachment, or using a hand mixer, cream the butter until fluffy and pale yellow, about 2 minutes. Scrape down the sides of the bowl and the beater. Add the sugars and continue to beat until smooth, 1 to 2 minutes. Add the egg and the vanilla and beat on low speed to incorporate.

3. Gradually add the flour at low speed and beat just until incorporated. Add the chocolate chunks and beat or stir to incorporate them into the dough.

4. Place a piece of parchment paper or wax paper on your work surface. Using clean hands or a spatula, scoop up bits of the dough and form two logs about 2 inches in diameter on the parchment. Roll them up in the parchment, wrap the parchment in foil, and refrigerate for at least 2 hours and for as long as a week.

5. To bake, preheat the oven to 350°F with the rack on the lower setting. Line baking sheets with parchment. Cut the logs, using a serrated knife, into slices ¼ to ⅛ of an inch thick. Place the cookies on the parchment-covered baking sheets about 1 inch apart. Bake 10 to 12 minutes, reversing the pans front to back halfway through. The cookies are done when they are brown around the edges and brown on the bottom. Remove from the oven and cool on racks, or just slide the parchment off onto a surface for the cookies to cool. Store airtight.

Classic Holiday Butter Cookies

MAKES 2 TO 3 DOZEN

Everybody needs a good sugar cookie recipe for holiday cookies, whether we're talking Christmas, Valentine's Day, or Halloween, and this one couldn't be easier. The dough is not at all finicky, so kids can have fun making all sorts of shapes. All you need here is a good rolling pin and a selection of cookie cutters. I like to bake these until golden brown; I think that gives them a better flavor than the traditional pale sugar cookies.

3	cups all-purpose flour		1¼	cups sugar
½	teaspoon baking soda		2	eggs
¼	teaspoon salt		1	teaspoon vanilla extract
½	pound (2 sticks) unsalted butter, cut into ½-inch pieces			

1. Sift the flour, baking soda, and salt together in a medium bowl.

2. Place the butter in the bowl of a standing mixer or in a medium bowl if using electric beaters, and cream until smooth and fluffy, about 1 minute. Scrape down the sides of the bowl and add the sugar. Beat until smooth and fluffy, about 1 minute.

3. Add the eggs, one at a time, scraping down the sides of the bowl after each addition. Add the vanilla and beat in.

4. At low speed, beat in the flour a cup at a time. Beat only until well incorporated, about 1 minute.

5. Scrape the dough out of the bowl, divide into two pieces, and press each piece into a 1-inch thick disk. Wrap tightly in plastic and refrigerate for at least 1 hour and for as long as a week.

6. Preheat the oven to 350°F with the rack in the lower third. Line baking sheets with parchment paper. Roll out the dough between pieces of parchment or wax paper until it is about ¼ inch thick. To facilitate cutting, place in the freezer for 30 minutes. Cut desired shapes, gathering up scraps and rolling out again to get as many cookies as you can. Place 1 inch apart on baking sheets.

7. Bake the cookies for 15 to 20 minutes, or until light brown and the bottoms are golden, reversing the trays front to back halfway through the cooking. Remove from the heat and cool directly on the parchment or on racks.

Banana Spring Rolls with Two Dipping Sauces

MAKES 8 SERVINGS

This is a dessert I developed about twenty years ago, when I opened my first Chinois restaurant and was playing around with desserts that would appeal to Western tastes but have an Asian twist. One afternoon at Spago, while I was enjoying one of my favorite childhood desserts, apple strudel, it occurred to me that I could use a spring roll wrapper to enclose a similar filling, then deep-fry it. I would change the fillings with the seasons, but the one that was always the most popular was the banana filling below. Bananas are delicious hot, as anybody who has ever eaten the famous New Orleans dessert bananas Foster knows, and they're available year-round. Their firm, smooth consistency requires no precooking, which makes assembling these spring rolls very easy.

Wolfgang's EASY TIPS

➤ You can easily give a banana filling all kinds of interesting twists by adding chopped crystallized ginger or candied lemon or orange peel, ground cinnamon or allspice, nuts such as almonds or pecans, bittersweet chocolate chips—whatever your imagination tells you.

➤ You'll find commercial packages of spring roll wrappers or "skins" not only in Asian markets but also in the refrigerated cases or freezers of well-stocked supermarkets. Made from wheat flour and water, they generally measure between 6 and 7 inches on a side. You can also use egg roll wrappers of the same size, which are made from flour, eggs, and water and tend to be thicker and coarser in texture.

➤ You can serve these with just one of the sauces if you don't want to make two. The chocolate sauce is the easiest, and I've never met a person who doesn't like the combination of bananas and chocolate.

For the caramel-rum sauce:

1	cup granulated sugar
½	cup water
1	cup heavy cream
2	tablespoons unsalted butter
2	tablespoons rum

For the chocolate sauce:

¼	cup granulated sugar
¼	cup water
½	pound bittersweet chocolate, cut into ¼-inch pieces
½	cup heavy cream
2	tablespoons unsalted butter

For the spring rolls:

4	ripe bananas
1	cup dark brown sugar
16	spring roll wrappers
1	egg white, beaten
2	ounces unsalted butter, melted (if baking only)
	Peanut or vegetable oil for deep frying
	Confectioner's sugar for garnish
	Assorted fresh berries for garnish (optional)
	Fresh mint sprigs for garnish (optional)

1. Make the caramel-rum sauce. In a clean, medium-heavy saucepan that holds at least double the volume of the sugar and water, combine the sugar and water and stir together with a clean spatula or your hands. Put the pan over medium heat, cover, and bring to a boil. Uncover, and using a clean, damp pastry brush, brush down any sugar crystals that may be adhering to the sides of the pan. Turn the heat to medium and, watching carefully but without stirring, boil until the mixture forms a golden-brown syrup and measures 325°F on an instant-read thermometer. Meanwhile, heat a pan of water and place a whisk in it.

➤ You can also bake the spring rolls, but the wrappers will not be as crisp. If baking, preheat the oven to 400°F. Melt 2 ounces unsalted butter and lightly but evenly brush all the spring rolls. Place them seam down on a parchment-lined baking sheet. Bake in the middle of the oven until golden brown, about 15 minutes.

2. Immediately remove the caramel from the heat and let rest for 1 minute, or until the bubbles have subsided. Slowly and carefully stir in the cream with the warm whisk. Stir vigorously until well blended, then stir in the butter and rum. Cover and keep the sauce warm by setting it inside another pan filled with hot water.

3. Make the chocolate sauce. Combine the sugar and water in a small saucepan and bring to a boil over high heat. Reduce the heat to medium and simmer for 5 minutes. Remove from the heat, measure out ⅓ cup of the simple syrup, and set it aside (if you have more, it makes a great sweetener for iced tea).

4. Place the chocolate in a heatproof bowl. In a small saucepan over medium heat, or in a microwave, bring the cream and butter to a boil. Remove from the heat and pour over the chocolate. Tap the bowl on your work surface to make sure all of the chocolate is submerged, and wait for 1 minute. Using a heatproof spatula, slowly stir the mixture until the chocolate is melted and the mixture is well combined. Add the simple syrup and stir until smooth. Cover and keep the sauce warm by setting it inside another pan filled with hot water.

5. Make the banana spring rolls. Peel the bananas and cut each in half crosswise and lengthwise to make four pieces per banana. Spread the brown sugar on a plate. Place a spring roll wrapper in front of you on a work surface with one corner pointing toward you. Roll a piece of banana in the brown sugar, and then place the piece on the wrapper across its lower third. Fold the point nearest you up over the banana, and roll the banana even with the wrapper's two side points. Fold the points in over the ends of the banana. With your fingertip or a pastry brush, brush the remaining exposed edges of the wrapper's top half with beaten egg white. Continue rolling up the banana toward the top tip and press down gently with your finger to seal the moistened edges. Repeat with the remaining banana pieces, brown sugar, wrappers, and egg wash.

6. Heat the peanut oil or vegetable oil to 350°F and fry the rolls until they are golden brown, turning over once, about 2 minutes on each side. Drain on paper towels. Cut each spring roll diagonally in half, using scissors or a sharp knife. Arrange four halves decoratively on each serving plate. Spoon or drizzle some of the warm sauces around the rolls. Place some confectioners' sugar in a fine-mesh sieve and tap the sieve over each serving to dust the rolls. Garnish, if you like, with berries and mint sprigs. Serve hot, passing extra sauce in serving bowls or sauceboats for guests to help themselves.

Making Banana Spring Roll

1.

2.

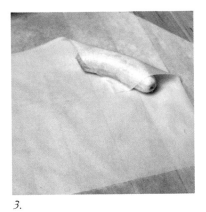

3.

4.

5.

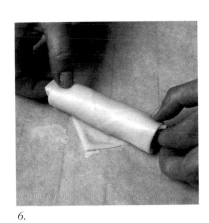

6.

Chocolate Mousse

MAKES 6 SERVINGS

Wolfgang's EASY TIPS

➤ Use the best chocolate you can buy. I prefer bittersweet Valrhona, but any respectable brand will do.

➤ Don't overbeat your egg whites or your cream. If the egg whites are beaten too dry, they'll fall apart; if the cream is overbeaten, it won't blend evenly through the mousse.

➤ The base for this mousse is a simple combination of chocolate melted in cream called ganache. Ganache is the foundation for chocolate sauces, truffles, icings, ice cream, and many other confections.

There are many reasons to have a great chocolate mousse in your repertoire. First of all, everybody loves it. Second, it's one of the easiest desserts to make. Because it takes so little time and can be made a day ahead, it's a great dessert to make for a dinner party.

6	ounces bittersweet chocolate		Pinch of salt
¾	plus ¾ cup heavy cream	⅛	teaspoon cream of tartar
4	egg whites	¼	cup sugar

1. Cut the chocolate into ¼-inch pieces using a serrated knife. Make sure your pieces are small. Place in a medium-size, heatproof bowl. Bring ¾ cup of the cream to a boil in the microwave or in a saucepan over medium-high heat. When it comes to a boil, pour it over the chocolate. Tap the bowl on your work surface so that all of the chocolate settles into the cream. Wait 1 minute, then slowly stir the chocolate and cream with a heatproof rubber spatula until the chocolate has melted and the mixture is smooth. Transfer to a large bowl and set aside.

2. In the bowl of a stand mixer fitted with the whisk attachment, or in a large mixing bowl with electric beaters, beat the egg whites until they begin to foam. Add the salt and cream of tartar and continue to beat at medium speed until they form soft, slightly drooping peaks when the beaters are lifted. Still beating, add the sugar and continue until the whites form stiff, but not dry, peaks.

3. Fold the egg whites into the chocolate mixture using a rubber spatula until fully blended.

4. In the same bowl in which you beat the egg whites, beat the remaining ¾ cup cream on medium speed until it forms soft peaks, 1 to 2 minutes. Do not overbeat. Gently fold the whipped cream into the egg white and chocolate mixture.

5. Spoon the mixture into individual parfait glasses, martini glasses, wine glasses, or ramekins. Cover with plastic wrap and refrigerate until the mousse is well chilled and firmly set, at least 2 hours.

Making Chocolate Mousse

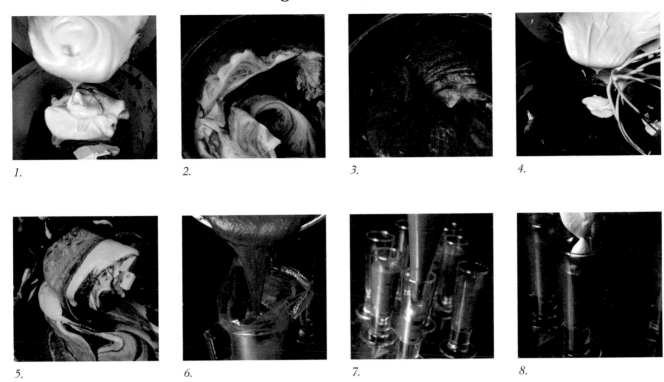

1. 2. 3. 4.

5. 6. 7. 8.

Granny Smith Apple Pie with Cheddar Cheese Crust

MAKES 8 SERVINGS

Wolfgang's EASY TIPS

➤ Put the butter into the freezer for about 15 minutes before you begin the pastry. It's important that it stay very cold and hold its shape in the pastry. Handle the pastry as little as possible with your hands.

➤ You can also use a standing mixer to make the pastry. Sift the flour into the bowl of your standing mixer. Add the cold butter and salt. Mix for 2 minutes at low speed, then stop and pinch flat any large lumps of butter. Add the cheese, beat at low speed for 15 seconds, then add the water and vinegar. Mix until the dough comes together and proceed with the recipe.

➤ To cut neat apple wedges, cut the apple in half through the core. Lay the cut side down and cut in half. Cut each quarter into three wedges, then lay each wedge down flat and cut the core edge away.

In England it's traditional to accompany apple pie with a slice of sharp cheddar cheese. In this recipe I've put the cheese in the pastry, and the tangy result is perfect with the simple apple filling.

For the cheddar cheese pastry:

2¼ cups all-purpose flour

½ teaspoon salt

6 ounces (1½ sticks) unsalted butter, cut into 1-inch pieces and frozen for 15 minutes

1½ cups shredded extra-sharp cheddar cheese

¾ teaspoon apple cider vinegar

⅓ to ½ cup ice water, or as needed

For the Granny Smith apple filling:

6 plus 1 tablespoons unsalted butter

8 medium Granny Smith apples, peeled, cored, and cut into ½-inch wedges

½ cup sugar

4 tablespoons Calvados (apple brandy) or applejack

1 large egg, beaten

Vanilla ice cream or whipped cream for serving (optional)

1. Prepare the pastry dough. Put the flour and salt in the bowl of a food processor fitted with the stainless steel blade. Pulse the machine 5 or 6 times to combine them. Add the frozen butter and process for 5 seconds. Add the shredded cheddar and pulse the machine four times to mix it in. In a measuring cup, combine the cider vinegar and ⅛ cup ice water. With the motor running, pour the vinegar-water mixture through the feed tube and continue processing until a ball of dough forms. If the dough doesn't come together, add another tablespoon or two of ice water.

2. Turn out the dough onto a lightly floured work surface, form it into an even ball, and cut it into two pieces, one slightly larger than the other. Pat each piece into a flattened disk, wrap it in plastic wrap, then chill the disks in the refrigerator for at least 2 hours.

3. Prepare the filling. Heat a large skillet or sauté pan over medium-high heat and melt 6 tablespoons of the butter. When the butter is light brown, add the apples and sprinkle with the sugar. Cook, stirring frequently, until the sugar has turned a golden-brown caramel color, 10 to 15 minutes. The apples should still be firm. Stir in the Calvados and remove from the heat. Transfer the apple filling to a sheet pan lined with foil and set aside to cool to room temperature.

4. Preheat the oven to 400°F. On a lightly floured work surface, use a floured rolling pin to roll out the smaller disk of chilled dough to an even circle with a diameter of 11 inches. Gently fold the dough in half or into quarters and transfer it to a 9-inch pie pan. Unfold the dough and gently ease it into the contours of the pan. Roll out the larger disk of dough to a circle about 12 inches in diameter.

5. Fill the lined pie pan with the cooled apple mixture. Dot the apples with the remaining 1 tablespoon of butter. Carefully place the larger disk of pastry over the pie. Tuck the edges of the top pastry under the rim of the bottom pastry and press down with your fingers to seal together and decoratively flute the pastry edges all around the pie's rim. With the tip of a small, sharp knife, cut three slashes about 2 inches long in the center of the top crust.

6. Place the pie on a baking sheet and bake in the lower third of the preheated oven for 30 minutes. Reduce the heat to 375°F and bake for 20 minutes more. Remove the pie from the oven, brush its top with the beaten egg, return to the oven, and bake until golden brown, about 5 minutes more. Serve hot, warm, or at room temperature, accompanied with vanilla ice cream or whipped cream if you wish.

Meringue Nests
with Lemon Curd, Chocolate Mousse, or Ice Cream

Wolfgang's EASY TIPS

➤ A stand mixer or handheld mixer makes the job of making meringues easy.

➤ Make sure all of your ingredients are at room temperature.

➤ Crisp meringues have up to 2 cups of sugar for each cup of egg whites. They are baked in a very low oven (200°F to 225°F) for up to 2 hours, then cooled in the turned off oven.

➤ Crisp, dry meringues will keep for several weeks if stored in an airtight container at room temperature.

➤ Do not fill the meringues until just before serving, or they will become soggy.

Meringues are one of the easiest pastries in the world to make, yet they always impress. I like to substitute them for classic pastry shells and fill them with lemon curd (page 238) or chocolate mousse (page 232). Good quality ice cream also makes an easy and much appreciated filling. However they are filled, garnish the nests with your choice of fresh berries and small sprigs of fresh mint.

4	large egg whites, at room temperature
¼	teaspoon cream of tartar
1	cup superfine sugar
2	cups Fresh Lemon Curd (page 238), Chocolate Mousse (page 232), or good-quality ice cream or sorbet

Assorted fresh berries for garnish

Fresh mint sprigs for garnish

1. Preheat the oven to 225°F. Line a baking sheet with parchment paper. Using a glass, jar, or bowl as your guide, draw eight circles on the paper, each about 3½ inches in diameter. Turn the paper over; you should still be able to see the circles. Fit a large pastry bag with a ½-inch plain tip.

2. In the bowl of a stand mixer fitted with the whisk attachment, or in a large stainless steel bowl with a handheld beater, beat the egg whites on medium speed until they begin to foam. Add the cream of tartar and 1 tablespoon of the sugar and continue to whip the egg whites at medium-low speed until they form soft, slightly drooping peaks when the beaters are lifted out. Turn the speed to medium-high and continue to whip the egg whites as you gradually add the superfine sugar a tablespoon at a time. Beat until the meringue is shiny and holds stiff, upright peaks when the beaters are lifted out. Take care not to overbeat.

3. Drop spoonfuls of the meringue onto the circles on the parchment, and using an offset spatula, spread them using a back and forth windshield-wiper motion into even circles ¼ to ½ inch thick. Spoon the remaining meringue into a pastry bag fitted with the plain tip and pipe a rim around each base. Spoon or pipe any extra meringue onto the baking sheet to use as tests for doneness (and for extra cookies for the kids).

4. Bake the meringue nests in the oven for 1½ hours. Remove a test piece to check for doneness. It should be stiff and crisp to the bite after a 5-minute rest. If it is still moist in the middle, leave for another 30 minutes. Turn off the oven and leave the meringues inside for 1 hour more. Remove the meringues from the oven and, when they are completely cool, pack them carefully in an airtight container and store at room temperature until ready to use.

5. Shortly before serving, place the nests on individual serving plates. Fill each one with a filling of your choice. Garnish with berries and mint sprigs and serve immediately.

Fresh Lemon Curd

MAKES ABOUT 2 CUPS

Wolfgang's EASY TIPS

➤ You can also make curd with blood orange juice. Use one-third lemon juice and two-thirds blood orange juice to get the acidity you need for curd. The result will have a dramatic color and wonderful flavor.

➤ Use an instant-read thermometer when you make curd so that you won't allow it to get too hot and curdle.

Like a tangy lemon pudding, this simple custard makes a wonderful filling for Meringue Nests (page 236), single-crust pies, Savory Crêpes (page 12), cookies such as Linzer cookies (page 224), and any number of other pastries. You could even eat it on its own or, as they do with lemon curd in England, spread it on a fresh-baked scone, crumpet, English muffin, or toast. Feel free to vary the citrus juices to your liking.

⅔ cup sugar	¾ cup freshly squeezed lemon juice, strained
2 tablespoons finely grated lemon zest	
3 large eggs	4 tablespoons (½ stick) cold unsalted butter, cut into small cubes
4 large egg yolks	

1. Fill a large bowl with ice and water for cooling the curd. Fill a medium saucepan two-thirds full with water and bring to a simmer over medium heat.

2. Combine the sugar and lemon zest in a food processor fitted with the steel blade and pulse the mixture until the sugar is yellow and fragrant with lemon.

3. Beat together the eggs and egg yolks in a nonreactive, heatproof bowl that will rest on the rim of the medium saucepan. Add the sugar mixture and whisk for about half a minute, then place above the simmering water. Whisk continuously until the sugar is dissolved, about 15 seconds.

4. Check with your fingers to make sure the sugar has dissolved, then add the lemon juice and whisk over the simmering water without stopping until the mixture thickens, about 5 minutes, or until it has the thickness of sour cream and measures 160°F on an instant-read thermometer. Whisk in the butter a little at a time. Wash out and dry the heatproof bowl you used for the curd, and strain the curd back into the bowl. Immediately place the bowl in the ice bath to cool. Stir occasionally. When it has cooled completely, refrigerate. Place a sheet of plastic wrap directly over the surface of the curd to prevent a skin from forming, then cover the bowl. The curd will keep for one week in the refrigerator.

Making Lemon Curd

1.

2.

3.

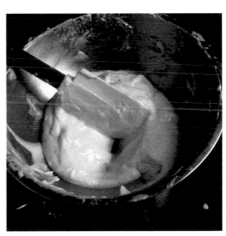

4.

Warm Strawberries
with Baked Meringues and Vanilla Ice Cream

MAKES 6 SERVINGS

Briefly cooking berries in a warm berry sauce is an easy, unexpected, and beautiful way to serve them, and the sauce itself can be made up to three days ahead. This is also a smart strategy when you find that berries you've bought are less sweet than you had hoped for since the sugar in the sauce helps bring out their natural flavor. The warm berries just beg for good vanilla ice cream. To add a touch of crunch and complete a beautiful presentation, I also like to include discs of crisply baked meringue, a variation on the traditional French dessert shells called vacherins (vahsh-RAN), which you can easily prepare several days ahead. The meringues are identical to the Meringue Nests on page 236, but they are made without the rim. Just bake the flat discs.

1	recipe meringues (page 236)

For the strawberry sauce:

1	pound fresh ripe strawberries, hulled
½	cup dry white wine
⅓	cup sugar
1	tablespoon fresh lemon juice
½	teaspoon grated orange zest
⅓	cup fresh orange juice
1	whole star anise

For the final presentation:

½	cup cold heavy cream
½	pound strawberries, hulled and cut into quarters, plus 4 for garnish
1	pint good-quality vanilla ice cream
	Whipped cream for garnish
	Fresh mint sprigs

1. Make the meringue discs following the directions for Meringue Nests on page 236. Do not pipe a rim around the edges of the discs.

2. Make the strawberry sauce. Combine the strawberries, wine, sugar, lemon juice, orange zest, orange juice, and star anise in a medium, nonreactive saucepan. Over medium-high heat, bring to a boil, stirring occasionally, then reduce the heat and simmer for 5 minutes. Remove from the heat, cover, and let the ingredients steep for at least 10 minutes. Remove and discard the star anise and transfer the mixture to a blender. Blend until smooth. Place a fine-mesh strainer over a nonreactive bowl and, using a rubber spatula, press the purée through the strainer. Cover the bowl with plastic wrap and refrigerate until ready to use.

3. For the final presentation, first whip the cream in a chilled mixing bowl with a chilled whisk or a handheld mixer with chilled beaters. Beat at medium-high speed until soft peaks form.

4. Pour the sauce into a medium saucepan. Over medium-high heat, bring it back to a boil, lower the heat, and simmer until it thickens slightly, 3 to 5 minutes. Gently stir in the hulled, quartered berries and cook just until heated through but still firm, about 3 minutes more.

5. Place a meringue disc on each of four dessert plates. Top each disc with a scoop of ice cream. Spoon the sauce with the berries around the ice cream and meringue. Top with another meringue disc. Garnish with whipped cream and fresh mint sprigs. Serve immediately.

Pink-and-White Baked Alaska

MAKES 8 SERVINGS

Baked Alaska, that impressive creation of ice cream and oven-browned meringue, was named by the chef at Delmonico's in New York in 1876 to commemorate America's purchase of the Alaskan Territory. In France it has always been known as *omelette à la Norvégienne* (Norwegian omelet). I've simplified the traditional recipe by leaving out the layer of sponge cake that usually sits under the ice cream. After all, who notices it anyway? The final browning of the meringue can be done in a 500°F oven or with a small butane kitchen torch available in most gourmet shops and kitchen supply stores. Both are described here.

1 quart good-quality strawberry ice cream, softened	6 large egg whites, at room temperature
1 quart good-quality vanilla ice cream, softened	¼ teaspoon cream of tartar
1 quart good-quality raspberry sorbet, softened	1½ cups superfine sugar
	Raspberry Sauce (page 30, optional)

1. Lightly spray a 5 x 9-inch loaf pan or an 8-inch-deep, 2-quart glass or stainless steel mixing bowl with nonstick cooking spray and line with plastic wrap. Fill a third of the bread pan or bowl with a thick layer of strawberry ice cream, using the back of the spoon to press it into an even layer covering the bottom and sides of the bowl, or one flat layer in a bread pan. Fill another third of the pan or bowl with a generous layer of the vanilla ice cream and smooth the surface. Make a third layer, filling the bowl or pan to the top with the raspberry sorbet. Cover the bowl with plastic wrap and freeze until the ice cream is solid, 2 to 3 hours or longer.

2. Remove from the freezer and allow to sit for 10 minutes at room temperature. Run a knife around the edges of the pan or bowl. Invert a heatproof serving platter over the bowl or pan and, holding the bowl and platter firmly together, turn them over and lift off the bowl or bread pan and the plastic to unmold the ice cream. If the ice cream won't come out, briefly dip the bowl or pan into a large bowl of hot water and repeat the process. Put the platter with the ice cream back in the freezer to chill while you make the meringue.

3. In the bowl of a stand mixer fitted with the whisk attachment, or in a large stainless steel bowl with a handheld beater, beat the egg whites on medium speed until they begin to foam. Add the cream of tartar and 1 tablespoon of the sugar and continue to whip the

egg whites at medium-low speed until they form soft, slightly drooping peaks when the beaters are lifted out.

4. Turn the speed to medium-high and continue to whip the egg whites as you gradually add the superfine sugar a tablespoon at a time. Beat until the meringue is shiny and holds stiff, upright peaks when the beaters are lifted out. Take care not to overbeat.

5. As soon as the meringue is ready, remove the ice cream from the freezer and use an icing spatula or the back of a large spoon to spread the entire batch of meringue evenly over its surface. This is done most easily if you spoon the meringue onto the top of the ice cream and spread it down the sides. Return the dessert to the freezer once more until serving time.

6. Browning the meringue using the oven: Preheat the oven to 500°F. Remove the Alaska from the freezer and place it on a sheet tray. Place the tray in the oven for no more than 5 minutes, until the Alaska is nicely caramelized and browned. Remove from the heat and serve at once.

    Using a butane torch: Light a small butane kitchen torch following the manufacturer's instructions, with the flame set to medium. Holding the flame about 1 inch from the surface of the meringue, move it slowly across the surface to lightly brown its peaks.

7. To serve the baked Alaska easily, use the butane torch to warm a metal serving knife and cut the dessert into wedges or slices; alternatively, dip the knife into a glass of hot water before each cut. Put a spoonful of raspberry sauce on each plate, if desired. Transfer each wedge to a chilled serving plate and serve at once.

Sabayon with Fresh Berries

MAKES 6 SERVINGS

Wolfgang's EASY TIPS

➤ Make sure that the bowl with the egg yolks is not touching the simmering water in the pot. This will cause the eggs to scramble.

➤ This is a last-minute preparation, but you can have your egg yolks and other ingredients ready before you sit down for dinner. The time it takes to make the sabayon will be a perfect break between dinner and dessert. However, if you do want to have most of it done in advance, make the gratinéed variation that follows the recipe.

➤ **VARIATION:** Gratin of Fresh Berries with Sabayon. Preheat the broiler. Prepare the berries and sabayon as directed above. Whip 1 cup of cream and fold it into the sabayon. Place the berries in an attractive gratin dish or in ovenproof ramekins and spoon the sabayon over the top. Place under the broiler for a few minutes until lightly browned. Take care to watch the gratin closely as it will brown quickly. Serve at once.

The name of this French dessert comes from its Italian version, zabaglione, which in turn derives from an old Neapolitan word for foam. That makes sense, since sabayon consists of a warm, sweet froth of egg yolks and wine, a perfect topping for fresh berries. Elegant though sabayon may be, its preparation is simplicity itself: the yolks and sugar are beaten with a wire whisk in the top of a double boiler or a stainless steel bowl over a pan of barely simmering water. The gentle heat keeps the eggs from scrambling. Your choice of the robust Sicilian fortified wine known as Marsala, full-bodied merlot, or light and brisk Moscato d'Asti will give the sabayon three different but equally pleasing personalities.

3	cups fresh berries of your choice, stemmed, rinsed, and drained	8	large egg yolks
⅓	cup sugar	1½	cups Marsala, merlot, or Moscato d'Asti
1	teaspoon lemon juice	6	sprigs fresh mint for garnish

1. If you are using large strawberries, cut them into thick slices; otherwise, leave the berries whole. Put them in a nonreactive mixing bowl with 2 tablespoons of the sugar and the lemon juice. Toss gently to combine, taking care not to bruise the berries. Cover with plastic wrap and chill in the refrigerator for at least 1 hour. Shortly before serving, spoon the berries and their juices into large wine goblets or other attractive glass serving dishes.

2. Fill a medium saucepan about one-third of the way up with water and bring to a simmer. Put the egg yolks in a stainless steel or copper bowl large enough to sit comfortably on the saucepan without touching boiling water inside. Add the remaining sugar and beat together until thick and lemon-colored. Whisk in the Marsala, merlot, or Moscato d'Asti. Place the bowl on top of the pan of water and whisk briskly and continuously, taking care to constantly scrape the bottom and sides of the container until the yolks form a foam with the consistency of lightly whipped cream, about 5 minutes. Watch carefully or the eggs will scramble. Remove from the heat and quickly taste the sabayon; if it does not taste sweet enough, return to the heat and whisk in another 1 or 2 tablespoons of sugar. Continue whisking over the simmering water until the mixture is thick and foamy, another 3 to 5 minutes. Remove the foam from the heat and spoon it over the berries. Garnish with mint sprigs and serve immediately.

Making Sabayon

1.

2.

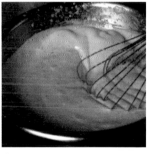

3.

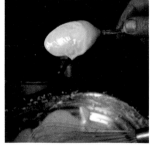

4.

Lemon and Watermelon Granitas

MAKES 8 SERVINGS

Granitas require no special equipment, are easy to make, and highlight the fresh natural flavors of the season's ripe fruit.

For the lemonade granita:

3	**cups water**
1	**cup sugar**
	Grated zest of 2 lemons
1	**cup fresh lemon juice**

For the watermelon granita:

2	**pounds peeled seedless watermelon (about half of a round melon), cut into 1-inch chunks**

½	**cup sugar**
½	**cup water**
2	**tablespoons fresh lemon juice**
1	**tablespoon fresh lime juice**
⅛	**teaspoon salt**
	Fresh mint sprigs for garnish (optional)

1. Make the lemonade granita mixture. In a nonreactive saucepan, stir together the water, sugar, and lemon zest. Bring to a boil over medium-high heat and continue boiling for 3 minutes. Remove from the heat and stir in the lemon juice. Set a fine-mesh sieve over a mixing bowl and pour the mixture through the sieve to strain out any pulp. Set aside to cool.

2. Make the watermelon granita mixture. Working in batches, in a food processor fitted with the stainless steel blade, combine the watermelon chunks, sugar, water, lemon juice, lime juice, and salt. Process until puréed. Place a fine-mesh sieve over a mixing bowl and pour the purée through the sieve to remove the pulp from the juice.

3. Pour each granita mixture into its own small, shallow, nonreactive metal baking pan (9-inch round or rectangular cake pans are a good size). Cover each pan with plastic wrap and freeze until the granita mixtures begin to set, about 45 minutes. Using a clean fork for each mixture, scrape the granitas to break up the ice crystals, and mix them well. Cover the pans, return them to the freezer, and repeat the process every 20 minutes, pushing the ice crystals on the outside of the pan toward the center so that the unfrozen liquid in the center will go to the edges. Do this until the granitas are completely frozen but not a solid block.

4. To serve, chill large wine glasses or individual glass bowls in the freezer. Scrape up each granita with a fork once more and scoop the watermelon granita into each glass or bowl. Top with a scoop of lemon granita. Serve immediately, garnished with mint sprigs if you like.

Wolfgang's Easy Tips

➤ The granita mixture, which you can make using a juicer or just by puréeing the fruit, should taste rather sweet to you at room temperature; freezing-cold temperatures will mute the sweetness.

➤ Less acidic fruits such as melons, strawberries, and stone fruits benefit from a touch of lemon or lime juice.

➤ If you can get your hands on some Meyer lemons, try these for the lemon granita.

➤ If the granitas freeze into solid blocks, break them up by pulsing in a food processor filled with the steel blade until icy.

Pineapple Upside-Down Cake

MAKES 10 SERVINGS

Wolfgang's EASY TIPS

➤ To peel and cut the pineapple, first cut the ends off using a large sharp knife. Stand the pineapple up on a cutting board and cut away the skin in wide strips, cutting down from the top. Now trim away the eyes. You can use a pineapple corer to cut out the core, or just slice the pineapple crosswise, stand a few slices one on top of the other, and using the tip of a paring knife, cut out the core.

➤ Be sure to reverse the finished cake onto a plate while it is still hot so the caramelized sugar doesn't cool and stick to the pan.

➤ My favorite accompaniment for this is coconut sorbet.

This classic American cake is always a hit with Europeans. It's easy enough for a child to make, yet it will please the most sophisticated diners.

For the cake:

1¼ cups all-purpose flour

1½ teaspoons baking powder

¼ teaspoon salt

¼ pound (1 stick) unsalted butter, at room temperature if using a hand mixer

½ cup sugar

2 eggs, at room temperature

1 teaspoon pure vanilla extract

¾ cup milk

For the topping:

3 tablespoons unsalted butter

¾ cup firmly packed light brown sugar

5 to 6 slices fresh pineapple, cored, or 1 cup drained pineapple chunks

1. Preheat the oven to 350°F. Spray a 9½-inch or 10-inch cake pan or buffet server with cooking spray.

2. Sift together the flour, baking powder, and salt three times and set aside.

3. Melt the 3 tablespoons butter in the pan and spread evenly over the bottom. Sprinkle in the brown sugar and press down in an even layer. Arrange the pineapple in an even layer on top of the sugar, breaking up the pieces if necessary.

4. Make the topping. In the bowl of a stand mixer fitted with the paddle attachment, or with a hand mixer, beat the butter on high speed until light and fluffy, about 1 minute. Scrape down the sides of the bowl and continue to beat at high speed while you gradually add the sugar. Add the eggs, one at a time, scraping down the sides of the bowl after each addition. Beat in the vanilla. At low speed, slowly add the sifted dry ingredients alternately with the milk. Beat until smooth.

5. Spread the batter over the pineapple. Bake for 35 to 40 minutes, or until a tester comes out clean. Remove from the oven and allow to cool on a rack for 5 to 10 minutes.

6. Using oven mitts, reverse the pan onto a large serving plate and allow the cake to cool before serving (it can be served warm but not hot). If you wish, serve with whipped cream, vanilla ice cream, or coconut sorbet.

Ginger Crème Brûlée

MAKES 4 TO 6 SERVINGS

Here's another Asian twist on a classic French dessert. In any given restaurant, crème brûlée will always top the list of favorite desserts. Literally "burnt cream," this preparation conceals creamy vanilla custard beneath a translucent, amber, brittle topping of caramelized sugar. The custard's simplicity allows for seemingly endless variations. It can be infused with spices like cinnamon, or with violet or rose petals, or fortified with espresso or butterscotch or chocolate.

3	cups heavy cream	3	thin slices fresh ginger root
⅓	plus ½ cup sugar for the custard and the topping	6	egg yolks

1. Combine the cream, the ⅓ cup sugar, and the ginger root in a medium saucepan and bring to a simmer. Remove from the heat, cover, and let steep for 15 minutes. Meanwhile, preheat the oven to 300°F with the rack in the center. Place six ½-cup ramekins or four 1-cup ramekins in a baking dish that is at least ½ inch deeper than the ramekins.

2. Beat the egg yolks in a medium-size bowl. Whisking the egg yolk mixture continuously, slowly pour in the hot cream. Strain through a fine strainer into a bowl and discard the ginger slices. Fill the ramekins to the top with the custard. Fill the baking dish with enough hot water to come two-thirds of the way up the sides of the ramekins. Cover loosely with foil and place in the oven. Bake 40 to 45 minutes, until the custards have set but have not browned. They should jiggle slightly.

3. Remove the ramekins from the baking dish and chill for at least 2 hours or for up to 2 days.

4. Shortly before serving, make the caramel topping. Sprinkle half the remaining sugar (¼ cup) over the custards in an even layer. Ignite a kitchen torch and move the flame back and forth over the sugar until it melts and forms a glossy, deep-brown mahogany caramel. Repeat the process with the remaining ¼ cup sugar. Do not let the caramelized crème brûlée sit for more than an hour.

Wolfgang's EASY TIPS

➤ The custard part of crème brûlée is easy. All you have to do is use gentle heat to keep the eggs from curdling. Some versions accomplish this by stirring the custard over simmering water in a double boiler, then spooning it into individual ramekins. In others, like the one below, the mixture is poured into ramekins while still liquid, then oven-baked at low heat in a water bath.

➤ "Burning" the sugar to caramelize it can be easily accomplished using a butane kitchen torch, now available in any well-stocked retail or Internet kitchen supplies store. Look for a model that lets you adjust the flame and that also includes a childproof locking device.

Cherry Cobbler with Shortcake Topping

MAKES 6 TO 8 SERVINGS

Wolfgang's EASY TIPS

➤ When buying cherries, look for plump, shiny fruit with green stems, indicating the fruit has been picked recently. Store cherries unrinsed in the refrigerator, loosely wrapped in plastic. Rinse just before using.

➤ Use a handheld cherry pitter to pit the cherries. These are easy to find in housewares and kitchen supply stores.

➤ I like to cut the topping into squares that approximate the size of a serving before placing them on the cobbler and baking. This makes the finished cobbler neater to dish up, and it gives it a beautiful surface resembling a cobblestone street.

➤ If the dough is too wet to roll out, then spoon it onto the topping in side-by-side dollops.

Cherry season is one of my favorite times of year, especially when I get a chance to pick them myself. If you've ever walked through a cherry orchard in full fruit, you'll know how magical ripe cherries look hanging from the trees like miniature Christmas ornaments. No matter where they grow, cherries have a short season, usually no longer than a month. That's probably why we don't use them that often in cooked desserts; we just love to savor them as they are. But don't be deterred from making this easy cobbler. The only time-consuming part will be pitting the cherries. The topping is put together in minutes, so the whole thing can be assembled and baked in just under an hour.

For the shortcake topping:

2	cups cake flour
¼	cup sugar
2	teaspoons baking powder
½	teaspoon salt
6	tablespoons chilled unsalted butter, cut into small chunks
¾	cup heavy cream

For the filling and garnish:

2	pounds fresh cherries, pitted
¼	cup mild flavored honey, such as clover or orange blossom
¼	cup brown sugar

¼	teaspoon ground cinnamon
1	tablespoon cornstarch
2	tablespoons lemon juice
2	tablespoons Kirsch
1	tablespoon butter, softened
2	tablespoons chilled unsalted butter, cut into small pieces, plus butter for the pan
2	tablespoons heavy cream
2	tablespoons sugar
	Powdered sugar for dusting
	Good-quality vanilla ice cream for serving

1. Make the shortcake topping. Put the cake flour, sugar, baking powder, and salt into a food processor fitted with the stainless steel blade; turn the machine on and off a few times to combine. Add the chilled butter and pulse the machine several times until the butter is chopped up into small pieces the size of gravel. With the motor running, pour the cream through the feed tube; stop processing the moment the dough barely begins to form a ball. Gather the dough together and transfer to a lightly floured work surface. With a lightly floured rolling pin, gently press or roll out the dough to an 8-inch square. With a large, sharp knife or pastry trimmer, neatly trim the edges of the square, then cut it into eight equal squares. Line a baking sheet with parchment paper, transfer the squares to the baking sheet, and refrigerate at least 30 minutes or until needed.

2. Preheat the oven to 375°F while you make the filling. In a medium bowl, stir together the cherries, honey, brown sugar, and cinnamon. Dissolve the cornstarch in the lemon juice and Kirsch, and stir into the cherry mixture. Mix thoroughly. Grease an 8 x 8 x 2-inch baking pan or a 2-quart baking dish with the soft butter. Spoon the fruit mixture into the buttered pan. Dot its surface with the chilled butter.

3. Arrange the chilled shortcake squares neatly on top of the filling in the pan. Brush the shortcake with the heavy cream and sprinkle with the granulated sugar. Bake in the preheated oven until the shortcake is golden brown and the fruit is bubbly, 35 to 40 minutes. Remove from the oven and let it settle at room temperature for at least 10 minutes.

4. To serve, use a large spoon to transfer each square of shortcake and the filling beneath it to an individual dessert plate. Spoon some powdered sugar into a fine-mesh sieve held over the cobbler and tap the side of the sieve to dust each portion. Add a scoop of ice cream for each guest who would like one, and serve.

Grilled Summer Fruit with Fresh Raspberry-Grape Sorbet

MAKES 4 SERVINGS

Wolfgang's EASY TIPS

➤ If you don't want to go to the trouble of making the sorbet, buy a good brand of raspberry sorbet and serve that with the grilled fruit.

➤ Other fruits can be substituted for the peaches and plums when they're not in season. Try mangos, apricots, or pears.

Grilling fruit is easy to do and gives you surprisingly delicious and attractive results whether you use an outdoor or indoor grill, a stovetop grill pan, or even the broiler. The sorbet that accompanies the fruit in this recipe is also simple to make, either in an ice cream machine or just with a blender or food processor as a granita. Be sure to start with peak-of-season, ripe but firm, sweet summer fruit.

For the sorbet:

2	cups white grape juice
1	cup water
½	cup sugar
4	cups raspberries, rinsed and dried on paper towels

For the fruit:

2	ripe, sweet peaches, halved and pitted
4	ripe, sweet plums, halved and pitted
2	ripe, sweet nectarines, halved and pitted
2	tablespoons unsalted butter, melted
	Fresh mint sprigs for garnish

1. Put the grape juice in a small saucepan and bring to a boil over medium-high heat. Boil until it reduces to 1 cup, 7 to 10 minutes. Make a simple syrup by combining the water and sugar in another saucepan and boiling until the sugar has dissolved. Combine the syrup and grape juice and chill, either in an ice bath or in the refrigerator.

2. Purée the raspberries in a blender or a food processor fitted with the stainless steel blade. Set a fine-mesh strainer over a mixing bowl and pour the purée through the strainer to remove the seeds, pressing down with a rubber spatula to force all the purée through and scraping any purée into the bowl from the underside of the sieve. Stir in the chilled grape juice mixture.

3. If you have an ice cream or sorbet maker, transfer the berry mixture to the machine and freeze, following the manufacturer's instructions. Pack it into a freezer container with a lid and freeze until solid. If you do not have an ice cream or sorbet maker, make a granita. Transfer the mixture to a shallow baking dish or bowl, cover it with plastic wrap, and place it in the freezer. Leave the mixture until it begins to set, about 25 minutes. Using a clean fork for each mixture, scrape the granita to break up the ice crystals, and mix well. Cover the pan, return it to the freezer, and repeat the process every 20 minutes, pushing the ice crystals on the outside of the pan toward the center so that the unfrozen liquid in the center will go to the edges, until the mixture is completely frozen but not a solid block. About 15 minutes before serving time, remove the container of sorbet from the freezer to soften slightly for scooping.

4. Preheat an indoor or outdoor grill or the broiler. Brush the fruit halves all over with the melted butter and cook them on the grill or under the broiler until golden brown, 3 to 5 minutes per side.

5. Use an ice cream scoop or a large serving spoon to scoop the sorbet onto the centers of individual serving plates. Arrange the fruit around the sorbet, garnish with mint sprigs, and serve immediately.

Chocolate and Pistachio Biscotti

MAKES 3 DOZEN

Wolfgang's EASY TIPS

➤ You can make biscotti dough by hand, but it's easiest to make it in a stand mixer.

➤ Use a knife or a cleaver to chop the pistachios. If you use a food processor, they will be coarsely ground instead of chopped, and the texture won't be right for the cookies.

➤ If you wish, substitute blanched peeled almonds for the pistachios.

Biscotti means "twice-cooked" in Italian, because these delicious, crisp cookies bake once as large logs of dough and a second time after the logs have been cut into individual slices. The result is a wonderfully crisp cookie that goes perfectly with iced desserts, fruit desserts, or simply a glass of sweet wine or a cup of coffee. The cookies will keep for weeks in an airtight container.

2	large eggs		½	cup cocoa powder
1	tablespoon amaretto		1½	teaspoons baking powder
¼	cup dry white wine		1	cup pistachios, coarsely chopped
1	cup sugar			
	Pinch of salt		1	large egg white, lightly beaten
2¼	cups all-purpose flour (more as needed)			

1. Preheat the oven to 350°F. Line a large baking sheet with cooking parchment. Lightly spray the parchment.

2. In a medium mixing bowl, beat the eggs with a fork until foamy. Whisk in the Amaretto and white wine. Gradually beat in the sugar and salt. When the ingredients are well blended, set the mixture aside.

3. Sift the flour, cocoa powder, and baking powder into the bowl of a stand mixer fitted with the paddle attachment. Turn the machine on low and add the egg mixture. Turn the speed to medium and beat until a dough forms on the paddle. If the dough is very sticky, add up to ¼ cup additional flour. Change to the dough hook and continue to beat while you gradually add the pistachios. When all of the pistachios have been added, scrape the dough out of the machine and knead the mixture for about a minute by hand, until smooth.

   If you do not have a stand mixer, sift the dry ingredients into a large mixing bowl. Make a well in the center of the dry ingredients. Add the egg mixture, stirring with a fork until the flour is evenly moistened and the mixture is crumbly. Turn the flour mixture out onto a lightly floured work surface. Gently knead the dough until it is smooth, gradually incorporating the pistachios as you do so.

4. Shape the dough into a log 12 x 4 inches long and place it on the prepared baking sheet. Brush the log with the beaten egg white. Bake the log in the preheated oven until it has expanded and

turned dark brown, 25 to 30 minutes. Transfer the baking sheet to a wire rack and leave the log to cool for 15 minutes. Meanwhile, reduce the oven temperature to 300°F.

5. Using a serrated knife, cut the log on the diagonal into ½-inch-thick slices. Lay the slices cut side up and side by side on the baking sheet. Bake for 20 minutes, or until the cookies are dry and dark brown. Transfer the baking sheet to the rack and let the biscotti cool completely to room temperature before serving or storing in an airtight container.

Easy Marjolaine

MAKES 8 SERVINGS

Marjolaine is one of my favorite pastries. It's a sort of layer cake, except the "cake" layers are dacquoise, meringue enriched with nuts. Hazelnuts are traditional, but almonds or pistachios would also work. In this version I use a chocolate ganache and tangy whipped cream filling and top the cake with chocolate glaze. The contrasts between the very sweet dacquoise with the bitter chocolate and slightly sour whipped cream are wonderful.

For the meringue:

6	egg whites, at room temperature
¼	teaspoon cream of tartar
1½	cups superfine sugar
1	cup toasted, skinned hazelnuts (see step 1 page 224, except omit the flours), finely chopped

For the ganache glaze and filling:

½	pound bittersweet chocolate
1	cup heavy cream
2	tablespoons light corn syrup

For the whipped cream filling:

1	cup heavy cream
½	cup crème fraîche
1	tablespoon sugar

1. Make the meringue. Preheat the oven to 325°F. Coat a 12 x 15-inch baking sheet with nonstick cooking spray and line with parchment. Lightly spray the parchment. In the bowl of a stand mixer fitted with the whisk attachment, or in a large stainless steel bowl with a hand held beater, beat the egg whites until they begin to foam. Add the cream of tartar and continue to whip the egg whites at medium speed until they form soft, slightly drooping peaks when the beaters are lifted out. Turn the speed to high and continue to whip the egg whites as you gradually add the superfine sugar a tablespoon at a time. Beat until the meringue is shiny and holds stiff, upright peaks when the beaters are lifted out. Take care not to overbeat. Fold in the chopped hazelnuts.

2. Scrape the meringue onto the baking sheet and, using an offset spatula, spread in an even layer over the entire surface of the pan. Place in the oven on the middle rack and bake for 30 to 35 minutes, or until light brown and crisp. Turn off the oven and leave the meringue for 1 hour with the heat off. Remove from the oven and allow to cool. When completely cooled, remove from the baking sheet and, using a serrated knife, carefully cut crosswise into three equal pieces. Set aside on sheets of parchment paper.

3. Make the ganache. Chop the chocolate into ¼-inch pieces and place in a heatproof bowl. Bring the cream to a boil in a saucepan or in the microwave and pour over the chocolate. Gently tap the bowl on your work surface so that the chocolate settles into the cream and allow it to sit for 1 minute. Using a plastic spatula, stir the mixture, scraping the bottom of the bowl until the chocolate and cream are nicely blended and completely smooth. Divide the ganache into two equal parts. Add the corn syrup to one half and set aside. Fill a large bowl three-quarters full with ice cubes and water and place the bowl of remaining ganache in the ice bath to cool. Stir over the ice water, using a rubber spatula, until the ganache is thick.

4. Place one piece of the meringue on a serving platter and spread the cool ganache over it in an even layer. Top with another sheet of meringue.

5. Make the whipped cream filling. Combine the heavy cream and créme fraîche with the sugar and beat until fairly stiff. Spread in a thick, even layer over the second sheet of meringue. Top with the last sheet of meringue. Stir the glaze, and if it has cooled too much to pour freely, heat at 50% power in a microwave for 25 seconds. Pour the glaze over the top layer of the marjolaine and spread it in an even layer. Allow the glaze to drip down the sides. Set aside the marjolaine and allow the glaze to cool and set. If you wish, trim the edges with a serrated knife. Your marjolaine is now ready to slice with a serrated knife and serve. If not serving right away, store in the refrigerator.

Wolfgang's Sachertorte

MAKES 1 (9-INCH) CAKE, SERVING 10

Wolfgang's EASY TIPS

➤ If you want a slightly sweeter cake, add another tablespoon of sugar to the egg whites.

➤ Because there is so much batter, folding will be easier if you transfer the chocolate mixture to a large, wide bowl before you fold in the egg whites.

➤ Use the best chocolate and cocoa you can find. I like Valrhona.

➤ To cut the cake in half horizontally, use a long, serrated knife. It should be at least 10 inches long.

For the cake:

¾	cup all-purpose flour
1	teaspoon baking powder
6	ounces bittersweet chocolate, cut into ¼-inch pieces
6	tablespoons (¾ stick) unsalted butter, at room temperature
4	tablespoons confectioners' sugar
1	teaspoon vanilla extract
5	egg yolks
3	tablespoons cocoa powder
6	egg whites
⅛	teaspoon cream of tartar
6	tablespoons plus 1 teaspoon granulated sugar

For the filling:

¾	cup apricot preserves
1	tablespoon apricot brandy or amaretto (optional)

For the glaze:

6	ounces bittersweet chocolate
6	tablespoons (¾ stick) unsalted butter
1	tablespoon light corn syrup
	Whipped cream for serving

1. Preheat the oven to 350°F. Cut a piece of parchment to line the bottom of a 9-inch springform pan. Coat the pan and the parchment with nonstick cooking spray or butter. Sift together the flour and baking powder three times and set aside.

2. Place the chocolate in a heatproof bowl over a saucepan of simmering water and stir gently to melt. Or melt it in the microwave by cooking it for 2 minutes at 50% power and again for 30 seconds, then stir until melted.

3. In a standing mixer fitted with the paddle, or with a hand mixer, cream the butter and confectioners' sugar at medium speed until light and fluffy. Add the vanilla and the egg yolks one at a time and beat until the mixture is light and fluffy, about 5 minutes. Beat in the cocoa and the melted chocolate.

4. In a separate, clean bowl, using a whisk attachment or electric beaters, whip the egg whites until they begin to foam. Add the cream of tartar and continue to beat until the whites form medium peaks. Continue to beat while you gradually add the granulated sugar, one tablespoon at a time. Beat until the mixture is stiff.

5. Stir one-fourth of the egg whites into the egg yolk mixture to lighten it. In three additions, fold in the remaining egg whites, alternating with the flour. When the mixture is thoroughly amalgamated, gently scrape it into the prepared pan.

6. Bake 35 to 45 minutes, or until the top is firm when gently pressed with your fingers and a tester comes out just about clean. Remove from the oven and allow to cool 10 minutes in the pan on a rack. Then carefully remove the ring and allow to cool completely on a rack.

7. Make the apricot filling. Purée the preserves in a food processor fitted with the steel blade, or put through a sieve. Transfer to a pan, stir in the apricot brandy or amaretto and warm slightly so that you can spread it easily over the cake. When the cake is cool, slice it in half horizontally to make two layers. Spread the bottom layer with two-thirds of the apricot filling and top with the second layer. Spread the top with an even layer of the remaining preserves. Chill.

8. Make the chocolate glaze. Combine the chocolate and butter in a heatproof bowl and melt over simmering water, or in a microwave at 50% power for 2 to 3 minutes. Stir in the corn syrup. Allow to cool slightly (it should be at 90 to 95°F).

9. Remove the cake from the refrigerator. Place it on a rack above a sheet of parchment paper or a newspaper. Pour the glaze over the top all at once. Turn the cake and spread the glaze over the sides. Allow to cool for 5 minutes, then transfer the cake to a cake plate or a cardboard round and refrigerate for 15 minutes. Serve with whipped cream.

Zesty Lemon Bars

MAKES 2 DOZEN

Wolfgang's EASY TIPS

➤ To remove the zest from a citrus fruit, first wash the fruit with a small amount of detergent if it has been waxed. Rinse well and dry its surface completely with a kitchen or paper towel. The tool you use will determine how big or small you want the pieces to be, which will be dictated by how you are going to use the zest. Rub the fruit lightly over the pointy rasps of a grater or, even better and easier, a microplane (see page 274), to get fine particles of zest that can blend in and suffuse a recipe like my Zesty Lemon Bars with their fresh, lively flavor. Drag the small, sharp-edged holes of a special tool called a citrus zester, available in cookware stores, to get attractive, thin little strips that provide small bursts of flavor when you bite into them. For slightly larger strips, draw a swivel-bladed vegetable peeler across the fruit, then use a small, sharp knife to cut those ribbons of zest into pieces of the desired size. Or leave the ribbons of zest whole to simmer in a braise, stew, or sauce, and then remove them before serving. Whatever method you use, however, always take care not to dig into the peel so deeply that you remove any of the bitter white pith along with the zest.

I call these "Zesty Lemon Bars" because there is zest both in the shortbread crust and in the custard filling. Citrus zest refers to the thin, brightly colored outer layer of any citrus fruit's peel. It's packed with intensely flavorful oils that can liven up the taste of a wide range of sweet dishes and savory dishes like seafood, poultry, meat, and vegetables.

For the lemon shortbread crust:

1½	cups all-purpose flour
¾	cup confectioners' sugar
3	tablespoons cornstarch
⅛	teaspoon salt
1	tablespoon grated lemon zest
6	ounces (1½ sticks) unsalted butter, cut into ½-inch pieces

For the lemon custard topping:

4	eggs
1	cup granulated sugar
¼	cup all-purpose flour
	Pinch of salt
¾	cup fresh lemon juice
¼	cup milk
1	tablespoon finely grated lemon zest
	Confectioners' sugar for decorating

1. Preheat the oven to 350°F. Adjust the rack to the bottom third of the oven. Spray the bottom and sides of a 9 x 12-inch baking pan. Cut a piece of cooking parchment to fit the bottom of the pan and line the pan with the parchment. Spray the parchment.

2. To make the crust, put the flour, sugar, cornstarch, salt, and lemon zest in the work bowl of a food processor fitted with the stainless steel blade. Pulse several times to combine them. With the machine running, gradually drop in the pieces of butter through the feed tube and continue to process until you have a slightly crumbly dough. Transfer the mixture to the prepared baking pan and, with your fingers, press it into the bottom to form an even layer of crust. Bake in the lower third of the oven until the crust is light golden in color, 25 to 30 minutes. Remove from the oven and allow to cool. Turn the oven down to 325°F and adjust the rack to the middle.

3. Prepare the topping. In a medium mixing bowl or an electric stand mixer, whisk the eggs until smooth. Combine the sugar, flour, and salt in a bowl and stir until well blended. Whisk this mixture into the eggs. Stir in the lemon juice, milk, and lemon zest.

4. Pour the topping mixture over the prebaked crust. Return the pan to the oven and continue to bake until the custard is set,

jiggling only slightly when the pan is moved, about 30 minutes. Remove the pan from the oven and leave it at room temperature until completely cooled. Cover the pan with plastic wrap and chill in the refrigerator for at least 2 hours.

5. Before serving, use a sharp knife to cut them into rectangular bars. With a small spatula, starting at one edge, carefully begin to pry them up and out from the baking pan; they'll become easier to remove as you have more room to insert the spatula. Arrange the bars on a platter. Just before serving, dust them with confectioners' sugar.

Fresh Peach Melba with Raspberry Sauce

MAKES 6 SERVINGS

Peach Melba has definitely seen better days—too often we find it made with canned peaches and ordinary vanilla ice cream. But when peaches are at their height, so sweet that you can't bite into one without the juices running down your face, this can be a terrific dish. Try to find freestone peaches for this, the ones that come away easily from the pit.

Wolfgang's EASY TIPS

➤ Let your nose lead you to good, tree-ripened peaches. You should be able to smell their sweet perfume almost before you can see them. If you want to eat or cook with the peaches the same day, buy them fully ripened, still firm yet soft enough to yield slightly to gentle pressure from your fingers. Buy them a little firmer than that if you want to keep them for a few days; they'll continue to ripen when left in a bowl at room temperature (never in the refrigerator).

➤ To peel peaches, bring a pot of water to a full boil and fill another bowl three-fourths full with ice and water. Meanwhile, with a small, sharp knife, score a shallow X in the skin at the blossom end of each peach. Carefully add the peaches to the boiling water and boil until their skins start to wrinkle, about 20 seconds. With a slotted spoon, remove the peaches and transfer them to the bowl of ice water. When they are cool enough to handle, drain them and, starting at the X, peel away the skin.

For the poached peaches:

3	large ripe, firm, freestone peaches
2	cups water
2	cups sugar
¼	cup lemon juice
	Grated zest of 1 lemon

For the fresh raspberry sauce:

1	pound raspberries
½	cup sugar
2	tablespoons lemon juice

For serving:

1	cup sliced almonds
1½	pints good-quality vanilla ice cream
1	cup heavy cream, whipped to soft peaks

1. Prepare the peaches. Bring a saucepan of water to a boil and skin the peaches as directed in the tips.

2. In another saucepan, make a simple syrup. Stir together the 2 cups water, the sugar, and the lemon juice and zest. Over medium-high heat, bring the mixture to a boil, then reduce the heat to low. Add the peach halves to this syrup and continue simmering until tender, 5 to 7 minutes. Remove from the heat and let the peaches cool in the syrup. Transfer the fruit and syrup to a nonreactive bowl, cover with plastic wrap, and refrigerate until serving time.

3. Make the fresh raspberry sauce. Put the berries, sugar, and lemon juice in a blender or a food processor and process until puréed. Place a fine-mesh strainer over a nonreactive bowl and, with a rubber spatula, pass the purée through the strainer to remove the seeds. Cover with plastic wrap and refrigerate.

4. Before serving, toast the sliced almonds in a small, dry skillet over low heat, stirring almost continuously, until they turn light golden, about 3 minutes. Transfer immediately to a bowl to cool.

5. To serve, scoop the ice cream into six attractive, chilled serving bowls. Remove the peach halves from their syrup and place them cut side down on top of the ice cream. Drizzle each serving generously with the raspberry sauce, garnish with whipped cream and toasted almonds, and serve immediately.

Crêpes with Vanilla Ice Cream and Warm Chocolate Sauce

MAKES 6 SERVINGS

Pancakes, whether thin crêpes of thick raised cakes, make surprising and satisfying desserts. One of my favorite desserts as a child was a crêpe filled with vanilla ice cream and topped with a warm chocolate sauce. I don't know a grown-up who doesn't also love this utterly simple combination.

1 recipe crêpes (page 12)	1 recipe chocolate sauce (see step 3 page 230), warmed
1 pint good quality vanilla ice cream	

1. Make the crêpes as directed on page 12.
2. Place a couple of spoonfuls of ice cream on a crêpe, flatten the ice cream down a little with the back of your spoon, and fold the crêpe in half over the ice cream. Fold the crêpe in half again so that it is a quarter circle. Fill all of the crêpes and place two or three on each plate.
3. Drizzle on the warm chocolate sauce and serve.

Wolfgang's EASY TIPS

➤ You can make the crêpes ahead and heat them in a microwave. Just make sure you serve them right away once you've folded the ice cream into the warm crêpes.

Dessert Pancakes

MAKES 25 MINI-PANCAKES

I like to make small blini-size pancakes and serve them with apricot jam and whipped cream or crème fraîche. You could also serve this dish for breakfast.

1½ **cups all-purpose flour**	¼ **cup melted unsalted butter**
2 **teaspoons baking powder**	1 **teaspoon vanilla extract**
1 **teaspoon baking soda**	1 **cup Dried Apricot Jam (page 29)**
¼ **cup sugar**	½ **cup whipped cream or crème fraîche**
⅛ **teaspoon salt**	
2 **eggs**	
1½ **cups buttermilk, or 1 cup buttermilk and ½ cup milk**	

1. Heat an electric griddle or a stovetop griddle or heavy pan over medium-high heat. Sift together the flour, baking powder, baking soda, sugar, and salt into a medium bowl.

2. In another medium bowl, beat the eggs and whisk in the buttermilk (or buttermilk and milk), the melted butter, and the vanilla extract. Quickly whisk in the flour mixture and stir only until it is combined.

3. Ladle the batter onto the griddle by tablespoons for small, 2-inch pancakes. Cook until bubbles break through and turn over. Cook another 30 seconds to a minute, until nicely browned on the other side and transfer to a plate.

4. Serve the pancakes hot with dried apricot jam and whipped cream or crème fraîche.

Wolfgang's EASY TIPS

➤ Use a table-top griddle for these if you have one. Otherwise use a heavy stovetop griddle or cast iron pan.

APPENDIX

Kitchen Equipment

The home cook should be able to do everything a restaurant cook can do, but on a smaller scale. In restaurants we're used to working with large, heavy pots and pans that we set over high heat. In the home kitchen, pots and pans need not be as large as restaurant equipment, but they should be heavy and of good quality. In addition to cutlery, pots and pans, and baking equipment, the home cook can take advantage of gadgets such as food processors, mixers, pressure cookers, and indoor grills. Carefully chosen equipment will help you to be a better cook. The list below covers everything you will need to make the recipes in this book.

CUTLERY

Confidence in the kitchen begins with good knives. When the knife you use is well suited to the job and has a good, sharp blade and a comfortable, safe handle, chopping, slicing, and carving become a breeze.

Knife Basics

Choosing the right knives depends on several factors. Obviously, price will affect your choice, because some of the best cutlery can be costly. In the long run, however, spending more money now can save you money later. High-quality knives that you care for properly are a smarter choice than cheap knives that you have to keep replacing. Good design and quality materials also bring better performance. Whether you're a home cook or a professional chef, keep the following important factors in mind.

Blade Materials

• *Carbon steel*. This carbon-iron alloy used to be the chef's blade material of choice because it takes and holds an extremely sharp edge. But carbon blades corrode over time, and they discolor on contact with acidic foods like lemons, tomatoes, or onions. They can also impart a metallic taste to these reactive ingredients.
• *Ceramic*. Made from zirconium oxide, a material that can stay razor-sharp for years, this rela-

tively new material is manufactured through a long firing process to create a dense material that does not corrode, rust, or alter flavor. It is designed especially for slicing. Heavy-duty chopping can damage the blade. Most ceramic knife manufacturers recommend sending these knives out to professionals for sharpening.
• *High-carbon stainless steel*. Not surprisingly, this is the preferred blade of most professionals today. High-carbon stainless steel combines stainless steel's strength and carbon steel's ability to take a super-sharp edge. It is durable, doesn't rust or discolor, and doesn't interact with foods.
• *Stainless steel*. Resistant to corrosion and stronger than carbon steel, stainless may, in fact, be too strong; blades made from it are harder than most sharpening tools, so they're more difficult to maintain. However, stainless steel is great for other types of cutting tools, such as poultry shears.

Blade Manufacture

• *Sharpness*. How sharp a blade is and how long it stays sharp are key to a knife's quality. See page 270 for instructions on how to keep a knife sharp.
• *Balance*. Simply holding a knife by its handle tells you a lot. Look for a well-balanced knife with weight evenly distributed to ensure that the knife will cut efficiently, with minimal exertion.
• *Forged versus stamped*. When you buy metal blades, ask if they have been forged (shaped under intense heat) or stamped (pressure-cut

from sheets of metal). Most experts prefer forged metal knives, which tend to be heavier, more durable, and better balanced.

- *The tang.* This strip of metal extends from the blade into the handle and affects both sturdiness and balance. A full tang that is the same length and shape as the handle and visible between the two handle halves is generally preferable for most heavy-duty knives like the chef's knife. Lighter knives, such as the paring knife and the boning knife, work fine with partial tangs.

The Handle

- *Comfort, efficiency, and safety.* A knife's handle must feel good in your hand, providing a comfortable, secure grip that facilitates safe, efficient work.
- *Aesthetics, materials, and construction.* Attractive handles can add to a knife's aesthetic appeal. More importantly, they serve a practical purpose. Handles made of hard rubber or from hard-woods infused with plastic usually last longer and are less likely to splinter or warp. Slick plastic handles, by contrast, attract grease and may cause a knife to slip around in your hand. If you are purchasing a knife with an integral stainless-steel handle, be sure it has ridges or grooves along the side of the handle to help reduce the chance of slippage. Non-integral handles, whatever they are made from, should be securely attached to the blade's tang with metal rivets.

Caring for Your Knives

Sharp knives do the job efficiently and safely, with beautiful results. Dull knives make cutting harder and slower and yield less attractive results. They are also more dangerous. A dull blade requires more pressure to cut, which can lead to awkward movements, careless cutting, and accidents.

A note of warning: If you ever see the words "never needs sharpening" on a knife's package, stay away from it. Such statements usually mean, "No matter what you try, you'll never be able to successfully sharpen this knife."

Keeping it sharp
- Every time you cut with a knife, on a microscopic level the blade's edge rolls back a little. Over time, the edge grows too dull to cut effectively. More than contact with tough or hard foods, constant impact with cutting board surfaces leads to dulling. Even the act of pulling a knife from a storage block dulls a sharp edge, which is why I recommend storing knives in a block with horizontal slots or, if you have vertical slots, with the cutting edge facing up.
- *The sharpening steel.* Resembling a blunt, cylindrical dagger, this essential tool helps maintain keen cutting edges. To work effectively, it must be composed of a harder substance than the blades that are sharpened on it. Many knife sets include a steel. If you purchase knives and steel separately, however, you will need to know their Rockwell Hardness Rating (see sidebar on page 271) so you can buy a steel that is harder than the knives.
- *Using a steel.* To maintain a knife's edge, I recommend that you stroke it along a sharpening steel before each use. To steel a blade safely, point the steel away from your body with one hand, firmly gripping the steel's handle with your fingers well clear of the sharpening surface (a good steel will include a perpendicular metal guard collar between the steel and the handle). With your other hand, grip the knife so its cutting edge points upward and rests at its hilt near the steel's point, at a 20-degree angle to the steel. Slowly but surely, draw the blade toward you while simultaneously swiping the blade lengthwise across the steel,

forming a slight circular motion. Repeat on the other side of the blade's cutting edge, on the underside of the steel. Five or six such swipes on each side of the blade will suffice. For safety's sake, avoid quick, jerky strokes.

• *Ceramic sharpeners.* You may also want to look for one of the new ceramic sharpening devices, which are harder than any traditional steel around. Shaped like a normal steel, only smaller, a ceramic sharpener is used by holding the knife steady and drawing the sharpener across the blade. If you find that over time the sharpening steel does not produce a fine edge, then the next step is to actually sharpen the blade.

In my restaurants, we send our knives out to a professional once a year to have them sharpened. That gets expensive for the home cook. There are also electric knife sharpeners on the market, but I find that they actually spoil the edge of the knife. Besides, for much less money you can get exceptional results using a traditional sharpening stone.

• *Sharpening stones, or whetstones,* are slender rectangular blocks made of super-hard materials that have a wide surface to draw the knife over. Diamond-embedded stones are excellent to use with stainless-steel or high-carbon steel knives.

To properly use a stone, lay it on a flat surface with the coarse side up. Some stones require light oil or water for lubrication. Place the knife firmly on the stone, holding the edge at a 20-degree angle. Pressing evenly and gently, draw the blade over the stone from heel to tip. Sharpen in one direction only and do not over-sharpen. Finish the job with a few strokes on a sharpening steel, and then wipe the blade with a clean, dry towel. These stones don't last forever; replace them when their surfaces become pitted or uneven.

• *Serrated knives.* These must be professionally sharpened.

ROCKWELL'S RATING

The Rockwell scale is an internationally recognized measurement scale that determines the strength and hardness of a substance, including the metals used in knives. The professional's choice for a metal blade's hardness usually lies between 55 and 58 degrees on the Rockwell scale. This strength takes a sharp edge and holds it for a long time. (Ceramics are not metal and so are not judged on a Rockwell scale.) A sharpening steel and sharpening stone should be at least 8 degrees harder than whatever knife they are sharpening.

Keeping knives clean

Even if a manufacturer specifies that a knife is "dishwasher safe," I always hand wash my knives. Wash cycles strong enough to dislodge food from dishes can also chip or dull knife edges and loosen handles.

Instead, wash each knife individually after use with warm, soapy water. Never leave knives standing in a sink full of water, where you might forget about them and accidentally cut yourself. Towel-dry knives before returning them to storage.

Storage

Never throw your knives into a cluttered kitchen drawer. Not only could you damage the blades, but you may very well cut yourself the next time you search through the drawer.

Freestanding hardwood blocks are practical and attractive. When storing knives in a block, always slide them in their slots sharp edges up so that the blades don't get dull rubbing against the wood. There are also magnetic strips that can be mounted on the wall near the work area that hold the knives tightly by the blades. This makes retrieval very simple. Magnetic strips are not recommended for homes with small children and pets, since some amount of tapping can loosen the knives.

If you choose to keep knives in a drawer, make sure each has a strong polystyrene sheath to protect it from being nicked by other knives and utensils. The sheath also safeguards your fingers from the blade when you reach into the drawer.

The Knives You Will Need

Sometimes I wish there was just one knife to do every chore. But I know that a great painter would never be limited to just one brush, so I always appreciate the variety of highly specialized knives that make cooking so enjoyable.

Boning knife

You can give the butcher the day off if you have a high-quality boning knife at home. Keep in mind that a wider, stiffer blade should be used on larger cuts of meat, like a leg of lamb, because you'll need lots of power. Thinner, more flexible blades are ideal for filleting fish, maneuvering through small chickens, and tackling other delicate jobs.

Bread knife

Sometimes called a serrated slicer, the bread knife has scalloped teeth that cleanly saw through breads, whether hard-crusted or soft and fluffy. The 8- to 10-inch blade also neatly slices cake layers and may be used to cut delicate tomatoes without crushing them.

Chef's knife

Aptly named, the chef's knife is the workhorse of the bunch because its size, shape, and blade style (wide at the heel while tapering to the point) allows it to accomplish many different large-scale tasks, especially chopping, dicing, mincing, and slicing. An 8- to 10-inch blade suffices for nearly every job.

Clam or oyster knives

These short, rigid blades separate tough shell halves easily. Choose one with a comfortable, sturdy grip.

Cleaver

With its broad rectangular blade, this heavy knife delivers blows powerful enough to cut through bones. It does a great job butterflying whole chickens or cutting a rack of lamb into individual chops, and its size and weight also make short work of chopping hard, dense ingredients like baking chocolate. The wide, flat blade also helps you to scoop up pieces from the cutting board and move them to a bowl or pot. A good cleaver for home use will have a blade 6 to 9 inches long and about 3 to 4 inches wide.

Paring knife

The highly useful paring knife closely resembles a chef's knife, only it's smaller. The 2- to 4-inch blade is sharp and strong enough to swiftly take off the tops of strawberries, trim garlic, and slice delicate mushrooms. Over time, you'll find many, many uses for your paring knife.

Slicing knife

Although a high-quality slicing knife is sharp enough to glide through a ripe tomato, this knife is made especially for tough jobs like carving through a chicken breast or a rib roast. The blade is long (8 to 10 inches), strong, and narrow. Some models are more flexible for confident tableside carving; others are more rigid to deal effectively with cold, tough cuts of meat.

Utility knife

As its name implies, the utility knife has quite a few uses. Depending on the manufacturer, the narrow pointed blade is 6- to 8-inches long and often has mixed blade surfaces (partially serrated, partially flat, for example). This combination makes the knife indispensable for prepping vegetables for salads and slicing sandwiches. It is also precise enough to make crinkle cuts in carrots, cucumbers, and radishes.

Special Cutlery

These items will help you with carving, peeling, and cutting poultry and shellfish.

Carving fork

Even the best carving knife needs a carving fork as its partner. The heavy, two-pronged fork, complete with a long handle to provide a firm grip, is used for lifting and turning large chunks of meat and for holding them steady while you carve.

Poultry shears

Tougher than scissors, poultry shears easily cut through the wing joints of a chicken or quickly section a bird into four portions. I also use mine for cutting open lobster tails along the underside of the shell. One of the blades should be notched for cutting bones, and the other blade should be serrated to grip flesh.

Vegetable peeler

Peelers come in several forms to suit particular jobs. Some you draw toward you to peel, while others you push away. Swivel-action blades peel in both directions to follow the contours of potatoes and cucumbers; there are harp-shaped

peelers that remove the slimmest portion of a radish's surface; there are rigid peelers with double blades for right-hand or left-hand users. But I feel the most essential aspect of a quality peeler is the handle grip. When you peel as many potatoes as I do, less stress on the hands is very important.

UTENSILS

Chinois Sieve or Strainer

Chinois is a French word meaning "Chinese hat" (although I think that the cone-shaped kitchen tool by that name resembles a dunce cap). There is little difference between a sieve and a strainer; both are used for straining fruits, vegetables, sauces, and stews. They are both also great for dusting desserts with cocoa powder or powdered sugar. Each tool has a tight mesh colander at the end of a handle. The mesh is so tight that almost nothing except for liquids can pass through. They should be made of durable stainless steel. Most home cooks prefer strainers, which cost less than chinois and can also be used for sifting.

Colander

This wide-brimmed bowl punctuated with holes drains cooking liquids from vegetables or pasta and may also be used for rinsing produce under cold running water. Stainless-steel colanders are sturdier than plastic; large ones are more versatile than small ones. Look for a colander that will fit inside the rim of your largest stockpot so you can also use it to steam foods.

Food mill

A food mill is a hand-cranked tool that strains or purées fruits and vegetables, removes seeds from berries, squeezes out skin and seeds from cooked tomatoes, and mashes potatoes with ease. I also use mine to grind seafood and poultry for soups and sauces. A rust-resistant, stainless-steel mill with a one-quart capacity works just fine for the home.

Mandoline

This tool is used in restaurant kitchens for very thin, uniform slices and other special cuts. Normally, you slice ingredients by holding them still on a cutting board while moving a knife up and down. The mandoline reverses that principle. It secures a sharp blade in a fixed position on a board across which you move the ingredient up and down in a strumming action similar to that used when playing the instrument that gives this utensil its name. If you do invest in a mandoline, choose a sturdy model that includes a finger guard.

Microplane

The tool I use for such tasks as grating Parmesan and zesting citrus is a microplane. This looks like a long (twelve-inch) carpenter's file with raised edges and teeth. Gently rub the food along the stainless-steel grating area to produce flavorful shavings.

Pasta fork

This long, sturdy fork helps to separate strands of pasta and to remove pasta from cooking liquid while doubling as a serving fork. Stainless steel works best since plastic will melt and bend while stirring pasta in the boiling water.

Spatulas

• Rubber spatulas are perfect for scraping the bottoms of pans without scratching and for folding ingredients into one another. Always buy heat-resistant rubber spatulas.

• Stainless-steel spatulas with slotted faces help turn foods cleanly while straining out grease. The unslotted variety is sturdy enough to turn over pancakes or burgers without incident. I prefer offset spatulas, with the handles set higher than the faces.

• Wooden spatulas look elegant and don't scratch pans, but they absorb color and odors from foods, and some will splinter with age.

Spoons

• Wooden spoons are easy on nonstick coating and their handles stay cool. Softwoods, like pine, however, are very porous and absorb odors and stains. For wooden spoons, I prefer olive wood because it's not as porous and it lasts longer without splintering.

• Stainless-steel spoons are sometimes slotted for straining vegetables from their cooking liquids. They are also the best tools for removing a large turkey or roast from a roasting pan without piercing the skin. They won't absorb flavors and they stay relatively cool.

• Skimmers are large, flat, slotted spoons that easily lift off the foam from soups or stocks and are exceptionally useful for clarifying butter. Skimmers are made from different materials, but I prefer sturdy stainless steel.

• Ladles are long-handled spoons with deep, wide bowls. Stainless steel is important here because this tool is used most often to scoop up boiling liquids, such as soup, and the handles tend to stay cool. A two-ounce ladle is great for serving gravy or sauces; a four-ounce ladle works nicely for soups and stews. Try to find a ladle with a hooked end; it can hang from a pot rack when not in use and the hook prevents the ladle from sliding down inside the stockpot in between servings.

Tongs

This gripping tool allows us to grab and retrieve hot food or turn food while it's sautéing or grilling without piercing it. Look for stainless-steel tongs that are at least eight inches long with a locking mechanism at the end, so they don't take up as much storage when placed in a drawer.

Whisks

Whisks are used to whip air into foods like eggs and cream and to combine ingredients for sauces, batters, and doughs. Different sizes of whisks are appropriate for different tasks. A large balloon whisk has a huge head with flexible wires that add a great amount of air, perfect for whipping egg whites and cream. Smaller models have stiffer wires that cut through and mix pastry creams and custards. I recommend that you have both.

You might be holding a whisk for a considerable amount of time, so choose a comfortable grip with wires made from rust-resistant stainless steel.

MEASURING TOOLS

Even if you like to experiment with quantities and proportions—something I encourage home cooks to do—you need to begin a dish with some precision, and you need measures for this. Here are the items you'll need to get started.
• A set of six measuring spoons that range from ⅛ teaspoon through 1 tablespoon.
• A set of four dry measuring cups that range from ¼ cup to 1 cup.
• A set of tempered glass liquid measuring cups in 1-cup, 2-cup, and 4-cup sizes.

BOWLS

Bowls are commonplace items, but that doesn't mean that any old container will help do the job of mixing, holding, and organizing prepped ingredients, storing, and sometimes even cooking. The better your selection of bowls, the better the results of your cooking.

When serving food, beautiful, brightly glazed earthenware bowls help show off what's for dinner. But when it comes to cooking, you need other materials.

For most of my prepping and mixing, I prefer stainless-steel bowls that come with matching plastic lids. These are lightweight and don't react with flavors or aromas. Purchase a set with 1-pint through 5-quart capacities.

Stainless-steel bowls are used for cooking as well. These bowls can be used directly on the stovetop if necessary, such as when preparing a custard or hollandaise sauce. They can be placed over a matching saucepan of water to make the Sabayon on page 244 or to temper chocolate (a simple process of melting and cooling chocolate that makes it easy to work with). In fact, I find that stainless-steel bowls fitted atop saucepans make better double-boilers than the specialty pan sold for that function. The bowl wins because the pan usually has straight sides and squared corners, tough territory for a whisk. Stainless steel is also ideal for chilling desserts in the refrigerator.

The one specialty bowl that I always recommend is a 12-inch unlined copper bowl. This is the essential bowl for whipping egg whites: its size and shape allow for proper aeration during the whipping, and a chemical process takes place between the copper and the egg whites that produces a stable foam and incredible volume when the egg whites come into contact with heat. Many copper bowls today come with a tin lining to protect the food from copper's unique properties, but be sure to choose an unlined bowl for this purpose.

Finally, I think home cooks should also have a set of heatproof glass bowls. Select sizes ranging from 4-ounce custard cups, perfect for *mise en place* (arranging your ingredients before you begin to cook), to a 6-quart mixing bowl that is large enough to use for a double batch of chocolate chip cookies. Make sure you buy tempered glass, which is safe for both the oven and microwave.

BLENDERS, GRINDERS, AND PROCESSORS

In the past few decades, technology has given us wonderful, timesaving kitchen equipment. With newer models being added all the time, it's good to know what to look for when purchasing. The information below should help with your choices.

Blenders
From fruit smoothies to frozen margaritas, puréed soups to crushed ice and ground nuts, blenders perform a wide range of basic tasks that call for speed and power. With a wide range of choices available, keep the following in mind:
• Weight. The base should be fairly large and heavy, so the blender won't wobble while in use.
• Power. To perform heavy-duty tasks like crushing ice, look for a motor that is at least 350 watts.
• Blade. For the best chopping action, look for a model with a four-blade mechanism.
• Carafe material. A heat-resistant, heavy-duty glass jar lets you keep an eye on ingredients. Avoid plastic jars, which scratch and wear more quickly.
• Carafe shape. V-shaped jars feed ingredients down to the blade more easily, facilitating the crushing, chopping, or puréeing action. Those

that also are fairly wide at the base allow ingredients more room to move around.
• Lid. It should fit snugly and include a removable center piece that allows steam to escape when puréeing hot soups and lets you add ingredients during blending.

Coffee Grinders
Nothing compares to freshly ground coffee. Coffee mills are also useful for grinding spices. There are two types.
• Burr grinders process beans at slow speeds, which preserves more of the coffee's aroma. The finished grounds are suitable for drip coffee makers, French press machines, percolators, and espresso/cappucino makers.
• Blade grinders spin at much higher speeds to produce grounds that should only be used in drip coffee makers. I have a separate blade grinder that I use to grind fresh spices. The grinder is washable, so the aromas don't linger. Always use separate mills for coffee and spices.

Food Processors
These days, food processors are almost as common as toasters. These powerful, well-built machines are invaluable for slicing, shredding, and mixing ingredients. They purée in seconds and make pasta dough, piecrusts, and some breads a breeze.
• Since the food is dropped down a chimney tube to be processed, look for wide plastic tubes that can handle different sizes of ingredients.
• The best machines have motors directly under the bowl and blade, not off to the side (where the belt is more likely to be strained).
• Look for a 400-watt (or higher) motor for adequate power.
• The machine should weigh between 10 and 13 pounds and not wobble around while processing.

- A 7-cup capacity mixing bowl is adequate for many jobs, but it is possible to find bowls that hold up to 16 cups, or the equivalent of three pounds of bread dough.
- Some food processors come with many attachments. Make sure yours has a stainless-steel, multi-purpose blade, a dough blade, a slicing disk, a shredding disk, and a julienne disk.
- Since the blade choice is what determines the cut, the "on/off" and "pulse" settings are all you really need on your machine, although some come with up to twelve speed settings.
- Look for machines whose mixing bowls are safe for boiling liquids, the microwave, and the dishwasher.

Hand Blenders

The first handheld blender I can remember seeing was some four feet in length. It was large and awkward, but it performed magical tasks, like puréeing twenty gallons of soup right in the pot.

Modern hand blenders, sometimes called immersion blenders, are much more ergonomic and manageable. They're slender and lightweight, with a powerful rotary blade at one end. The blender is immersed right into the pot or container. The home cook can quickly emulsify vinaigrettes and mayonnaise, blend a breakfast smoothie, and even get the lumps out of gravy.
- Look for a 100-watt (or higher) motor.
- Since you'll be holding the blender for brief periods of time, find a comfortable handle.
- Variable speeds are great. Blending big chunks of fruit takes more speed and power than puréeing hot soups.
- A stainless-steel base is better than plastic when using it to purée hot soups and gravies.
- Attachments, such as a mini-chopper for herbs and a whisk for whipping cream, always come in handy.

ELECTRIC MIXERS

Depending on your needs (and space), electric mixers can make life in the kitchen much easier, especially if you like to make pastry and bread.

Hand Mixers

Not a serious baker? You probably don't need a standing mixer. A hand mixer is probably more useful. It performs many of the same tasks as a standing mixer, such as mixing, whipping, beating, and blending. But it works on smaller quantities with less power and more portability. The beauty of a hand mixer is that you take the mixer to the task. For example, you can mix egg whites over a pan of boiling water for French meringue, or mash potatoes right in the pot they were boiled in.

Key features to look for when selecting a hand mixer include:
- Power. It needs at least 200 watts for effective whipping and beating.
- Comfort. Look for a mixer that isn't too heavy and is easy to hold for long periods of time.
- Toughness. Strong stainless-steel beaters (without a center post) facilitate adding in chips and candies when making cookie dough.
- Extras. Some mixers include a dough hook attachment, which can be used for kneading biscuit dough or mixing up meatloaf and meatballs. However, hand mixers are not powerful enough for bread dough.

Standing Mixers

Standing mixers are heavy-duty machines that help cooks and bakers do everything from whipping an eight-egg-white meringue to kneading bread dough. They are heavy and require a lot of counter space. But if you are serious about baking, you'll be amazed at how essential a standing mixer is.

- Look for a motor that has at least 500 watts of power, especially if you'll be kneading bread dough.
- The mixer should be heavy, with its weight evenly distributed to remain stable during the mixing process.
- High-quality mixers have one paddle, whisk, or dough hook attached to a head that rotates above the bowl in an orbital motion. Older and less expensive models have spinning mixing bowls, which are less effective.
- In addition to the large whisk, paddle, and dough hook attachments, standing mixers should have a utility hub for additional attachments, such as a meat grinder, pasta maker, and citrus juicer.
- Choose a heavy-duty, stainless-steel mixing bowl with at least a 5-quart capacity. Anything smaller will restrict the types of jobs you're able to do.

TRIPLE BEATER HAND MIXERS

New to the marketplace is the triple-beater hand mixer. The third beater adds even more stability to the mixing process, so it's fabulous for whipping up meringues and creams quickly.

COOKWARE

Pots and pans are available in so many different materials that it's tempting to just buy a full set made from one material and be done with it. However, I think that you should build your cookware collection with specific tasks in mind. That way you'll get the best performance.

Materials
Cookware comes in aluminum and stainless steel, triple-ply stainless steel and cast iron, enameled cast iron and copper, earthenware and nonstick. I do most of my cooking on triple-ply stainless steel and enameled cast iron. For omelets and crêpes, I always use nonstick cookware.

Aluminum
Aluminum is one of the best heat-conducting metals. It is also lightweight and generally inexpensive. However, it is a softer metal and because of that it reacts with foods. Have you ever made a tomato sauce in an aluminum pot? The metal can change the color of the sauce and give it a tinny taste.

To solve that problem, some aluminum cookware is lined with stainless steel, eliminating any problems of taste and appearance. There is also anodized aluminum, in which the surface is sealed and won't react to foods. This version of aluminum is extremely durable and still provides excellent heat conduction. But along with being more expensive, this seal turns the surface very dark, making it difficult to tell the colors of your sauces when preparing them.

Cast iron
Many cooks have childhood memories of favorite dishes cooked in these dark, heavy pans. From fried chicken to catfish to corn bread, food takes on a nostalgic feeling when prepared in cast iron. This heavy metal is perfect for searing and frying because once it's hot it stays that way for a long time.

Unfortunately, cast iron has drawbacks. Iron reacts with acidic foods, so it's not recommended for use with wine or lemon juice. It adds its own taste and color to other foods, such as spinach and tomato sauce. Because it's prone to rust it must be washed, dried, and seasoned with oil (heated to open the pores and then sealed to prevent rusting) after each use. And, boy, are cast-iron skillets heavy.

The solution to most of these problems is coated or enameled cast iron. The coating is designed to sustain high temperatures without chipping or peeling and stands up to frying, roasting, and braising. Unlike uncoated cast-iron, it does not need seasoning, and it will not rust. This cookware is usually a lot more expensive than basic cast iron, but it's worth the price. And by the way, it's just as heavy.

Ceramic and glass

Ceramic and tempered glass don't conduct heat effectively, but they retain it very well. Both are good choices for casserole dishes, and most models can go from oven to table to dishwasher without problems. The materials don't react to the food and are quite sturdy.

Copper

Many chefs prize their copper cookware as if it were a trophy. Not only is copper elegant and durable, this metal is by far the best conductor of heat.

Copper cookware is very expensive and very heavy. There is also quite a bit of maintenance involved to keep it clean and polished. Unfortunately, copper reacts with many foods. In the case of egg whites, that's a good thing because it helps produce stable foam. (I have one unlined copper bowl just for my eggs. See "Bowls" above.) But for other cooking tasks, look for copper pots that are lined with either stainless steel or tin. These thin metal linings help protect the pot and the food.

Nonstick surfaces

All cookware is nonstick to some degree, if you use it properly. For instance, when a cast-iron, stainless-steel, or aluminum skillet is preheated over high heat, and then a film of oil is added to it and allowed to heat as well, a steak or chicken breast or fish fillet will not stick to it if left to brown undisturbed.

Nonstick pans don't require as much diligence on the cook's part. They also make some traditional cooking tasks so much easier that many professionals, myself included, will turn to them when making omelets or crêpes, for example. Obviously, they make cleanup easier, too. But unlike conventional cookware they don't promote the formation of a glaze on the pan bottom that you can deglaze to form the basis for a flavorful sauce.

Today's highest quality brands of nonstick coatings are actually imbedded in or bonded to the metal for longer-lasting results. I have been using my heavy-duty pans for years; I make sure never to put them in the dishwasher and to use only wooden or plastic spoons and spatulas so they won't scratch. These resist scratching and some can even be used with metal utensils, though wood or plastic remain smarter choices for longer wear. Less expensive nonstick coatings are little more than sprays applied to the metal in the factory, and can scrape or flake off with repeated use.

Stainless-steel cookware

The sturdy nonporous stainless steel used in cookware is made from a combination of steel, chromium, and nickel. This alloy is noncorrosive and does not react with ingredients. It won't rust, it's nontoxic, and it doesn't leave a metallic taste. It's virtually indestructible: you can put it in a dishwasher and it will stay shiny forever. Sounds perfect doesn't it? It would be except for the small problem that it's not a great conductor of heat.

The solution is called "cladding," in which another metal that conducts heat better, like aluminum or copper, is joined to the pan's stainless-steel bottom, combining the benefits of both metals. This style of cookware is sometimes referred to as triple-ply because the aluminum or copper layer will be completely encapsulated between two sheets of stainless steel.

Handles

Handles are quite important when considering cookware. I choose stainless-steel handles that are riveted directly onto the pans. The connection is secure and stays intact when the cookware goes through different temperature changes. Stainless steel also stays cooler than other metals.

Not to be dismissed, however, are phenolic handles, those common hard-plastic black handles. The change in materials (metal pan, plastic handle) reduces the transfer of heat to handle, so you can grasp the handles without using an oven mitt. But the handles won't withstand high-temperature ovens.

Finally, hold the pot in your hand for a while before purchasing it. A comfortable grip is essential for comfortable cooking.

Lids

Lids should fit securely down into the pan and be heavy (to stay in place over boiling liquids). Metal lids work just fine, but I like to see the food during the cooking process (for instance, to know if the water has evaporated from the rice), so I like tempered glass lids. Although they can break if dropped, normally they're durable enough for a long life. The lid handle should be raised just enough so that you can securely grasp it while wearing a potholder.

YOUR COOKWARE COLLECTION

Once you have decided on the materials you want, here are the different types of cookware you'll need to build a strong foundation.

Casserole

This heavy, high-sided dish is designed for slow oven or top-of-the-stove cooking. Models range in size from 1 pint to 10 quarts and should have two easy-to-grasp side handles and a lid with a raised handle. (Test them while using a potholder.) Casseroles are meant to go from oven to table, since they retain heat effectively.

If you choose a metal casserole, it can also be used safely on a stove burner; those made of earthenware, ceramic, heatproof glass, and stoneware cannot, unless a flame tamer is set between the burner and the casserole. Choose an 8-, 10-, or 12- to -15-inch casserole depending on your needs.

Chicken Fryer

This large high-sided frypan with a long straight handle and a small helper handle on the opposite side is good for much more than frying chicken. Any dish that is browned and then braised will cook in one of these. Either a 10-inch or 12-inch diameter fryer will work at home. Make sure it has a domed lid that fits snugly on the pan. Because of its heat-conducting ability, cast-iron is a great choice for a chicken fryer. However, these items are very heavy.

Griddle

I use my griddle for pancakes, scones, crumpets, and even bacon and eggs. The key word is speed, since the heat from the flame is transferred quickly through the griddle's thin surface to the food. Round or rectangular are equally effective. Aluminum and cast iron are the best heat conductors.

Grill Pan

With the raised ridges found on grill pans, you can get attractive grill marks on foods year-round.

Choose a pan with a thick bottom so that it sits firmly on your stovetop while you flip and move foods around. A 12-inch cast-iron grill pan is quite useful for most kitchen uses.

Roasting Pans

Roasting pans are made both deep and shallow, with lids and without, and in a variety of materials. As always, picking the right pan depends on individual needs and preferences.

• Roasting pans can be as large as 28 x 22-inches. So before you shop for a pan, measure the inside of your oven. You'll want to have at least 2 inches between the oven walls and the pan's sides.

• A shallow roasting pan allows plenty of warm oven air to reach the sides of the roast. The 16 x 13-inch pan is usually ideal for most cuts of meat, but there should be at least 2 inches between the sides of the pan and the roast for proper air circulation.

• Deep roasting pans are usually 2 inches taller on all sides than what you are roasting.

• Many deep roasters come with vented lids, which make the roaster act a lot like a steamer. This results in very moist meat, but not crisp skin. (Deep roasters are also the perfect tools for making exquisite custards.)

• I prefer roasting pans made of stainless steel. This metal conducts heat sufficiently for roasting, even when I move the pan to the stovetop to finish my gravy or sauce. Whatever metal you choose, remember that the pan should carry between 10 and 20 pounds without bowing. A heavy-gauge metal, like stainless steel, resists warping over time; lightweight aluminum does not.

• Finally, do yourself a big favor and insist on pans with sturdy metal handles riveted to the sides. They should be large enough to accommodate oven mitts, not just bare hands.

Roasting Rack

Once you have a roasting pan, be sure to get the right supporting players for the job. Roasted foods should be elevated away from the fats at the bottom of the pan so that heat circulates underneath. I recommend a nonstick, V-shaped rack to accomplish this. With the rack in the pan, make sure before cooking that there is room to safely dip a spoon around to retrieve basting juices. And remember to buy a rack with handles. Removing the rack without them can be a messy job.

Saucepan

This small pan is ideal for making sauces, melting butter, reheating soups, and cooking rice. Look for a large circumference at the base and sides that aren't too deep (to promote even heating). I like stainless-steel-lined copper saucepans. Saucepans are available in 1- to 4-quart capacities. Since they're probably the most-used pans in the kitchen, I recommend you have at least 2 different sizes.

Sauté Pan

This is a shallow, wide skillet with sloping sides and a long handle. It browns meats, stir-fries vegetables, and poaches eggs with great efficiency. Lined copper is great for sautéing, but so are aluminum, stainless steel, and heavy-duty, high-quality nonstick. A 10- or 12-inch pan is ideal for most homes.

Stockpot

A stockpot is very useful—not just for soups and stocks—but for lobster, pasta, and corn-on-the-cob. Most pots range in size from 1 gallon to 20 quarts. I recommend buying at least a 10-quart capacity because there is no sense in buying a big pot that is too small for the job. It should have a thick bottom (thicker than the sides in order to support heavy bones) and two riveted handles. Consider buying an aluminum stockpot for its heat-conducting properties and its lightweight material. Some models have convenient steamer inserts.

Thermometer

Rarely do you see a chef without an instant-read thermometer in his chef jacket pocket. These gadgets allow quick readings of meat's internal temperature. But I prefer the digital probe thermometers with heatproof cords. The probe is left inserted in the roast during the entire cooking process. The cord runs to an easy-to-read monitor that's left outside the oven; you can check the temperature at any time without opening the oven and releasing its heat. When the meat reaches the desired temperature an alarm will go off.

Wok

A wok is designed to cook food quickly with little fat. It has a small base and large fluted sides that make tossing food around easy. A 14-inch model with heat-retardant wood handles works best for home cooking. Make sure you purchase one with a stabilizing ring that fits over a stovetop burner.

BAKING AND PASTRY EQUIPMENT

Pastry is more scientific than any other type of cooking. The intricacies of mixing ingredients, rising doughs, and the reaction to indirect heat is less free-form than stovetop cooking. To avoid blunders, it's important to follow a baking recipe from start to finish, with no variations, until you have mastered it.

I also think that having high-quality equipment is of great value. Just like cookware,

bakeware comes in different materials and styles. Here are recommendations for some essential pieces for your home baking.

Baking Sheets

The first step in buying any baking sheet is to measure the inside dimensions of your oven. I've lost count of the number of home cooks who have told me that they've bought a wonderful professional-quality baking sheet, only to find it didn't fit! Ideally, there should be 2 inches of clearance all around the sheet's front, back, and sides to allow the oven's heat to circulate freely for even baking.

Lightweight aluminum sheets will warp over time. Heavy tinned steel sheets are sturdy and conduct heat well for even baking. They also darken over time, an advantage because darker surfaces absorb heat better.

Baking sheets with nonstick surfaces can be helpful. But my pastry chefs and I prefer simply to line our baking sheets with virtually nonstick parchment paper, available in well-stocked supermarkets and kitchen supply shops.

Although most home cooks can certainly get by with just two baking sheets, if you want to bake often and in quantity I suggest you have four good-sized baking sheets. That way, you can have a full batch of cookies ready to go into the oven on two room-temperature sheets the moment another batch comes out of the oven.

Bundt Pan

The Bundt pan is a popular choice for dense cakes and frozen desserts. It has a heating tube in the middle for even baking. A standard Bundt is 8½ inches in diameter and has a 9-cup capacity. Most are made from cast aluminum. Don't confuse it with a tube pan (page 283).

Cake Pan

The common cake recipe calls for 9-inch round pans. I recommend getting two aluminum 9-inch rounds with at least 2-inch-high sides.

8-inch Square Pan

This is ideal for making brownies, gingerbread, and coffee cakes. They are manufactured in both heat-tempered glass and nonstick aluminum. I prefer the aluminum because it heats up more quickly.

Jelly-Roll Pan

This standard pan doubles as a baking sheet. It becomes a jelly roll pan when you use it for roulades and jelly rolls. It measures approximately 12 x 7 inches and has slightly rolled edges. Heavy-gauge aluminum is the standard material.

Loaf Pan

I recommend 5 x 9 x 4-inch aluminum bread pans. Have at least two.

Muffin Pan

Personally, I like mini-muffins. You can purchase pans that hold anywhere from 24 tiny muffins to 6 jumbo ones. Tinned steel is the most popular material for these pans. I like heavy nonstick pans.

Pie Pan

Pie pans come in 8-, 9-, and 10-inch diameters, as measured from the inside top rim to the opposite side. The most common recipes call for a 9-inch pan, so I recommend buying two of these. I choose tempered glass since knives will often be used to cut pies in the pan and because the glass effectively browns crusts evenly.

Springform Pan

Everyone who loves cheesecake and intends to make it at home needs to have at least one 9-inch springform pan. I also use mine for Sachertorte (page 260). The unique design of the heavy-gauge aluminum springform makes for uniform heating. It gets its name from the side, which is spring-loaded and when released pulls away from the bottom of the pan.

Tart Pan

This wonderful pan can make elegant tarts as well as perfect quiches. There is no crimping necessary to form fancy sides; the pan's shape does this for you. There are actually two parts to the pan: the side ring and the bottom. When the tart cools, the outside ring drops off. Since most crust recipes require a great deal of butter, there is no need for a nonstick surface. I recommend a stainless-steel tart pan.

Tube Pan

Not to be confused with a Bundt pan, the tube makes archetypal angel food cakes and traditional marble pound cakes. The tube conducts heat evenly to all sections of the batter. It has high sides and a removable bottom. A 10-inch diameter with 4 ½-inch depth is ideal for most recipes. All pieces are lightweight aluminum.

PRESSURE COOKERS

It seems as though everyone has a pressure cooker horror story that ends with pea soup dripping from the ceiling. I remember walking into a restaurant in France where a chef was preparing risotto from scratch in a small stovetop pressure cooker. When the pot was left unattended for too long, the results were something like a bomb: the lid was launched across the room and risotto stuck everywhere.

Today's pressure cookers are modified for safety, and those explosive incidents, thankfully, are behind us. When I first started working seriously with pressure cookers, I was amazed at the quality of the food's flavors, aromas, and textures. Although these appliances are known mainly as timesaving devices (steam is a very efficient heating source), they can also be used for fine cooking.

The Science of Steam

When liquid comes to a boil, steam is produced. If this steam is prohibited from escaping by the securely sealed lid of a pressure cooker, it is driven back into the liquid, raising the boiling point by 40°F.

The pressure also drives the steam into the food itself. With the lid fastened securely, the steam's pressure begins to break down the fibers of the food, tenderizing tough meat quickly and delicately infusing vegetables and grains with the flavors of the seasoned cooking liquid. Vegetables also keep their bright colors and retain high levels of nutrients.

Finding the Perfect Pressure Cooker

• Safety first. Pressure-cooking can be somewhat tricky at first, which is why it is vital that you follow all the safety precautions. The lid should be tightly fastened and sealed; a safety clamp (or two) on the lid is reassuring, too. There should be one valve that vents excessive steam to control internal pressure and a second valve that prevents the cooking vessel from opening if there is still too much pressure inside.
• Size matters. You can always cook one chicken breast in a large pressure cooker, but you can't put eight breasts into a small one. Try to find

one with a 4- to 6-quart capacity. You'll want the room to make stocks and soups. Sturdy hard plastic handles make for a sure grip no matter what the size.
• Heavy metal. Whether the cooker is stovetop or electric, I prefer the pot to be made from heavy stainless steel, which doesn't react with the foods during cooking. I would not want a softer metal like aluminum to be in contact with my food at those extreme temperatures. A nonstick surface saves time during cleanup, but only if it is of high quality, like Excalibur.
• Several settings. I like pressure cookers with more than one pressure setting so I have greater control over the food. Look for the options of 5, 10, or 15 pounds of pressure during cooking.

Keys to Successful Pressure Cooking

1. It is essential to read the instructions that come with your pressure cooker before operating it.
2. Keep the steam vent clean to prevent any buildup of pressure.
3. Always use an ample amount of liquid. For larger cookers you need at least two cups of liquid to generate steam. Please note: Liquid is not a heavy substance like barbecue sauce or tomatoes or oil. Liquid is water, stock, or wine.
4. Always cut meat and vegetables into uniform sizes so all the pieces cook evenly.
5. Never fill the cooker more than two-thirds full. The more room steam has to do its job the better the results.
6. Avoid foods that foam as foam clogs up steam vents.
7. The timing on pressure cooking begins when high pressure is achieved. This is usually indicated by a raised knob or button on the top of the cooker.

8. When using a stovetop cooker, turn the flame to high until the pressure in the vessel is at the right setting. Once the correct pressure is achieved, turn the heat down to medium-low. Failing to do this can result in unnecessary escape of liquid, which might lead to burned ingredients.

DEEP FRYERS

It's no mystery why people love to eat crisp, crunchy, golden-brown fried foods. And when you cook them at home you have more control over the ingredients, the equipment, and the cooking techniques, making it possible to enjoy fried foods that are cleaner tasting and less greasy than most of those that you can buy.

But many home cooks typically shy away from frying. They don't want the guesswork of heating the oil to the right temperature, the smell that permeates the kitchen, the mess, and the splattering, and they fear the remote possibility of accidents.

Fortunately, today's electric deep fryers have turned deep-frying into an easy, pleasurable task that is free of mess and odor. If you love fried foods and don't mind giving up just a little bit of your kitchen storage space, an electric deep fryer is a great investment.

The Right Fryer
Look for a machine with the following qualities:
• The fryer basket should be completely enclosed and have a lid to protect against hot oil splatters.
• The frying basket should have a removable handle, and it should be able to be raised and lowered in and out of the oil by an outside lever.
• Newer models have the heating element and thermostat submerged in the oil to automatically regulate the temperature and adjust the heat accordingly.

Tips for Frying
The type of oil you use, the temperature of the oil, and safety are all keys to successful frying.

Types of oil to use
When it comes to deep-frying, cooking oils are not created equal. Choose an oil that has a high smoke point, meaning that it doesn't begin to break down as quickly and generate smoke. Corn, canola, peanut, soy, and safflower oils are all excellent choices. Olive oil, while being a heart-healthy oil, is never recommended for deep-frying.

When is it time to change your oil?
The quick answer is: Almost every time you fry. And here's why. When cooking oil is old, its chemical composition starts to change due to the amount of air it has been exposed to as well as the tiny crumbs of food from previous cooking sessions. This causes the oil to react differently with food and reduces its ability to make things crisp and crunchy. Even more importantly, it introduces unhealthy substances called free radicals into your food. For these reasons, I recommend changing the oil each time you fry, and I certainly recommend using the same cooking oil no more than twice. If you do use it a second time, you should pour off at least a third of it and add an equal amount of fresh oil. If you are going to use the oil again, strain it into a clean, airtight container and keep it refrigerated.

Taking the oil's temperature
Another significant factor for successful frying is the temperature of the oil. I do most of my frying between 350°F and 375°F. Doughnuts and other pastries are the only items I fry at lower temperatures. Note that when you place the food in the oil, the temperature drops, so you may

have to turn the burner up slightly, and you must wait for the temperature to come back up between batches.

The best way to monitor the oil's temperature when cooking is with a deep-fat thermometer. This is sometimes also called a candy thermometer. Find a thermometer that registers up to at least 400°F. The best models have a stainless-steel frame and a plastic handle at the top, as well as easy-to-read numbers. Digital thermometers with the heatproof cord will also work well.

Elbow room

The last factor for the best frying results is to avoid overcrowding the fryer or fry pan. For example, if you drop two cups of French fries into two cups of oil, the fries won't have room to move around, and the oil has a hard time heating all the surface areas.

Since frying takes only 2 to 3 minutes for most foods (other than large pieces of chicken), it's easy and convenient to fry many small batches instead of one big crowded one. This ensures even cooking and the crispy results we all love.

Prepare for frying

Before you deep-fry most foods, you coat them with breading or batter to retain moisture and flavor. The coating also protects food from absorbing too much fat while adding texture. Here is an easy-to-follow guideline for coating foods:

1. Set up three shallow bowls on the counter. Place flour in the first bowl. Place a mixture of eggs and either water or milk in the second bowl. Place the breading of choice (see below) in the third bowl.
2. Clean the food to be fried, shake off excess water, and blot dry. Season the food if you like with salt and pepper.
3. Dip the food in the flour and shake off excess flour.
4. Dip the food in the egg mixture and drain off any excess.
5. Dip the food in the coating, pressing gently to make sure it is coated completely. Shake off excess coating.
6. Leave the breaded food on a plate or baking sheet until you are ready to fry it.

Common and uncommon breading options

Many starchy foods can be used as breading. Each will have its own unique texture and appearance. Here are some options:

Breadcrumbs (fine dry, or fresh)
Cornmeal
Cracker meal
Panko (Japanese-style wheat breadcrumbs)
Rice flour

After frying

Drain the food in a fryer basket and shake the basket a few times to get rid of excess oil. Dump the fried food onto a plate lined with clean paper towels for more draining. Don't leave too long on the paper, or you will lose flavor. Season the food while it's hot. The food will not hold the seasoning if you wait until it cools. Do not season while deep-frying because this will damage the oil and could cause flare-ups.

ELECTRIC GRILLS AND SPECIALTY IRONS

Modern kitchen appliances have taken giant steps forward in recent years. New indoor grills and griddles make all kinds of kitchen adventures possible.

Contact Grill

As popularized by George Foreman's line, the contact grill is really an excellent cooking tool.

It's smaller than other indoor grills, but it cooks meats and fish on both sides at once, searing the outside and sealing in moisture. This means that there is no need to turn the food, and cooking times can sometimes be reduced by half.

Key points to look for are multiple temperature settings, 1400 (or higher) watts of power, fat or grease catchers, dedicated cleaning implements, and embedded heating elements.

Indoor Grill

With an indoor electric grill, weather can never stand in the way of delicious grilled fish, steaks, and vegetables. These grills are much smaller than outdoor grills, so find the size that best suits your general needs and fits your kitchen storage area.

Wattage is important, too. The higher the wattage, the hotter the grill can get. Some grills barely heat up enough to cook meats evenly all the way through, so look for 1500 watts or higher. The heating element should be imbedded into the cooking surface to cut back on smoke and increase the heating and cooking capability.

As for materials, cast aluminum conducts heat very well. With a good nonstick surface, you should be very happy with an indoor grill's performance.

Panini Grill

Similar to the contact grill is the panini grill. Panini is Italian for "bread" or "sandwich," so this appliance is sometimes called a sandwich maker. That makes sense because it's the perfect size for making quick grilled sandwiches, complete with appealing grill marks. The heating elements run through the top and the bottom plates, and there are raised nonstick surfaces on both sides. A model with a "floating hinge" can adjust to cook various thicknessess of crostini, sandwiches, and other snacks. Look for a cast-aluminum body, adjustable heating, and 1400 watts of power. The panini grill can double as a contact grill.

Pizzelle Iron

This kitchen tool is an indulgence, but if your family loves pizelles, those traditional crispy Italian cookies, then a pizzelle iron is a great investment. A traditional pizelle iron is handheld, with long handles and a cast aluminum body that is placed over a fire or hot stove burner.

Modern irons are electric and come with nonstick surfaces. The dough is placed on the surface and in less than a minute, amazing cookies emerge to be enjoyed right away or used as the foundation for fantastic desserts.

Waffle Iron

Weekend breakfasts are so special when waffles are served. Today's waffle irons have an astounding number of settings to suit a wide range of waffle styles (from thin and crisp to thick and cakelike). Make sure your iron has nonstick plates, indicator lights for when it's ready to cook and for when the waffle is done, and a cast-aluminum body. A Belgian waffle iron is deeper and allows the batter to rise to a magical thickness while retaining a fluffy texture inside. Try putting chocolate cake batter in the waffle iron to make chocolate dessert waffles, served with vanilla ice cream and hot fudge.

Kitchen Helpers

These are the ingredients that will come up often in the recipes. Stock your pantry—which includes the refrigerator and spice cabinet—and you won't be spending hours at the supermarket shopping for ingredients. Then you can give your full attention to the best produce, meats, and fish that you can find.

OILS, BOTTLED SAUCES, AND CONDIMENTS

All-purpose flour
Asian style toasted sesame oil
Balsamic vinegar
Barbecue sauce
Mayonnaise (Best Foods, Hellmans, or homemade, page 218)
Bread (have a crusty loaf in the freezer and one on hand)
Breadcrumbs
Canned tomatoes
Capers
Dijon mustard
Dried fruit, such as apricots, raisins, prunes, cranberries, and cherries
Dried pasta (penne, fusilli, spaghetti, angel hair, linguine, fettucine, rigatone)
Dry white wine
Eggs
Extra-virgin olive oil
Frozen peas
Gherkins
Good quality canned or boxed beef stock
Good quality canned or boxed chicken stock
Hoisin sauce
Honey
Imported green and black olives
Ketchup
Madeira
Panko (Japanese breading mix)
Peanut oil

Port
Prepared marinara sauce (I recommend the boxed Italian import called Pomì)
Prepared pesto
Red wine, such as pinot noir
Rice (basmati, long-grain, Arborio, and wild rice)
Roasted red peppers
Russian dressing (preferably homemade, page 220)
Seasoned rice wine vinegar
Sherry (both sweet and dry)
Sherry vinegar
Soy sauce
Sugar (white, light brown, superfine, and confectioners')
Sun-dried tomatoes
Sun-dried tomato pesto
Teriyaki sauce
Thousand Island Dressing (preferably homemade, page 219)
Tomato paste
Unsalted butter
Walnut or hazelnut oil
Wasabi powder or paste (I prefer the paste)
Wine vinegar

HERBS AND SPICES

Black peppercorns
Bay leaves
Caraway seeds
Cayenne
Chili powder
Cinnamon sticks

Herbs and Spices Cont.

Coriander seeds

Cumin seeds

Ground cinnamon

Hot red pepper flakes

Italian seasoning

Kosher salt

Lemon pepper seasoning

Oregano

Paprika (sweet and hot)

Sea salt

Star anise

White peppercorns

FRESH FOODS

Carrots

Celery

Fresh ginger

Garlic

Mushrooms

Onions

Parsley

Lemons

Shallots

Red onions

CHEESES

Fontina

Goat cheese

Gruyère

Mozzarella

Parmesan

FRESH HERBS I LIKE

Basil

Chives

Cilantro

Marjoram

Mint

Parsley

Oregano

Rosemary

Sage

Tarragon

Thyme

FINDING THE BEST

Produce

Shopping at a farmers' market is the best way to ensure that your produce is locally grown and seasonal. Most of the produce sold at these markets is also organically grown. If you can't fill your produce needs this way, look for quality supermarkets and whole foods stores with good turnover. The shorter the distance the food has traveled to get to your store, the more recently it has been picked.

Meat and Poultry

Gone are the days when there was a butcher in every town. Most of us buy our meat at the supermarket, and it has often been packaged by the time you get to it. But this doesn't mean that you can't seek out the supermarket butchers. You may not see them, but they're in the back, and will often accommodate you with cuts of meat that you can't find on the refrigerated meat shelves. If

you need a rack of pork, for instance, because you want to make the Rack of Pork with Dried Fruit Stuffing on page 196, ask the butcher at your market if he can save you a rack before he cuts it into chops. Ask him to butterfly it for you too while he's at it, if you don't want to do it yourself.

Seek out supermarkets and whole foods stores that actually have meat counters. You'll be more likely to find naturally raised beef, prime or choice beef, free range chickens, and quality cuts at these stores.

Fish and Shellfish

It really pays to find a good fish market with heavy turnover. The next best thing is a quality supermarket that has a good reputation for fish. Wherever you buy your fish, the place should never smell "fishy." That's an obvious sign that the fish is not fresh. The fish should look shiny, whole fish should have clear eyes, and there should be no discoloration. Avoid packaged fish if you can. You want to be able to inspect it.

MENU PLANNING AND ADAPTING RECIPES TO SEASONAL AVAILABILITY

Both the size of the dinner, whether you are preparing a family meal or a dinner party for guests, and the season should play a role in determining your menu. In the middle of summer you probably won't want to heat up your kitchen or weigh yourself down with a long-roasting braised meat like the Wine-braised Brisket of Beef on page 178; but what a perfect main dish this would make on a cold winter night. On the other hand, a chilled, light starter like Scallop Ceviche (page 42) might not appeal to you in the dead of winter, when you're more likely to make a comforting soup like the Root Vegetable Soup on page 64. If you are preparing a dinner party for four, you could take on dishes that require last minute cooking and plating, like the Pan-fried Trout with Lemon and Caper Sauce on page 152 or the Pan-Seared Ahi Tuna with Wasabi Cream Sauce on page 147. But if there will be eight at your table, you might want to go with a roast or a braise, be it beef, pork, or lamb shanks, and start the meal with a soup or a salad. The same considerations apply to dessert. Make it easy on yourself and do something that can be accomplished ahead of time, like a sachertorte (page 260) or Chocolate Mousse (page 232) if you're serving a crowd; but try a last-minute treat like the Sabayon with Fresh Berries (page 244) or Banana Spring Rolls with Dipping Sauces (page 229) for a smaller number of guests.

Family meals require much less planning, because one course will usually suffice, and that could be as simple as a soup or a roast chicken or a pasta accompanied by a salad. You'll have a lot of fun with the grilled panini on pages 83-98, which will open up a range of possibilities for quick and easy family dinners.

The availability of ingredients is of course your other consideration. If an ingredient in a recipe is not in season, always ask yourself if something else can be substituted. You wouldn't be able to make a fresh peach Melba in the late fall or winter; however you could always substitute pears for peaches and frozen raspberries for fresh in the sauce. If you're craving Straw and Hay Pasta with Fresh Peas and Prosciutto (page 111) and you've missed that two-week window when fresh English peas are available, by all means use frozen peas. Can't find pattypan squash on a winter's day when you'd love to make the Braised Lamb Shanks with Squash and Peas on page 184? Substitute winter squash; it'll still be a wonderful dish. Although you wouldn't want to make a gazpacho with anything other than fresh tomatoes, there's not a pasta sauce or hot soup in this book that won't be just as good if you use quality canned tomatoes. Good quality canned tomatoes or a good prepared marinara sauce like the Italian import Pomì is always a better solution than out of season fresh tomatoes.

Talk to your suppliers. Tell them what you're cooking. If they don't have what you want, ask them what might work instead. This is one of the many advantages of shopping at farmers' markets and finding good butchers and fish markets. They know their products and can help you adapt your recipes if you need to.

CHOOSING WINES

To me, a dinner is not really a dinner without a glass of wine to go with it. Like the food, wine is an integral part of the dining experience. But also like the food, wine doesn't have to be fancy to be very good. You don't need an expensive bottle of Chateau Lafitte or Meursault to have a wonderful wine, any more than you need foie gras and truffles to make a great meal.

That's why choosing wine doesn't need to be a formal affair, even if it's for a formal meal. Today there are so many varietals—wines made from a single grape—from so many different parts of the world, that the choices are endless. It's not easy, or necessary, to pin down one country to focus on. Since I live in California, probably 75 percent of the wines I drink are from here; but I could just as easily be opening bottles from Australia or New Zealand, which have really come into their own over the last twenty years. Many of the new world wines are more affordable today than California wines, and are of excellent quality.

To find a perfect marriage for wine and food, first you have to know the food. Is it spicy? If it is, don't try to impress your guests by opening an expensive cabernet or Burgundy or pinot noir: the wine will be overwhelmed by the seasonings. Is it a juicy piece of red meat that can stand up to a robust, complex Bordeaux? Or a more subtle chicken or fish dish? If you're serving fish, don't think that you have to serve white wine, a notion that I believe is overblown. I love red wines, and often find myself drinking a glass of slightly chilled pinot noir with a good piece of fish. But that doesn't mean that a great chardonnay or a Riesling wouldn't also go well with a fish recipe.

With Asian-flavored foods, I often like beer or sparkling wine, because the fizz prepares your palate for the next bite. And I would never think of drinking wine with goulash (page 180); it has to be a nice, cold beer. I'm always puzzled when customers in my restaurant order this hearty, spicy Hungarian stew and a glass of wine in the middle of summer, when a good lager at the right temperature would be a perfect accompaniment. Today we have so many wonderful microbreweries that it's easy to find a style you like, be it a lager or an amber beer or a rich dark beer.

We have over six hundred labels on our wine list at Spago. But we also have the proper storage conditions for these wines. Unless you have a temperature controlled space for storing wines, don't buy expensive ones that require time to reach their peak. They will deteriorate quickly if you store them in your kitchen. Instead, focus on wines for everyday drinking that make good marriages with a range of foods. Ask your wine merchant for suggestions, read about wine in Robert Parker's books, or in *The Wine Spectator*, a magazine that reports on wine and food from all over the world. If your significant other is interested in wine, get them a subscription, and you'll benefit as well.

If you do buy upscale wines from Burgundy and Bordeaux, for example, it's important not only to know the producer but also the vintage, the year in which it was made. Some years are good, some are not. The wine literature and a knowledgeable merchant can help you with this.

Without getting into high-priced wines, which you can find relatively easily in good wine shops and upscale supermarkets, here are some of my favorite wines and Champagnes for everyday enjoyment. They will go well with the dishes in this book.

WOLF'S FAVORITE WINES

Sparkling Wines and Champagnes

Producer	Wine Type	Location
Perrier Jouët Fleur de Rosé	Champagne	Champagne, France
Veuve Clicquot Brut Yellow Label	Champagne	Champagne, France
Krug	Champagne	Champagne, France
Schramsberg	sparkling wine	Napa, California
Handley Brut	sparking wine	Anderson Valley, California
Crede di Valdobbiadenne	Prosecco	Italy

White Wines

Producer	Wine Type	Location
Qupe "Bien Nacido"	Chardonnay	Santa Barbara, California
Lewis "Reserve"	Chardonnay	Napa Valley, California
Babcock "Eleven Oaks"	Sauvignon Blanc	Santa Barbara, California
Garretson	Viognier	Central Coast, California
Patz & Hall	Chardonnay	Russian River Valley, California
Lis Neris	Pinot Grigio	Friuli, Italy
Bruna Giacosa	Arneis	Piedmont, Italy
Knoll	Gruner Veltliner	Wachau, Austria
Hirtzberger	Riesling	Wachau, Austria
Alois Kracher	all sweet wines	Austria

Red Wines:

Producer	Wine Type	Location
Hitching Post	Pinot Noir	Santa Barbara, California
Dumol	Pinot Noir	Russian River Valley, California
Ojai Vineyards	Syrah	Santa Barbara, California
Ridge	Zinfandel	Napa, California
Fontodi	Chianti Classico	Tuscany, Italy
Il Palazzone	Brunello di Montalcino	Tuscany, Italy
Vieux Telegraph	Chateauneuf-du-Pape	Southern Rhone, France
Tinto Pesquera	Tempranillo	Ribera del Duero, Spain
	Cabernets or Cabernet blends	Bordeaux

INDEX

Numbers in *italics* refer to pages showing preparation techniques

Z

Zucchini